The short guide to urban policy

Claire Edwards and Rob Imrie

D1093393

First published in Great Britain in 2015 by

Policy Press
University of Bristol
1-9 Old Park Hill
Bristol BS2 8BB
UK
t: +44 (0)117 954 5940
pp-info@bristol.ac.uk
www.policypress.co.uk

North American office:
Policy Press
c/o The University of Chicago Press
1427 East 60th Street
Chicago, IL 60637, USA
t: +1 773 702 7700
f: +1 773-702-9756
e:sales@press.uchicago.edu
www.press.uchicago.edu

© Policy Press 2015

British Library Cataloguing in Publication Data
A catalogue record for this book is available from the British Library.

Library of Congress Cataloging-in-Publication Data
A catalog record for this book has been requested.

ISBN 978-1-4473-0799-0 paperback

Contents

List of figures and tables

Figures

Tables

vii

Acknowledgements

We are indebted to Dr Sarah Fielder who copy-edited a draft of the book and compiled the references and index. Without her help, the book would have taken a lot longer to complete. We are grateful to Emily Watt, Laura Vickers, Jo Morton and Rebecca Tomlinson at Policy Press for their guidance and advice in the preparation and delivery of the book.

About the authors

Claire Edwards is a lecturer in the School of Applied Social Studies, University College Cork, Ireland. Her background is in urban and cultural geography and social policy. Her research interests include: urban regeneration and the effectiveness of urban policy, particularly in terms of its ability to provide benefit for excluded communities; the participation of disabled people in society and the disability rights agenda; and the politics of social research and the relationship between research and policy. She has published widely in urban geography, social policy and environmental planning, including many peer-reviewed journal papers.

Rob Imrie is Professor of Sociology in the Department of Sociology at Goldsmiths University of London, UK. His research interests include disability and design, urban regeneration, and urban policy and politics. He is author and co-author of several books, including *Disability and the city* (1996, Paul Chapman Publishing), *Inclusive design* (2001, Routledge), *Accessible housing* (2006, Routledge) and *Architectural design and regulation* (2011, Wiley-Blackwell). At present, he is directing a project funded by the European Research Council on the topic of universal design, disability and the designed environment.

Introduction

The objective of this book is to provide an overview of urban policy, or purposive interventions by government and non-governmental actors seeking to respond to a broad range of social, welfare, economic and ecological problems related to urbanisation. Urbanisation is fast becoming the dominant way of life for most people in the world, and many urban areas, particularly in countries of the global South, feature rapidly growing populations and greater demands for jobs, housing and basic services, and are spreading, rapidly, into fragile ecosystems. The urban challenges of the 21st century appear daunting and they range widely, from the deleterious ecological and environmental effects of urbanisation, including degraded landscapes, traffic congestion and air and water pollution, to problems of poverty and inequality, and responding to people's needs for access to good-quality jobs, housing, transport, education and other urban goods and services.

These manifold problems associated with urbanisation have given rise to urban policy, or systems of governance orchestrated by central and local government and a range of non-governmental, usually private sector, organisations and community groups. There are few cities without formal urban policy programmes, and their purported primary target is to enhance citizens' welfare by encouraging local economic development and job creation and providing people with the opportunities for access to the necessary means of life, such as good-quality housing. The broad remit of urban policy means that it is a difficult term to define, and, for Cochrane (2007, p 136), it comprises 'an overlapping patchwork without any clear or consistent overall unified agenda'. For some, there is little to differentiate urban policy from social and welfare policy, insofar that the objectives of both are to change people's lives through state intervention and social and economic support (Atkinson and Moon, 1994; Cochrane, 2007).

What appears to distinguish urban policy from other policy fields is its spatial or geographical focus on the city and, more specifically, on particular parts of cities characterised by government as problem places. Such places tend to be defined as locales with high numbers of people living in poverty and in conditions of relative need. They are, in government language, points of multiple deprivation in which people lack some of the basic means of livelihood, including jobs, a living wage and good-quality, affordable housing. Modern urban policy, in most Western developed countries, was primarily founded on seeking to solve the problems of people living in poor neighbourhoods, with the understanding that poverty was unjust and an affront to a civilised society. For instance, in 1964, US President Lyndon Johnson declared an unconditional war on poverty and racial injustice, and for the next decade, US urban policy focused on self-help programmes related to education, job training and community development.

Similar policy trends were evident in the UK and other Western countries, most notably, in the British context, a plethora of area initiatives, ranging from housing action areas to educational priority areas (see Atkinson and Moon, 1994; Cochrane, 2007). Later, from the early 1980s, the spatial focus for policy shifted towards urban regeneration and the encouragement of inward investment in stricken places, or areas previously abandoned by capital flight. Here, the solution to poverty and deprivation was identified as less about the provision of welfare and social support, and more about economic development and encouraging people to gain the education and skills most marketable to employers. Typical of the time was the London docklands regeneration, a model of property-led urban policy that has since come to dominate government approaches to the social and economic problems of cities (see Imrie and Thomas, 1999; Brownill, 2013).

The pursuit of economic growth as a means to boost jobs and incomes is subject to some challenge by those who question the viability of urban lifestyles and people's high levels of consumption in cities. This is reflected in many city administrations adopting greater sensitivity to issues of sustainable development, and seeking to create urban lifestyles that are less wasteful of energy, water and space. Thus, since the early 1990s, the continued encouragement of property-led regeneration by politicians and development actors has gone hand in hand with policy programmes to use urban space in efficient ways, by maximising the density of developments and by prioritising brownfield regeneration over urban expansion into suburban and greenfield areas. A whole series of policy concepts have emerged to describe new modes of urban living, from the compact city to the smart city, with a focus on creating socially inclusive places, or environments that cater for the needs of multicultural, cosmopolitan social structures.

The reality, as we recount in the book, is less than the ideal held up by some of the more optimistic commentators about urban futures. The city harbours some of the most intractable social and economic problems of our times, and, whatever the rhetoric of smart, eco or compact cities campaigners, much of urban policy today, like its predecessors, is implicated in maintaining the status quo and doing little to challenge the centrality of a capitalist growth ethic. For some, urban policy is no more than the deployment of the state's legal and governmental apparatus to promote speculator capitalism by encouraging global investments in land and property. For evidence of this, writers such as Lees (2012) and Slater (2013) point towards state-led gentrification in cities stretching from Istanbul in Turkey to Santiago in Chile, with outcomes described by Swyngedouw et al (2002, p 545) as 'perverse and pervasive processes of social exclusion and marginalization' set amid 'the greatest affluence, abundance, and pleasure'.

These authors suggest that in its pursuit of property development, urban policy is part of the problem in supporting global investment strategies that are pricing people out of low-cost housing areas, and extending socio-spatial divisions between the 'haves' and 'have nots'. This reflects a broader, problematical dynamic in which public policy is closely aligned with facilitating private investment activities, and there is much to support this understanding of urban policy. In this book, we develop the theme that urban policy is, first and foremost, shaped by economic and political objectives to pursue property development and to (re)capitalise land as a means to boost profits and wealth creation. Urban policy is a series of political and policy tools seeking to (re)produce the conditions for sustained economic development. This follows a broader logic, propounded by politicians, that people's well-being and welfare can best be maximised by disciplining individuals into an acceptance of the efficacy of the market.

In this book, we outline and evaluate different dimensions of urban policy, primarily from the late 1960s and with reference to the major Western developed countries, with the focus on the UK and the US. The book is organised around a number of key themes. Foremost, while urban policy can be described and understood as a technical process, of plan-making and implementation, and an administrative function of governing, it is important to see it as a form of political action and part of the politics of place-making. In other words, urban policy has to be understood as propagating specific visions and values of what the good city is or ought to be, and it is not politically neutral or value-free. Rather, urban policy is part of political contestation and conflict, and it is shaped by, and helps to shape, often deep-seated struggles between different social and cultural groups over the form and substance of urban space.

Such struggles reflect, in part, the inter-organisational nature of urban policy in which a mixture of public and private sector agencies, operating at a variety of spatial scales, are involved in its development and delivery. These agencies are characterised by different emphases, values and practices, and they operate across a diversity of substantive fields spanning housing, employment, education, training, infrastructure and other categories, including security, crime and disorder. There is, then, a complexity to urban policy characterised by a host of national and local government interventions and entanglements that make it difficult to draw generalisations about policy form, process and substance. This complexity highlights the significance of urban governance and the multi-scalar nature of policy design and implementation.

What can be said is that most agencies involved in different elements of urban policy, from transport to housing and street cleaning, are primarily characterised by privatised forms of provision and policy designed to generate profit. A question is how far placing profit at the centre of policy processes can facilitate a coherent urban policy able to resolve the problems of disadvantaged people living in cities. For writers like Anna Minton (2006), the answer is that a market-focused policy approach cannot resolve urban problems. She suggests that the dominant approach of urban policy in recent times – property-led regeneration – 'aims for higher property prices which displace local people, breaking up local cultures and communities' (Minton, 2006, p 4). In this book, we reflect on, and develop, Minton's observations, and evaluate how far urban policy is for people or profit and whether or not the pursuit of the latter is anathema to the objective of creating cities that cater for all.

As a contribution to the *Short Guide* series, the book is an introduction for students to key debates about the management of cities and the role and significance of urban policy in shaping the social and economic fortunes of those who both live in and depend upon urbanisation for their well-being. The aims of the book are sixfold:

1. to provide a concise description of the major social, economic, ecological and environmental problems and issues associated with different forms of urbanisation;
2. to describe and evaluate the main elements of urban policy responses to the problems and challenges posed by urban living and lifestyles;
3. to outline and evaluate the significance of national and local political processes as drivers of urban policy;
4. to identify and explore the different theoretical understandings of urban policy and the governance of cities;
5. to assess the future for cities and urban policy in a context of economic austerity and political pressures to create sustainable urban environments; and
6. to draw on some selective international examples and experiences to highlight the ubiquity, and mobility, of urban policy measures.

The rest of the book is divided into eight chapters and a postscript. In Chapter One, we outline the changing social, economic, ecological and political challenges posed, over time, by urbanisation. Urban settlement has been a defining feature of human civilisation, and it poses challenges as to how to secure the welfare of those that depend on the city for their livelihoods and well-being. Urban policy, as interventions by state, quasi-state or non-governmental organisations in the everyday lives of urban inhabitants, is a constant part of the functioning of cities, although its precise shape and raison d'être varies over time and space. This variation tends to revolve around common problems and challenges of governance relating to the social reproduction of populations, and seeking to resolve tensions and conflicts between different social groups and interests. In the chapter, we outline different periods of urbanisation, from the early pre-modern city to the mega-cities of the 21st century, and highlight the different challenges posed to policymakers in seeking to reproduce and secure the everyday conditions of urban habitation.

Chapter Two evaluates different interpretations and understandings of what urban policy is. Urban policy is not easy to define as it straddles many different branches of social and welfare interventions by governments and by non-governmental, third sector and voluntary organisations. It is characterised by a plethora of policy objectives that are presented by state officials as seeking to enhance the quality of life for those living and working in cities. As we have suggested, urban policy is not politically neutral or benign, nor does it operate for the benefit of all citizens. Rather, urban policy, like all forms of state intervention, is part of political contestation between different actors and interest groups with different stakes in accessing and using the socio-economic and ecological resources of cities. This understanding informs the chapter, where we suggest that urban policy is shaped by liberal values that primarily propagate economic growth and wealth creation as the paramount goal of policy, and governance as a tool to promote active citizenship or self-help.

In Chapter Three, we discuss who or what urban policy is for. In 1970, Ray Pahl (1975 [1970]) coined the term 'Whose city?' to highlight policy as a form of social control over the urban populace in favour of rentier classes or capitalists seeking to extract profit from urban development. For Pahl, the rationale of (urban) policy was to secure the city for investment, and to ensure that policing strategies and penal sanctions controlled counter-views and/or urban social disorder. This draws attention to social inequalities and poverty in cities as a powerful basis for unrest, and the challenge for governments of policing places and people characterised by societal values exhibiting deviant and immoral behaviour, or ways of living incommensurate with what the good society is or ought to be. In the chapter, we consider issues of social exclusion and marginalisation in the city, and the role of urban policy in managing 'difficult populations', or groups deemed to be a potential threat to the social order, usually defined in narrow terms to denote those who resist compliance 'with the norms of the market' (Dikeç, 2007, p 25).

In Chapter Four, we chart the changes in urban policy after the 1980s from a focus on government social and welfare programmes towards a post-welfare state, including the encouragement by ministers of the privatisation of state assets and the pursuit of private sector-led strategies of urban entrepreneurialism. This represented a shift from a political commitment to state investment in public infrastructure and public control of significant urban assets, to the sale of urban assets and their control and management by quasi-government and private sector organisations. The centrality of local government as providers of urban services and welfare has, allegedly, become less significant. Instead, flexible forms of 'soft governance' have purportedly emerged to enable greater investment opportunities for private investors, as part of a political rationale to rebuild cities (see Allmendinger and Haughton, 2009). The chapter considers the shift from state (welfare) programmes to the promotion of privatisation and urban competition as the basis of urban policy.

Chapter Five focuses on community planning and partnership as two of the significant themes of urban policy, particularly since the late 1990s. Ever since the writings of Ferdinand Tonnies (2001 [1887]) in the late 19th century on community and society, a concern of urban scholarship has been the role of communities in shaping the urban experience. Seeking to create a local, neighbourhood scale of urban living characterised by dense interpersonal ties has been a recurring feature of urban policy. A discourse of community and development is widespread, and the chapter considers how the notion of community is articulated in relation to national, racial, ethnic, gendered and other identities and how these inform and influence urban policy programmes and policies. A focus of the chapter is the evaluation of active citizenship and governments' deployment of community as part of the modernisation of systems of (urban) governance in which the restructuring of existing welfare states involves a shift in responsibilities (for the delivery of welfare) from the state to the individual.

In Chapter Six, we assess the contributions of urban policy promoting culture-led regeneration, and the impacts of cultural policies on the social and economic fortunes of cities. While cities have always been a focal point for cultural production and consumption, it is since the early 1980s that city officials, worldwide, have adopted strategies to rebuild urban economies through the pursuit of culture-led regeneration. The emphasis on culture as a mainstay of economic development is diverse in form, and includes anything from music festivals to the promotion of theatre, dance and sporting activities. In the chapter, we describe the rise of culture and creativity as the basis for urban policy, and evaluate the significance of the creative classes thesis, which has become the cornerstone of, and justification for, the pursuit of policies to enhance cultural (re)production and consumption (see Florida, 2002). We discuss debates about the relevance and impact of culture as a means of promoting socially just forms of urbanisation.

Chapter Seven explores the rise in popularity of sustainability as the dominant theme of spatial policy since the mid-1990s, which continues to shape urban policy discourses about what the good city is or ought to be. The notion of sustainable development is not straightforward and its entry into the policy field has not been without dispute about its meaning. In the chapter, we outline how urban policy discourse is entwined with the objective of pursuing sustainable development, primarily defined as a 'growth first' approach intent on boosting local economic development, albeit in ways commensurate with broader social and environmental objectives. We consider the different ways in which sustainable development has been interpreted and put into practice in cities, and evaluate how far urban policy shaped by principles of sustainable development is able to mitigate the impacts of city living on ecology and the environment. As we suggest, the deployment of sustainable development discourse in most cities is not able easily to change pre-existing patterns of production and consumption, and there is evidence that politicians are using the sustainable development banner to pursue policies that are exacerbating socio-spatial inequalities, including the deterioration of ecological and environmental quality.

In Chapter Eight, we evaluate the impact of the post-2008 global recession on cities, and the development of austerity planning, which revolves around what Raco (2012) describes as the pursuit of a growth agenda without growth. By this, Raco is pointing to government policy that seeks to prioritise economic growth in a context where growth has all but disappeared, or is unlikely to be generated with any ease. The paradox is that governments, worldwide, are crafting conditions of 'de-growth' as a precursor to the creation of economic growth, and, in doing so, appear to be exacerbating poverty and inequality within and between cities. This is creating new problems in cities, including, in the US and British contexts, higher levels of underemployment, the supplanting of full-time work with part-time jobs and the encouragement of an employment culture tolerating flexible working practices (see Donald et al, 2014). These include zero contracts, or a flexible form of working that does not guarantee employees fixed hours of work, that is, a new form of casualisation in the labour market.

In a postscript, we speculate as to what the form and substance of urban policy is likely to be by the mid- to late 21st century given the increasing scale and significance of urbanisation, and the shift towards fragmented, privatised forms of governance and policy development and delivery. Urbanisation is a global phenomenon and everyone is connected, in some way, to patterns and processes of urban change. A major challenge for policymakers is the doubling of the global urban population by 2050, and the pressures that this brings to bear to provide liveable places.

The Convention on Biological Diversity (2012, p 2) notes that urban sprawl will increase pressure on scare resources, 'including water, on a global scale, and will often consume prime agricultural land, with knock-on effects on biodiversity and ecosystem services elsewhere'. Others, such as the European Commission (2011), suggest that social polarisation and segregation will intensify as welfare retrenchment continues, and that mass migration will continue to transform the sociocultural mix of cities and intensify the cosmopolitan character of urbanisation.

1

the urban challenge

Introduction

This chapter describes the social, economic and human conditions of Western, modern cities and the problems related to urbanisation and urban habitation. The modern city is, as many writers acknowledge, a place of paradoxes and contradictions, a melange of lifestyles, economies and values that pose both opportunities and challenges to policymakers (see Jacobs, 1961; Sennett, 1996). Historically, urban spaces, and the social rhythms and relations of cities, are entwined with the actions of governors, and little of urban life occurs outside of government or policy programmes to regulate the activities of citizens. The urban historian Lewis Mumford (1961, p 656) described the city as a potentially civilising environment characterised by 'effective cooperation' between diverse people and the application of human ingenuity to create places that enhance 'all the dimensions of life'. For Mumford (1961), the city was an orchestrated or choreographed place, a social collective, and a place of socialisation and sociability in which the very best of human expression might occur.

However, like other commentators, he viewed the coming of the Western, modern city as the propagation of less-than-human values, noting that 'the increasingly automatic processes of production and urban expansion have displaced the human goals they are supposed to serve' (Mumford, 1961, p 648). Here, Mumford (1961, pp 651–2) conceives of the modern city as a paradox, simultaneously a place of opportunity and progress while also a locale that disrupts entire ecological systems and dehumanises people by 'abject dependence upon the machine'. This observation is part of a broader, continuing discourse about urbanism and its effects on people and nature, and writings have conjured up the notion of the city as unnatural, encompassing the separation of people from nature and a capacity to forge urban character in ways whereby people become estranged from one another (see Wirth, 1938).

Whether one accepts the positive or negative views of urbanisation outlined by Mumford, the city is the most dramatic imprint of people on the earth, and it poses some of the greatest challenges in society today. The collection of large numbers of people in urban areas has, since the inception of urbanisation over 3,000 years ago, created immense pressure on ecology and the environment, and required human ingenuity to respond to people's need for adequate shelter, water and basic services. Throughout the long course of urbanisation, there has been much variation between the fortunes of different cities, with the economic rise and fall of some urban centres, and the emergence, in recent times, of major mega-cities, whose populations exceed 20 million people. Amid this variation, wherever and whenever the city, the commonality of problems relating to the daily sustenance and reproduction of urban inhabitants is striking, ranging widely from people's struggles to gain access to good-quality, affordable housing, to the operation of urban labour markets that consign many people to low-paid work.

In this chapter, we foreground our discussion of urban policy by seeking to situate it within the context of the 'urban problem', or the different social, economic and ecological challenges that urbanisation has posed for both inhabitants of cities and policymakers. What are the features of urban problems that are deemed to require policy interventions, and how do these problems vary over time and between different urban contexts? We suggest that whatever the urban context, there are common, recurring challenges relating to the social reproduction of the urban populace, and the management and maintenance of the urban fabric, including its physical infrastructure. Particular persistent issues relating to the habitability of cities are also evident in debates about urban policy (Lefebvre, 1968; Cochrane, 2007). These relate to, among others, issues of equity, social justice and rights to the city, including access to clean water, health care and education.

We divide the chapter into five substantive parts, primarily dealing with different periods of urbanisation and the challenges posed by each in relation to urban habitation. The first outlines early or pre-modern urbanisation, and highlights that urban problems are not new and have been a feature of society since its earliest days. In formative settlements, the challenge was to provide places to protect and secure the population, and to maintain the urban fabric, including the provision of dwellings, clean water and sanitation. Pre-modern urbanisation was often highly planned, including the siting of buildings and controls on the forms and functions of spaces. In a second section, we describe the emergence of the industrial city in the late 18th and 19th centuries, and the rise in people's consciousness of the despoliation of the country as urbanisation began to spread. The main social concern was the state of urban life, characterised by Briggs (1965, p 23) as 'confused and complicated ... a jumble of sites and buildings with few formal frontiers [and] a social disorder with districts of deprivation and ostentation'.

The third part considers the 20th century, in which urbanisation has expanded to more than 50% of the world's population living in urban areas, a figure likely to rise to over 70% by 2050. For some, the period heralded 'the age of urbanisation', denoting a break point from past centuries, with the emergence of different economies, lifestyles and forms of sociability (see Davis, 1955).[1] During the 20th century, urbanisation became entwined with processes of globalisation, characterised by the insertion of urban economies and labour markets into global flows of people, finance, goods and services, the rapidly changing size and scale of the city, and the increasing complexity of their social structures. It was also a period of decline for many Western urban economies, suburbanisation and the hollowing out of cities, and, post-1945, a discourse of decline became a staple part of the politics of urban policy formation in many countries (see Beauregard, 2003 [1993]).

The discourse of urban decline began to change in the period from the late 1980s, and in the fourth section, we outline a revival in cities or, at least, the acceptance by politicians that urbanisation is the kernel of economic development and prosperity that needs to be nurtured. For organisations like the World Bank and the International Monetary Fund (IMF), the city has to be harnessed, and, as stated by Glaeser and Joshi-Ghani (2014, p 1), cities are 'growth escalators, offering the opportunity to lift millions out of poverty, and serve as centers of knowledge, innovations, and entrepreneurship'. Such understanding has been pivotal in major investment and infrastructure projects in cities, with city politicians seeking to pursue internationalising agendas by vigorous place promotion, and the provision of various incentives, including land and buildings, to attract major global investors. It has also been a period of heightened consciousness of the ecological limits of cities, and the rise of sustainable development as a clarion call to policymakers to reduce the socio-environmental effects of urbanisation.

In the fifth part, we note that by the early 21th century, urbanisation in Western countries was fast becoming defined by multicultural and cosmopolitan social structures, reflecting the hyper-mobile world of globalisation, including mass migration around the globe and the fast communications facilitated by the World Wide Web and air travel. The major challenge has been the biggest global recession since the Great Depression of the early 1930s, and fiscal austerity and government cutbacks on public spending have been significant in reducing the scale of urban service provision and expenditure. We suggest that the contraction of full-time jobs and the rise of part-time, flexible work, in conjunction with pay freezes and wage reductions, has combined with the truncation of public welfare support to create new forms of socio-economic instability in cities.

Early and pre-modern urbanisation

Why do urban policies exist and what are the specific problems of cities that require policy interventions? The settlement of people is a relatively recent phenomenon and up until **4000** BC, human culture was nomadic and based on a subsistence economy of hunting and gathering. The first settlements were not random or conceived without forethought for their location (see Smith, 2007). They were derived from deliberative, conscious decisions about where to locate, and the physical form and juxtaposition of shelter, including public and ceremonial buildings. Figure 1.1 gives the example of Hattusa in Turkey, the capital city of the Hittite empire, which controlled most of Anatolia from around 1640 BC to 1200 BC.

Figure 1.1: The Lion Gate, Hattusa, Turkey

Source: http://en.wikipedia.org/wiki/Hattusa#mediaviewer/File:
Hattusa.liongate.jpg

Mielke (2011, p 187) notes that 'Hittite cities were deeply influenced by administrative and religious parameters'. The city of Hattusha was founded in the early period of the second millennium BC and the photograph shows the Lion Gate, a grand entrance in the southern section of the city walls. Neve (2000) describes the walls on either side of the gate as a vestibule-like entranceway built of large blocks.

Archaeological evidence suggests that formative urban settlement was characterised by sophisticated systems of governance, including diverse policy interventions to assure the reproduction of the (urban) populace and their means of everyday sustenance (see Smith, 2007). Areas such as Mesopotamia in the Middle East developed an urban character as early as 3200 BC, and craft specialisation and industries, including ceramic pottery, metallurgy and textiles, were a staple part of early city living. Whatever, and wherever, the urban context, deliberative, conscious human interventions in the socio-spatial processes of urbanisation have been paramount in shaping the city from the earliest times. These interventions, as depicted in Figure 1.2, ranged from the supply of water to Roman settlements through the construction of a complex network of aqueducts, to the construction of sophisticated sewage systems in Greek cities, such as Knossos in Crete, around 1600 BC.

Figure 1.2: Pont du Gard, Nîmes

Source: http://en.wikipedia.org/wiki/Roman_aqueduct#mediaviewer/
File:Pont_du_Gard_Oct_2007.jpg

To solve the major challenge of urban living – the provision of water – Roman engineers designed and construction aqueducts. These were major feats of engineering and one of the best preserved examples is the Nîmes aqueduct in France. It was built in 1 AD and carried water 50 km from a spring at Uzes to Nîmes, a Roman colony.

In the earliest documented settlements, such as Memphis in Egypt, Banpo in China and Uruk in modern-day Iraq, urban planning was used to create defensive structures, while ensuring that there were clear delineations between religious and secular (domestic) spaces (see Van de Mieroop, 1997). In Mesopotamian cities, such as Nippur and Assur, the careful planning and construction of monumental buildings, such as temples and ziggurats, provided permanent meeting places in what were otherwise largely nomadic cultures. Complex forms of governance shaped the physical layout and fabric of such settlements, and the maintenance of social order was inscribed into the built environment in which 'rulers used urban architecture to communicate messages about power, wealth, legitimacy' (Smith, 2007, p 27). In some cities, such as Pompeii, Roman city design produced what Mumford (1961, p 267) described as a 'well ordered group of public buildings [and] the maximum provision for civic meetings and association'.

This is not to romanticise pre-modern settlement. Urban inhabitants led a precarious existence because of their dependence on rural hinterlands for the supply of food, and the sourcing and maintenance of supplies of fresh water. Many ancient cities did not survive due to the depletion of resources, and the Mayan city of Copan, in present-day Mexico, is one of many examples of a city that declined due to the inability to maintain a water supply (Bell et al, 2004). The precarious nature of pre-modern urbanisation was also reflected in the hazardous and poorly constructed nature of the built environment. The common experience was the construction of crude and unstable buildings, described by Pounds (2005, p 69) as 'built of unbaked clay, [that] could not support the structures imposed upon them or were undermined and weakened by the effluent of nearby cesspits'. Pavements were narrow or non-existent and roads turned to mud in inclement weather and prevented ease of movement. Fires were endemic and difficult to control or put out.

These problems spanned the different centuries of pre-modern urbanisation. For instance, medieval settlements in the period 800 AD to 1300 AD were beset by significant challenges to ensure the health and well-being of their populations. Sanitation, securing a water supply and risk of fires were upmost in governing the towns and cities of the time. In most medieval settlements, buildings were squeezed into small areas, and the use of wooden construction meant that most places were fire hazards. Pounds (2005) argues that urban diseases were rife due to cramped living, poor sanitation and the lack of clean water. Typhus and tuberculosis were endemic and polluted water supplies, found in most medieval settlements, were a source of gastric and pulmonary diseases. As Pounds (2005, p 28) describes it: 'Tuberculosis was rampant in damp houses with rotting timbers, and smallpox was spread "on the breath" when people were crowded together for warmth or shelter'.

City governors also had to address issues familiar to the management of 21st-century cities, including crime and disorder and tensions relating to social inequalities and ethnic segregation. Pounds (2005) shows that violent crime was common in many medieval settlements, and that crime prevention was poor. He conjures up a familiar theme within urban studies of the contrast between rural sociability and urban anonymity, or the lack of interpersonal ties in cities, and the scope for strangers to perpetrate crime 'because detection was less easy and the criminal could more easily melt into the anonymity of the crowd' (Pounds, 2005, p 142). Morbidity and mortality were more severe in the towns, and 'the ordinary hazards of life were greater' (Pounds, 2005, p 68). Medieval records of unexpected deaths in England show that personal safety was often compromised because of poor urban infrastructure, including an absence of pavements, crumbling buildings and obstructions and obstacles in streets that prevented ease of movement and added a layer of danger.

Such problems did not pass without social comment or government interventions, and the social and economic problems of cities were the stimulus to a major expansion of state policies and programmes throughout the medieval period and later. Mumford (1961, p 335) cites the example of the English Parliament in 1388 passing an Act to forbid 'the throwing of filth and garbage into ditches, rivers, and waters'. Sanitary regulations were widespread by the end of the medieval period, including the first public sewage-processing plant in Bunzlau, Silesia in 1543 (see Mumford, 1961). Other aspects of urban life, ranging from regulating building lines to refuse collection and street cleaning, also became an object of governance. In different parts of Europe, urban communes organised many social and welfare services, including police and fire, and town planning was evident in cities such as Siena, in Italy, where, as Bowsky (1981, pp 14–15) notes, 'governments laboured to lend uniformity and rationality to the town's contours and to beautify the city'.

These practices challenge preconceived notions of pre-modern cities as places of squalor, dirt and disease, and, instead, illustrate Crone's (1989) observation that urban societies across the pre-modern world were politically organised and not, as some popular histories convey, backward and superstitious. Geltner (2012, p 20) notes that medieval settlements contained a heterogeneous population with diverse needs, and 'in many towns, many services were delivered, from urban hospitals … to the designation of red light districts, to the foundation of municipal prisons'. These services were part of broader practical and moral responses to the needs of at-risk populations, and also highlight a perennial theme about urban problems and policy responses. In the medieval city, as in the late 19th century to the present day, the urban problem was no more than seeking to overcome problems of social reproduction and the sustenance of the population.

The rise of the industrial city

The onset of industrialisation, and major rural to urban migration from the late 18th century, precipitated modern-day urbanisation and changes in the scale and nature of social, economic and ecological problems associated with cities (see Briggs, 1965). The making of the major metropolitan centres, such as London, Chicago, Paris and New York, was stimulated, in part, by major immigration, and the social geographies of cities were characterised not only by social class inequalities, but also by religious and ethnic divisions (Riis, 1890; Robson, 1988). The city of this time was a mosaic of place-based differences, and it posed a challenge for urban government as to how to govern what were often perceived to be ungovernable spaces. These were places characterised by social tensions related to difficult living conditions, including poverty, people's lack of access to housing, sanitation and clean water, and social inequalities within and between diverse neighbourhoods.

The emergence of the industrial city reflected modernist values, or those attitudes and practices that regarded economic progress as the highest ideal of human kind. By the mid-18th century, Western Enlightenment thinking was paramount in equating human happiness with material consumption, a value system supportive of people's exploitation of natural resources for their own ends. Cities, as industrial–economic complexes, reflected the Enlightenment ideal and their physical structures resembled an industrial workshop of different interlocking parts required to process nature from its raw material state to the point of final consumption. The industrial city was a magnet for people seeking job opportunities, and over a short period of time, the populations of fledgling settlements grew to significant sizes (see Table 1.1). For instance, in 19th-century England, cities such as Liverpool, renowned for its port activities, grew from a population of 80,000 in 1801 to 552,400 by 1881, and Leeds, a centre of textiles, grew from 53,000 to 309,100 over the same period.

Table 1.1: Population growth of select urban settlements in England, 1750–1881

Town	1750	1801	1881
London	675,000	959,000	3,814,600
Bristol	45,000	64,000	206,500
Birmingham	24,000	74,000	400,800
Liverpool	22,000	80,000	552,400
Manchester	18,000	90,000	341,500
Leeds	16,000	53,000	309,100
Sheffield	12,000	31,000	284,400

Source: Census of Population, various dates.

The reactions to the growing industrial city were often awe and shock at the rapid spread of urbanisation and its visual intrusions on, and despoliation of, the landscape and habitat. A typical observation was made by Elizabeth Gaskell (1855, p 55) in the novel *North and South* in which, referring to the 'fictional' town of Milton, she describes the 'deep lead-coloured cloud hanging over the horizon ... nearer to the town, the air had a faint taste and smell of smoke'. Comments of this type were commonplace and highlighted perceptions of urbanisation as antithetical to nature and the basis of ecological and environmental degradation. One of the more pessimistic representations of urbanism was the celebrated poem by James Thomson, 'The dity of dreadful night', published in 1874, and described by Jane Desmarais (2004, p 1) as 'a hymn to urban dystopia, a bleak critique of the finite human value of Victorian expansionism' (see Figure 1.3).

Figure 1.3: 'The city of dreadful night' (Thompson, 1874, stanzas 6–7)

The city is not ruinous, although
Great ruins of an unremembered past,
With others of a few short years ago
More sad, are found within its precincts vast.
The street-lamps always burn; but scarce a casement
In house or palace front from roof to basement
Doth glow or gleam athwart the mirk air cast.

The street-lamps burn amidst the baleful glooms,
Amidst the soundless solitudes immense
Of rangèd mansions dark and still as tombs.
The silence which benumbs or strains the sense
Fulfils with awe the soul's despair unweeping:
Myriads of habitants are ever sleeping,
Or dead, or fled from nameless pestilence!

It was more than urban form and the aesthetics of urbanisation that commentators drew attention to; it was also the perception that habitation in the industrial city was based on stark social inequalities that were a source of political tension and unrest. Henry Mayhew (2008 [1851]), in *London labour and the London poor*, exposed major social inequalities in urban life by undertaking interviews with Londoners, including street traders, entertainers, thieves and beggars. The data show a city divided between rich and poor people. Later, in 1886, Charles Booth (1889) began to collect social data that were subsequently part of a Poverty Map of London. His motivation was to show that the incidence of poverty in London was not as bad as some social reformers had claimed. However, the data indicated that the situation was worse than previously reported, and that about one third of Londoners lived in poverty.

Booth's research identified that the problems of poverty were likely to be place-specific, and his observations resonate with contemporary urban policy and prognoses in defining the urban problem as, in part, the spatial concentrations of poor people and disadvantage. In one instance, Booth (1889) describes people's entrapment in place: 'In Battersea poverty is caught and held in successive railway loops south of the Battersea Park Road.... This is one of the best object-lessons in poverty-traps in London.' Booth was not alone in describing the urban problem as one of housing inequality, poverty and immiseration in particular places, and in Jacob Riis's (1890) classic text, *How the other half lives*, he highlighted the unjust and unequal nature of people's housing conditions in particular parts of New York City in the 1880s. For Riis (1890, p 3), the squalid tenements housing the poor were a risk to everyone: 'they [the tenements] are the hot-beds of the epidemics that carry death to rich and poor alike'.

The social conditions of urbanisation became a constant issue of popular journals and newspapers in the mid- to late 19th century, and a significant theme was the loss of rural sociability and the onset of uncivilised living in cities. The novelist Charles Dickens (1866) used his writings as social commentary on what he, and others, regarded as the horrors of the city. In the novel *Oliver Twist*, he describes urban life:

> Some houses which had become insecure from age and decay, were prevented from falling into the street, by huge beams of wood reared against the walls, and firmly planted in the road; but even these crazy dens seemed to have been selected as the nightly haunts of some houseless wretches. (Dickens, 1866, p 36)

Such sentiments were later picked up by Louis Wirth (1938), whose seminal article, 'Urbanism as a way of life', described the crisis of urban society as the fragmentation of social ties, the onset of depersonalised relationships and the decline of sociability and neighbourliness. For Wirth (1938), a distinctive urban personality was associated with urbanisation, or people that were distant from one another, and blasé and indifferent to their fellow human beings.

The emergence of an urban type was, for some, the outcome of the development of capitalism as the driving force of social and economic relations, and what Mumford (1961, p 475) describes as the 'emphasis on speculation ... [and] profit making innovations'. For Mumford (1961, p 475), the coming of capitalist urbanisation was simultaneously the dismantling of 'the whole structure of urban life' and the erosion of 'value conserving traditions' in favour of the pursuit of 'money and profit'. Here, the principles of capitalism encouraged a fluid transition of urban space, seeking to intensify land use and encouraging the construction of buildings of minimal quality, 'quick to construct, easy to replace' (Mumford, 1961, p 475). The incipient capitalist city was premised on 'maintaining a slum level of congestion' as part of a process to escalate land values and to maximise rental incomes (Mumford, 1961, p 477). For Mumford, commercial speculation went hand in hand with social disintegration and the degradation of people and place.

The shock of rapid urbanisation inspired a new genre of social-scientific research and writings inquiring into 'the urban condition', with attempts at diagnosing what could be done to alleviate its negative manifestations and consequences. For instance, the English social reformer Edwin Chadwick (1984 [1842], p 370) wrote a far-reaching report about the sanitary conditions of the urban poor, noting that 'the annual loss of life from filth and bad ventilation are greater than the loss from death or wounds in any wars in which the country has been engaged in modern times'. For Chadwick, the conditions of life in cities required public works, and this later translated into the Public Health Act 1848. Much effort to improve cities occurred at the local level, and from the 19th century, municipal reform was to the fore and arguably the first formal urban policy interventions in the industrial city began to emerge (see Briggs, 1965).

Reforms ranged widely from the inauguration of the first public parks, such as Birkenhead Park (1843), to the establishment of new layers of governance. An example was the London County Council in 1888, which, as described by Dennis (2008, p 1), was able 'to provide essential services irrespective of ability to pay and to redistribute tax revenues from rich to poor areas'. In the US, the Progressive Era typified social reform in cities, which, from 1890 to 1920, was a reaction against the social and economic problems of rapid urbanisation and industrialisation. Social reformers such as Jane Addams (1912), through her direct experiences of living in the poorer parts of early 20th-century Chicago, campaigned for better housing conditions for immigrants and called for democratic reform and public authorities to be active in alleviating social stress and poverty (see Figure 1.4).

Figure 1.4: First days at Hull House

Hull House was a mansion house constructed in 1856 in a poor part of downtown Chicago. In 1889, Jane Addams and Ellen Gates Starr converted it into the first social settlement in the US. Hull House was part of the 'settlement movement' that originated in the early 1880s and was a form of self-help urban policy that encouraged middle-class people to live in disadvantaged areas and to share their skills and culture with those people deemed to be less fortunate. Jane Addams (1912, p 64) described the area where Hull House was located:

> The streets are inexpressibly dirty, the number of schools inadequate, sanitary legislation unenforced, the street lighting bad, the paving miserable and altogether lacking in the alleys and smaller streets, and the stables foul beyond description. Hundreds of houses are unconnected with the street sewer.... Rear tenements flourish; many houses have no water supply save the faucets in the back yard.... [We have] to provide a center for a higher civic and social life; to institute and maintain educational and philanthropic enterprises, and to investigate and improve the conditions in the industrial districts of Chicago.

By 1910, Hull House had been reconstructed to include 13 buildings and a range of social facilities were provided, including a theatre, music school, gymnasium, art studio and various meeting and recreational spaces. Johnson (2005, p 1) notes that the residents attracted to Hull House 'established the city's first public playground and bathhouse, campaigned to reform ward politics, investigated housing, working, and sanitation issues, organized to improve garbage removal, and agitated for new public schools'.

For some observers, the attitudes and interventions of people like Addams were part of the problem of urbanisation because they blamed the victim for their poverty (Yelling, 2007). Addams (1912, p 64) observed that in one slum area of Chicago, 'there is little initiative among the citizens. The idea underlying our self-government breaks down in such a ward'. Policy prognosis was self-help, or changing the habits of residents, and providing moral support to enable them to break free from poverty. The slums, or poor parts of cities, were caricatured by policy and political comment as places apart and, in Yelling's (2007, p 112) terms, often described as 'parasitical on the outside world, dependent on crime and charity'.

The emergence of an urban world

The first half of the 20th century witnessed a significant increase in urban populations, and by 1950 there were more people living in cities than in rural or non-urban areas. The early period of the century was characterised by the demographic and economic expansion of cities in the industrial heartlands of Western countries, characterised by major inflows of migrants and the development of new social inequalities, often based on racial or ethnic differences. For instance, urbanisation in the US was fuelled, in part, by six million African-Americans moving from the rural southern states to the urban areas of the North-east, Midwest and West. This movement occurred in two main waves between 1910 and 1970. The first wave, between 1910 and 1930, was described as 'The Great Migration' and featured 1.6 million migrants moving to the northern industrial cities. The second, more substantial, wave occurred between 1940 and 1970, with five million black people moving into the major urban industrial heartlands of the US and, in doing so, radically reshaping the social and ethnic mix of the cities.

Similar processes were under way in European cities, although not to the same scale. In the UK, the docking of the ship the Empire Windrush on 22 June 1948 at Tilbury docks, London, was symbolic of the new reality of the post-war UK as dependent on migrant labour to boost national and urban economies. The ship contained 492 people from the West Indies, who were the vanguard of large-scale immigration into the UK. Likewise, in Germany, major labour shortages from the early 1950s led successive governments to sign recruitment treaties with Spain and Greece in 1955, and later with Turkey (1961), Morocco (1963), Portugal (1964) and other countries (see Pitkänen and Korpela, 2012). The immediate problems included providing family housing and schooling, and the pattern of urban inhabitation was segregation from the mainstream population, characterised by immigrants living in poorer housing areas.

In the interwar period, from 1918 to 1939, the staple industrial economic base of many Western cities began to decline, and this process intensified after 1945, leading commentators to coin the term 'deindustrialisation' (Rowthorn and Ramaswamy, 1997). The features of deindustrialisation included plant closures in major cities, leading to a major loss of manufacturing jobs. For instance, in the US, the share of manufacturing employment declined from a peak of 28% in 1965 to 16% in 1994, and in the EU, it fell from a peak of 30% in 1970 to 20% by 1994 (see Rowthorn and Ramaswamy, 1997). Much of the decline was attributed to the relocation of plants to cheaper, lower-cost locations, often to rural and urban fringe locales, and, more dramatically, the offshoring of employment to non-Western countries with an abundance of cheap labour.

The impact of deindustrialisation fell disproportionately on cities and was part of a process of counter-urbanisation that included major population losses. Typical was Liverpool in the UK, where the population declined from a peak of just over 800,000 in 1931 to just over 400,000 in 2001 (see Figure 1.5). Even more dramatic population losses were evident in US cities, with Detroit declining from 1.8 million people in 1950 to 700,000 in 2012, a decline of over 60%. Chicago's population declined from 3.6 million to 2.6 million people in the same period. These experiences were repeated across the Western world and were characterised by the flight of usually skilled, affluent, younger people to new suburban locations, leaving behind a mixture of poorer, dependent people, often unskilled, and disproportionately people from minority ethnic communities.

Figure 1.5: Liverpool's population (by numbers), 1801–2001

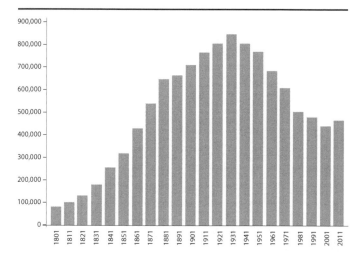

Source: http://en.wikipedia.org/wiki/Liverpool#mediaviewer/File:Liverpool_population_history.jpg

The decline of urban economies was intertwined with major social problems, and cities became increasingly known as 'places with problems, not opportunities' (Beauregard, 2003 [1993], p 4). Problems were manifest in many ways and were often highly visible, including abandoned and derelict land, deteriorating housing conditions, and growing urban inequalities. Such inequalities highlighted stark differences between the 'haves' and 'have nots', and the concentration of poverty in specific places and affecting particular groups, particularly minority ethnic communities and the working classes. For many, urban labour and housing markets were not providing opportunities for decent dwellings and jobs, and in some communities, such as the Watts neighbourhood of Los Angeles, the mixture of racist policing, poor job prospects and discrimination by employers combined to produce public protests and violent reaction (see Figure 1.6).

Figure 1.6: The Watts Riots, Los Angeles

Source: http://en.wikipedia.org/wiki/Watts_Riots#mediaviewer/File:Wattsriots-burningbuildings-loc.jpg

The Watts Riots took place in Los Angeles in August 1965 and were symbolic of the racialised and racist nature of public life and policy in the US. They occurred at the height of the US civil rights movement, and expressed black people's disaffection with mainstream society and disquiet with the unfairness perpetuated by a white culture that provided limited opportunities for minority racial groups to gain access to good-quality jobs, housing, education and social services. Rioting occurred over a six-day period, with 34 deaths, 1,032 injuries, 3,438 arrests and USD40 million of property damage.

Official reports noted that the riots were an expression of genuine social problems in South Los Angeles, yet, over the years, little has changed in any substantial sense, and many US urban neighbourhoods continue to be characterised by people living in poor and difficult conditions and exposed to different layers of institutionalised racism. The 2014 riots in the city of Ferguson, Missouri, highlight the continuing problems of racism and social inequality and the broader problems confronting black and minority ethnic people in relation to their exclusion from different strata of urban society.

The Watts Riots was only one of many such social protests that periodically occurred in inner-city locations, and throughout the 1960s until the mid-1980s, a wave of social and economic crises in cities reinforced the epithet of 'urban decline' as a more or less inevitable and irreversible process, leading to high levels of job loss and urban unemployment. Job loss was particularly concentrated among blue-collar workers, or those in semi-skilled and unskilled occupations, and there was a collapse in the value of inner-city land, including house prices. The inner-city crisis, as popularly understood, included fiscal retrenchment in major metropolitan areas, characterised in US cities by middle-class 'white flight' from inner cities reducing the local tax base and making it more difficult for local governments to raise funds to maintain local services and infrastructure, a phenomenon referred to by O'Connor (1973) as the fiscal crisis of the state.

By the end of the 1970s, various commentators were heralding the 'death of cities' and the inability of public policy to do much to solve the deeply entrenched socio-economic and ecological problems of urban areas (Dennis, 1978; Keeble, 1978); indeed, so much so that there were calls by politicians to abandon areas of cities and to let market forces take their course by people either gaining the skills and resources to compete in urban labour markets or to leave for places elsewhere. By the early 1980s, the political rhetoric of conservative ideologues, such as President Ronald Reagan in the US and Prime Minister Margaret Thatcher in the UK, was writing off cities, or at least not holding out any hope for significant resources or policy interventions to reverse urban decline. The period is best summed up by the Conservative politician Norman Tebbit, who, in 1981, advised people to abandon places without jobs and to 'get on their bikes' to search elsewhere (Tebbit, 1981).

This was a policy prognosis that regarded the problems of inner-city decline as a drain on public expenditure, and propping people up on welfare support as unlikely to solve high levels of unemployment and the attendant social problems. Instead, the urban problem was (re) defined as a problem of specific people living in particular places, relating to individuals lacking education, job skills and aptitude for work (see Chapter Two). There was an assumption embedded into Tebbit's understanding that people were largely responsible for their own misfortunes, and that they needed to price themselves into a job, to accept low pay and/or to acquire skills that employers wanted. This was a rejection of welfare or social support programmes to solve problems of poverty and social deprivation, and by the mid-1980s, unemployment in UK cities was as high as 50% in some wards at a time when welfare support was being withdrawn or reduced. By the end of the decade, the problems of the inner cities were, if anything, worse than at its beginning.

Post-industrial landscapes and the remaking of the city

The discourse of urban decline began to be challenged in the late 1980s with the realisation that cities were far too important to be written off or abandoned to market forces that might otherwise see places spiral into irreversible socio-economic decline. An important article by Robson (1994, p 131), entitled 'No city, no civilisation', highlighted the political ambivalence of government ministers and elite groups in the UK towards the cities, and he suggested that the 'political and intellectual elite' had scorned 'the concept of urban life'. By the early 1990s, most UK cities were still experiencing urban decline, particularly loss of population, and Robson's (1994) article was part of a growing realisation, not just in the UK, that cities were the kernels of invention and innovation and the focal point of human ingenuity and creativity; they could not be dismissed as anachronistic.

The cities were also the home for many of the nation's poor and dispossessed or people more or less abandoned by previous rounds of urban policy fixated on economic development at the expense of socially redistributive policy. For Robson, the imperative was for urban policy to pull back from the fundamentalist economic programmes of the 1980s, and instead focus on developing a social dimension. As Robson (1994, p 140) observed, the mark of a civilised society 'depends on the successful survival of its cities'. The Thatcher and Reagan years had exacerbated social divisions, and the main problem in cities was identified as social exclusion, or 'what can happen when people or areas suffer from a combination of linked problems such as unemployment, poor skills, low incomes, unfair discrimination, poor housing, high crime, bad health and family breakdown' (ODPM, Social Exclusion Unit, 1997, p 3).

The response of city politicians to such observations was to pursue a market-led approach to regeneration by encouraging new economic activity. In the period from the late 1980s, the changing economies of cities did little to reduce labour market inequalities or redress the sources of social exclusion. In seeking to pursue global growth and investment, cities began to open themselves up much more to flows of capital and labour, and the deindustrialisation of the post-1945 period was supplanted by an urban industrial structure characterised by the proliferation of advanced services and knowledge-based industries. The new knowledge industries, including finance, information technology (IT) and legal services, were part of the emergence of bifurcated labour markets. These were characterised by, on the one hand, highly skilled, well-paid, professional work and, on the other, low-paid and unstable unskilled jobs, primarily in catering, cleaning and a range of ancillary services.

City officials engaged in vigorous place-marketing to sell their land and cultural assets to global investors, and by the late 1990s, speculative investments by major global companies were fuelling house price rises beyond the incomes of many people. From London to New York and Paris, inner-city housing increasingly became the preserve of the affluent middle classes, and gentrification was the 'new regeneration' that, for many politicians, was the sign of successful urban renewal. For others, it was the reverse of urban revival and signalled the death of socially redistributive policy, or attempts to provide state welfare for vulnerable populations (Lees, 2003). The period was a speeding up of the rolling back of the state and the continuing privatisation of state assets, and with it the diminution of people's opportunities to gain ease of access to good-quality, affordable urban assets.

There was the expectation by many politicians that people living in cities had to adapt to the new realities of the post-welfare state by gaining the skills to compete in job markets and generating the means to look after themselves (see Atkinson and Moon, 1994). The revival of social pathology, or blaming people for their misfortunes, was to the fore throughout the 1990s, and there was broad consensus that people's problems, relating to social exclusion, poverty and low incomes, could be overturned by eliminating individual deficits of character, attitude and lack of readiness for work (see Chapter Two). Arguably, part of the urban problem in the period, which persists to this day, was state withdrawal of social support and its supplanting by rhetoric of self-help dressed up in a language that emphasised the importance of community support and development (see Chapter Four).

The period was also one whereby urban revival, through the pursuit of global economic growth, came up against contradictions related to the socio-ecological consequence of unfettered capitalism. By the early 1990s, the ecological limits of, and socio-environmental damage caused by, urbanisation had been discussed by the Brundtland Commission in 1987 and a follow-up summit in Rio de Janerio in 1993, which highlighted the major challenge of the times to be the unsustainable nature of urbanisation. While acknowledging that much had improved in cities since the 19th century with regard to water and sanitation, there was recognition of new challenges relating to the loss of species and habitat due to urban encroachment into often fragile areas, photochemical smog, the production of high levels of waste, and major traffic congestion.

The socio-ecological threats of urbanisation led some to claim that the city is a parasite on the environment as 'it makes no food, cleans no air, and cleans very little water' (Odum, 1989, p 17). For others, urbanisation despoils and degrades the natural world, or, as Bookchin (1979, p 26) suggests, 'the modern city represents a regressive encroachment of the synthetic on the natural, of the inorganic (concrete, metals, and glass) on the organic, or crude, elemental stimuli on variegated wide ranging ones'. Such sentiments are reflected, in part, in the notion of the ecological footprint, a popular concept that describes the amount of biologically productive land and resources that people consume and the waste that they produce. A plethora of research shows that the footprint of cities is proportionately greater than other, non-urban areas (see Wheeler and Beatley, 2004).

Such data highlight the disproportionate impact of urban lifestyles on ecosystems, and, for some, this reflects the contemporary crisis of urbanisation in which the challenges for policy are manifold and daunting. These include: securing local sources of energy as cities are too dependent on fragile supply systems; reducing dependence on energy and finding alternative means to provide power to cities; eradicating environmental inequalities and recognising that poorer people in cities are more likely than rich people to bear a disproportionate share of the negative environmental consequences of urbanisation; providing decent mobility for all and promoting the positive benefits of public transport; creating democratic systems of governance that can challenge corporate practice and a 'growth at all costs' mentality; and developing a culture of sustainability and transformation.

A new urbanism: urban austerity and the triumph of markets

The revival of cities is continuing apace, with demographic projections from both the United Nations (2014) and World Bank indicating that most of the world's population will live in cities by 2050. As Figure 1.7 shows, by 2050, it is estimated that a further 2.5 billion people will live in cities, with 90% of the growth occurring in Africa and Asia; this constitutes about 70% of the world's total population. The United Nations (2014) notes that by 2030, at least 41 urban agglomerations will contain at least 10 million inhabitants each, with some cities, such as Tokyo, in excess of 35 million people. These figures seem to answer Lewis Mumford's (1961, p 11) query, posed over 50 years ago, as to whether the city is likely to disappear or whether 'the whole planet [will] turn into a vast urban hive'. Demographic and other data suggest the latter scenario, as confirmed by rapid urbanisation in countries such as Nigeria, India and China, which, until recently, were notable for their high rural populations. Thus, between 2014 and 2050, China is expected to add 292 million urban dwellers and Nigeria 212 million (United Nations, 2014).

Figure 1.7: Percentage of population living in urban areas, 1950–2050

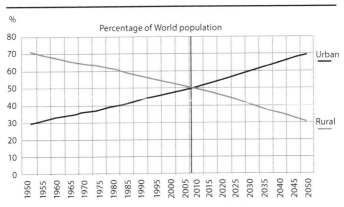

Data source: United Nations, http://esa.un.org/unup/psk0data.asp

The changing size and scale of urbanisation reflects the globalisation of local and national economies, and the concentration of economic opportunities and growth in urban centres. While cities have always been a magnet for people living in non-urban contexts, 21st-century urbanisation is accelerating the trend and, with it, new problems and challenges relating to the quality of life in cities. The United Nations (2014, p 3) *World urbanization prospects* report notes that the projected 'rapid and unplanned urban growth threatens sustainable development', and that uncontrolled population movements from country to city are likely to exacerbate problems of providing good-quality shelter and jobs in urban areas. Allen (2009, p 2) suggests that the greatest challenge is in the world's poorest countries, where the rate of urban population growth is likely to be the highest and yet where governments and governance systems are 'least equipped with the means to invest in basic urban infrastructure'.

This reflects a reality of 21st-century urbanisation: the withdrawal of governments from managing many urban services and the emergence of new systems of privatised urban governance. This trend has been exacerbated in the wake of the 2007–08 global financial crisis, in which debt management by governments has heralded a new era of fiscal austerity. This reflects the ascendency of neoliberalism, promoting policy approaches that include the reduction of public spending, the retrenchment of state welfare, the privatisation of public assets and the enhancement of corporate control over major infrastructure projects, such as the supply and maintenance of street lighting in British cities by the major corporate company Skanska. For some, the privatisation of urban services is exacerbating social inequalities and creating new pockets of poverty, while encouraging spectacular, speculator-led redevelopment characterised by the colonisation of urban space by corporate investors, and new waves of what Lees (2010) refers to as super-gentrification.

These trends are part of what Burkhalter and Castells (2009) describe as the transition from one economic model to another, in which city governments are seeking to create new ways to boost local economies, jobs and livelihoods. In the early 21st century, the challenge for city officials is managing public debt reduction while seeking to respond to the social and economic consequences of austerity. In cities such as London, austerity has been part of a broader political strategy by metropolitan governments to cut public welfare and to generate income by selling vast swathes of public land to speculative investors. This is a process repeated across cities worldwide, and it is implicated in producing new socio-spatial inequalities and extending and deepening existing ones. A report by O'Hara (2014, p 1) on the impact of cuts in housing and welfare benefits on communities living in British cities indicates that queues are 'lengthening for food handouts', with an increase in 'homelessness and a lack of opportunities for young people'.

The 21st-century city also appears to be characterised by a lack of opportunity for access to decent, affordable homes, with major Western cities experiencing unprecedented rises in house prices and rental levels, and the consequent rise in homelessness and reduction in people's housing choices. One of the starkest examples of the new housing crisis is Berlin, where rents have risen by 28% since 2007 and are continuing to climb at almost twice the national average. In London, the central city is unaffordable except to the super-rich, and new housing is sold primarily to international investors even before building has begun. This trend is part of the globalisation of cities, typified by many workers living at the margins, servicing the super-rich and subsisting on low wages, in contrast to global elites working in finance and professional services. The logic of austerity is to drive down wages and to attract labour to centres of work, and the challenge for the cities towards the mid- to end of the 21st century will be to break with the logics of neoliberalism premised on creating a society characterised by ever-widening material inequalities.

Conclusions

People have lived in urban areas for well over 3,000 years, and the management of urban problems has been an important part of human history. From the earliest pre-modern settlements in the Middle East to the mega-cities of the 21st century, urbanisation has posed problems relating to the social reproduction of people living in cities and to the management of large, diverse social groups and their needs. Urban areas have become complex assemblages of people, physical infrastructure and technologies, and the daily functioning of the city, from the operation of telecommunication systems to the movement of transport, has spawned diverse, socio-institutional systems of governance. They range from strategy steers from central government ministries to different service departments within local municipalities and an increasing range of private sector organisations that provide every conceivable form of product and service consumed by people living in cities.

The contradictions of urban life, as played out in the everyday functioning of cities, are part of the 'urban problem', or those conditions of life that pose a challenge to the social reproduction of people and to the integrity of the biological environment, including fauna, wildlife and habitat. The urban problem also relates to the economy, and here the reproduction of urbanisation, including the restructuring of urban space, the provision of new housing, the construction of physical infrastructure and the maintenance of transportation systems, are all, for Burkhalter and Castells (2009), prerequisites to assuring the growth of the capitalist system. Here, the urban problem is the sustenance of urban economic systems, including securing vital resources such as energy and water and providing the means for goods, services and people to move quickly and efficiently around cities. This draws attention to the efficiency of movement and mobility as a core theme of urban policy, which is the focus of our discussion in the next chapter.

Note

[1] A counter-view to the 'age of urbanisation' thesis is provided by Brenner and Schmid (2014), who note that urbanisation is much more omnipresent across time and space than many people acknowledge. We subscribe, in part, to this view, in that urbanisation, as part of a process of inhabitation, has always been a feature of humankind and is not easily definable in relation to discrete spaces or places, or reducible to a specific time period.

SUMMARY

From the inception of urbanisation, problems of habitation have persisted across different urban contexts, ranging from developing and maintaining a supply of clean water to ensuring human health and safety by reducing people's exposure to waste products and providing sanitary living conditions. Urbanisation, as a human artefact, is contradictory because it simultaneously leads to the disruption, even denudation, of ecology and the environment, while providing for people's livelihoods and means of sustaining life and well-being. Cities provide social opportunity while containing swathes of human degradation and poverty. Cities are also characterised by social inequalities and residential segregation, with places of relative affluence often sitting alongside places of relative poverty.

RECOMMENDED READING

Lewis Mumford's (1961) book *The city in history* is one of the best pieces of writing about urbanisation. Jane Jacobs' (1961) *The death and life of great American cities* has inspired and shaped different approaches to tackling urban problems. On pre-modern urban history, see Sjoberg (1965). For an overview of urban planning since the inception of urbanisation, see Peter Hall's (1988) *Cities of tomorrow.* Jacob Riis's (1890) text *How the other half lives* is a classic tract about urban poverty, deprivation and slum living in 19th-century New York City. On urban social inequality and marginalisation, Louis Wacquant's (2007) book *Urban outcasts* is excellent.

WEB LINKS

An excellent source of information about urbanisation and urban problems is the Brookings Institution (see: http://www.brookings.edu/research/papers/2002/07/urban-gale) and City Lab (see: http://www.citylab.com). The United Nations Environment Programme, Division of Technology, Industry and Economics, provides good insights into urban environmental problems, including water supply, sewage, solid waste, energy, loss of green and natural spaces, and urban sprawl (see: http://www.unep.or.jp/ietc/issues/urban.asp).

2

understanding urban policy

Introduction

In this chapter, we consider what urban policy is and what the underlying rationales are for government interventions in shaping urban economy and society. The argument is that urban policies are neither value-neutral nor apolitical, but, rather, contested and shaped through a complexity of socio-political processes (see Cochrane, 2007; Imrie and Lees, 2014). As urban policies have real, material consequences for different urban inhabitants, in which some people may benefit more than others, urban policy has to be understood through the lens of political processes and the interplay between diverse social and political interests. Here, the actions of the nation state, as well as private, corporate interests and locally mobilised social movements, including the local state, landowners, residents and class and community-based organisations, are important in shaping urban policy.

The chapter will seek to understand urban policy as part of the continuing struggle of states to respond to multiple, interconnected issues related to economic development and the social reproduction and welfare of people living in cities, particularly as they relate to job creation, housing opportunities and the provision of places conducive to well-being. From the popularisation of state welfare spending, driving public policy from the late 1930s to the end of the 1970s, to the (re-)emergence of neoliberalism in the early 1980s, urban policy programmes are intertwined with shifts in the balance of political forces and illustrative of deeply entrenched inequalities in society. Such inequalities, and the social and political tensions associated with them, draw attention to urban struggles arising from people's identities, particularly relating to gender, race, disability, class and the intersections between them.

We divide the chapter into five parts. First, we consider what urban policy is and how it has been defined and understood by different commentators. There is no singular definition or understanding, but rather a plethora of definitions that range from conceiving urban policy as policing people and social control, to policy as seeking to globalise local economies by inserting cities into broader global flows of investment and economy (see Blackman, 1995; Cochrane, 2007; Dikeç, 2007; Robson, 1988). Second, we outline the liberal discourses of government that shape urban policy, in which the primary policy objects have tended to be people defined as deficient in character, skills and aptitude and whose poverty and relative deprivation requires remediation through specific, targeted interventions. This is the so-called 'social pathology' definition of urban policy. We develop the argument by Imbroscio (2013a) that at the heart of urban policy is a moral imperative of government in encouraging self-improvement among segments of the population. Imbroscio (2012a, p 1) suggests that the paramount policy tool is mobility, 'marked by a strong emphasis on facilitating population movement as a means of addressing urban social problems'.

Third, we note that the dominant feature of urban policy is addressing problems of poverty and disadvantage in specific places, leading to area-based regeneration. The dominant theme and feature of urban policy initiatives is intervention in places and the development of local or neighbourhood scales. In this section, we outline the rationale and justifications for place-based policy interventions and evaluate their significance in redressing urban problems. In the fourth section, we describe and evaluate some of the theoretical approaches purporting to explain what urban policy is, with a focus on theories of urban politics (see Logan and Molotch, 1987; Stone, 1989). Finally, we outline how far urban policy is effective in achieving its objectives, and consider who gains and who loses from the process. Given our claim that urban policy is not neutral in its effects, but is shaped by political contestation, the outcomes of policy processes are never assured or guaranteed.

What is urban policy?

There is no simple answer to this question or any single definition of urban policy. The rest of the book will convey the complexities that make up what urban policy is, but suffice it to say that it is characterised by deliberative or purposive intervention by agents in different aspects of the functioning of cities. In other words, urban policy is a function of governing that may occur through government and non-governmental organisations or a combination thereof. Urban policy seeks to respond to social, economic, ecological and political problems in situ or that relate, first and foremost, to particular places. Some of the earliest forms of urban intervention were a response to what Glaeser (2011, p 10) describes as the negative consequences of proximity. These have historically included some dramatic events, such as the onset of contagious diseases spread by dense urban living. The remit of urban policy is potentially wide, and may include seeking to ameliorate the external effects of social, economic and/or ecological events, such as the impact of plant closures on local employment fortunes, or pollution caused by noxious industrial facilities located in close proximity to residential areas.

At its broadest, urban policy seeks to support people defined as in need who lack the necessary means to live in ways to guarantee their health and well-being. Here, urban policy targets processes of social reproduction by providing the basic necessities for life, including access to a minimum standard of housing and a bundle of welfare benefits. The objective is to ensure the reproduction of healthy bodies that may otherwise prevent people from full and productive lives as part of the workforce contributing to economic growth. This interpretation of urban policy conceives of it as driven by economic objectives, in which the productivity of labour needs to be guaranteed by the state through ensuring that minimum levels of consumption of food, clothing and shelter can occur. Some of the earliest state interventions in cities were reactions to the ill health and the malnourished state of the workforce, and provided a social policy response to the problems of people living in poverty and poor housing conditions. In some instances, the responses were private sector-led or a product of philanthropic gesture, including the development of company towns such as Bourneville in Birmingham, Saltaire in Bradford and New Lanark in Scotland (see Figure 2.1).

Figure 2.1: New Lanark

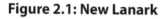

Source: http://upload.wikimedia.org/wikipedia/commons/d/d2/
New_Lanark_buildings_2009.jpg

New Lanark in Scotland was one of a number of model settlements that were constructed in the 18th and 19th centuries as responses to the poor quality of urban settlement and the health threats posed to people by the lack of sanitation and poor air quality. David Dale opened the New Lanark cotton mills in 1785, but it was his son-in-law, Robert Owen, who developed New Lanark into a model village or industrial community. Robert Owen believed that education, work, fair discipline, good housing and health care could overcome poverty and social disadvantage. The settlement contained well-equipped workers' housing, as well as community buildings, including the first infants' school. Robert Owen set out his radical social reformist views in *A new view of society: essays on the principle of the formation of the human character* (Owen, 1813).

Such illustrations show the spatial character of urban policy, or its primary objective in intervening in, and seeking to influence, the geographical distribution of social and economic opportunities, and enabling people to gain access to everyday resources, such as schools, transport and housing. It is the specific spatial or geographical component to urban policy that distinguishes it from other social welfare policy types. Some commentators note that the distinctiveness of urban policy relates to its focus on the city or an urban scale of intervention: that urban policy is seeking to resolve problems that are specifically urban. Thus, for Blackman (1995), the object of urban policy is to enhance the welfare of those who are part of urban society, while, for Cochrane (2007), the targets of policy are people who reside in places labelled as cities. In both instances, the issue of how far there is something that can be characterised specifically as 'urban' or that can be denoted with some precision as 'the city' is raised. This opens up a perennial debate in urban studies about what 'the urban' is or might be understood as, or whether or not problems associated with urban areas are, in Thomas's (2000, p 54) terms, 'distinctively urban problems'.

The shaping of urban policy depends, in part, on the answer to this question. There are two broad schools of thought that have dominated urban planning and policy. The first conceives of urban problems as outcomes of the characteristics of specific places, including the people and objects located in them. Here, the objective of policy is to remedy local deficiencies, such as people lacking the skills and education to compete in job markets, or housing of sub-standard quality, by targeted area interventions. The history of urban policy is replete with examples of such interventions, including, in the 1960s, UK policies relating to housing, education and social services. These included the Plowden

Report in 1967, investigating educational provision and attainment. The report recommended positive discrimination 'in neighbourhoods where children are most severely handicapped by home conditions' (Plowden Report, 1967, p 66). The outcome was the implementation of Educational Priority Areas in parts of London, Birmingham, Liverpool and Yorkshire in the late 1960s, which was described as a compensatory education policy 'intended to offset the effects of socio-economic disadvantage which may restrict the educational opportunities of children from socially deprived backgrounds' (Haggar, 2013, p 1).

The second school of thought notes that what are often defined as problems in places, such as a local skills deficit in a population, are symptoms, not causes, of urban problems. It is suggested that urban problems, and their specific spatial distribution, are created by processes that do not necessarily originate in cities or can be understood by an intra-urban scale of analysis. Rather, they are part of a broader, often global, scale of relations and the product of socio-economic, structural processes beyond the control of local people or city-level governance. As Massey (1984, p 56) says: 'it is not space itself which accounts for the impact ... but social and economic processes operating spatially'. For Robson (1988, p 42), this understanding brings into question the need for any urban policy given 'the general nature of the processes which work against cities'. The implication is that for policy to have impact, it needs to be constructed at a supranational scale as part of intergovernmental relations with the capacity to influence the activities of non-local actors, such as global conglomerates, whose actions in one part of the world may affect the socio-economic fortunes of people and places in other parts of the globe.

Many commentators, such as Haack (1996, p 14), agree that it is difficult to define a specifically urban policy and it may be regarded as a 'fuzzy notion' 'whose precise meanings vary according to context and conditions'. Cochrane (2007, p 13) notes that it is more or less impossible to pin down what urban policy is, or, as he says, there are 'many meanings, not just one' (see Figure 2.2). For Glaeser (2011), urban policies range from small-scale activities of urban government, such as the provision of grants and subsidies to local community groups, to large-scale, sometimes city-wide, initiatives driven by multi-agency partnerships. These might include initiatives such as the Thames Gateway regeneration, an ambitious plan conceived in the early 2000s to regenerate major tracts of land east and south-east of Central London, or major waterfront regenerations, such as London's docklands and the harbour areas of cities such as Baltimore and Boston in the US. For others, such as Dikeç (2007, p 26), urban policy is the exercise of the policing powers of the state, or 'the criminalization of the poor and the close surveillance of the population seen to be problematic'. Here, Dikeç (2007) regards urban policy as part of a class politics and intertwined with the (re)production of social inequalities.

Figure 2.2: Definitions of urban policy

- 'Urban policy is essentially about the welfare of local residents in an urban society' (Blackman, 1995, p 5).
- 'Urban policy includes any policy that is particularly relevant for cities' (Glaeser, 2011, p 111).
- 'Nothing more nor less than the cluster of initiatives aimed at dealing with the problem of cities or the inner cities' (Cochrane, 2007, p 1).
- 'Urban policy ... is a practice of articulation that constitutes space, and institutional practice that defines space' (Dikeç, 2007, p 4).
- 'State activity [which] affects the use of space and the built environment' (Fainstein and Fainstein, 1982, p 16).
- 'a loose collection of policies aimed at addressing or mitigating the effects of apparently distinctively urban problems' (Thomas, 2000, p 57).
- 'Urban policy is ... most fundamentally about places ... that is, urban settlements' (Imbroscio, 2013a, p 3).

Dikeç's (2007) understanding is far removed from the dominant, mainstream accounts that regard urban policy as a neutral, technical activity or part of an administrative, managerial function of governance.

Here, urban policy is treated as benign and operating for the benefit of all. The literature that reflects this is derived from neoclassical economics, which regards policy as part of a process to ensure the efficient operation of markets and the reproduction of socio-economic systems commensurate with the smooth operations of capitalism (Richardson, 1973). It is assumed that the role of government ought to be minimal and that policy interventions should only occur to remove impediments to growth and to ensure that the economic system is operating to enhance people's well-being. The justifications for urban policy include the pursuit of equity and efficiency goals. The former suggests that everyone ought to be provided with equality of opportunity to acquire jobs, goods and services, irrespective of who they are or where they live. This contrasts with the latter, in which the justification for policy is support for urban economies by making the best use of land and infrastructure to enhance productivity and wealth creation.

For much of the 20th century, equity concerns shaped spatial policy, including urban regeneration projects. The post-war period from 1945 saw an intensification of redistributive policy programmes in which an objective was to provide resources to poorer places to enable them to compete with richer cities and regions. The term 'Keynesianism', after the economist John Maynard Keynes, was coined to describe high levels of state intervention in planning the economy and society, and up until the mid-1970s, governments in the UK and elsewhere were committed to equity or seeking to reduce relative poverty and other indices of social deprivation. Urban policy reflected this broader understanding that the good city depended on the redistribution of wealth from richer to poorer people, and from richer to poorer places. The Keynesian settlement began to break down in the late 1970s, and, since then, urban policy has been primarily influenced by efficiency criteria, including the reduction of state involvement in spatial development, the privatisation of welfare and the supplanting of redistribution in favour of wealth creation.

Liberalism, the moral object and urban policy

The dominant political philosophy that shapes urban policy, particularly in Western nations, is classical liberalism or the view that the role of government is to intervene actively in people's lives to create the conditions of (their) freedom. Liberal views espouse a belief in free will, or the rights of individuals to live their lives more or less free from constraint (see Smith, 1776; Hayek, 1944). This is shaped, in part, by individuals' acculturation into the liberal ideals of good living as something to be attained by their exercise of self-discipline and responsible behaviour. Here, the role of government and public policy is to facilitate people's freedom from coercion as part of the process to ensure that their economic well-being, as the paramount objective of life, is guaranteed. For such guarantees to transpire, a minimal, steering role for the state is envisaged, with individuals taking responsibility to behave in ways commensurate with their acculturation into the values and lifestyles that reflect the objectives of liberal government.

These objectives tend to reflect traditional, conservative values of what society is or ought to be, and many commentators regard urban policy as part of a moral discourse seeking to shape citizens' lives. Thus, one interpretation of urban policy as a form of liberal government is as having a disciplining role, or the mobilisation of the state to acculturate people into mainstream society. The objective is to instil liberal values relating to good citizenship, revolving around the virtues of traditional, familial social structures. The subjects of policy are those people deemed to be deviant or operating outside of the norms of society; for Paul Boyer (1978, p viii), commenting on late 19th-century urbanism in the US, social reformers and philanthropists were imposing moral and civic virtue by 'controlling the behavior of an increasingly urbanized populace'. An example was the City Beautiful movement in the US, which, at the turn of the 19th century, was an approach to creating beautiful places as part of an attempt by social reformers to bring civilising sensibilities to poorer people, a process described by Wilson (1989, p 79) as propagating the restorative and 'ameliorative power of beauty' (see Figure 2.3).

Figure 2.3: City Beautiful

Source: http://en.wikipedia.org/wiki/City_Beautiful_movement#
mediaviewer/File:Coral_Gables_street_20100321.jpg

Conceived by middle-class reformers, such as Daniel Burnham, the City Beautiful movement in the US was led by certain architects and urban planners as a reaction to the ugliness of the growing US city. The movement was aimed at making the city more orderly, attractive and liveable in terms of buildings, cityscape and public space, and was influenced by European classical design, especially the Beaux Arts movement. The City Beautiful movement was prominent between the 1890s and 1920s in US cities such as Washington, Chicago and Cleveland. In 1893, Daniel Burnham led the construction of a temporary city at the World's Colombian Exposition in Chicago, which raised the profile of the movement. The height of the movement was in 1909, when the Plan for Chicago, or Burnham Plan, was published, including a network of avenues and parks, especially along the lakefront of Lake Michigan.

Much of urban policy has been shaped by a moral discourse of what the good citizen is or ought to be, with the focus on remaking the characters of individuals relating to their inabilities to function rationally within the world. The evidence of such irrationalities is the lack of participation in the labour market, the inability to acquire skills to compete for jobs and acceptance, by some, of a life at the margins of society, including participation in illegal activities. Analytical attention is focused on what O'Connor (2001, p 4) describes as 'cultural and skill "deficits" rather than the unequal distribution of power and wealth'. These ideas reflect a genre of writing about poverty and inequality in cities and their different explanatory emphases (see Harrington, 1962). The dominant discourse shaping policy interventions in urban problems defines poverty as cultural in origin, or what Harrington (1962, pp 22–4) describes as 'an institution, a way of life'. The prognosis, in policy terms, is the acculturation of the urban poor into mainstream life to assure their behaviour as moral, worthy and responsible citizens. The role of urban policy is to provide support for the (re)moralisation of the poor by instilling values of self-active and responsible actions commensurate with avoiding poverty and its attendant social problems.

This understanding of the urban problem, that is, the shaping of life opportunities by individual character, has been a binding theme in policy prognoses (see Chapters One and Three). It spans the early, classic writings of the urban condition, such as Jacob Riis's account of poverty in New York in the 1880s, the US government's 'War on Poverty' programmes of the 1960s and British neighbourhood renewal policies in the 2000s. At the crux of each is the understanding of the urban problem as beset by what Wilson (1987, p 256) describes as 'concentration effects'. These include the selective outmigration of skilled, affluent people from cities, leaving behind those without the human or social capital to withstand economic downturns or take advantage of economic growth. In his influential book *The truly disadvantaged*, Wilson (1987, p 256) draws attention to an urban underclass, or a category of people characterised by what Peterson (1991, p 617) refers to as their 'subjection, subordination, and deprivation'. Peterson (1991) notes that the urban underclass is understood by conservative commentators as people unable to care for themselves, exhibiting anti-social behaviour and creating reputational effects that contribute to the downward spiral of the places in which they live (see Chapter Three).

For advocates of liberal urban policy, the locational concentration of such people in pockets of poverty requires them to be moved out, or, alternatively, for other people, namely, the successful middle classes, to be moved in, thus exposing the underclass to the discipline of allegedly progressive ways of life (see, eg, DeLuca and Rosenbaum, 2010). Imbroscio (2013a, p 5) refers to this as exchanging one place for another in which what is redistributed 'is the advantage of place itself'. This understanding was evident as early as the 1890s, with Jacob Riis noting that the problem of the New York slums was the nature of the tenant. As Riis (1890, p 273) observed: 'they are shiftless, destructive, and stupid; in a word, they are what the tenements have made them'. Current renditions of this are evident in socially mixed neighbourhood policies, or the understanding that poor areas can be uplifted by bringing in a greater range of people, particularly those with high incomes and a mixture of attitudes and skill sets (see Lees, 2013).

Such processes define what is at the heart of urban policy, what Imbroscio (2012a) describes as the 'mobility paradigm', or the encouragement of people to move as the means to solve urban social problems. British urban and regional policy reflects such a paradigm, with formative regional policy in the 1920s diagnosing the problem of high unemployment as the reluctance, in part, of workers to move to areas of job opportunities. The remedy, in 1928, was the Industrial Transference Board, described by the *Glasgow Herald* (1928, p 13) as 'for the provision of employment for young workers by transference and their better training or alternative occupations'. While later phases of policy, such as the Special Areas Act of 1934, sought to redirect jobs to where people lived, the onus was on the mobility of people and/or things to redress and ameliorate the worst excesses of place-based deprivation. The problems of places, and of the people living there, were often understood as residing in the characteristics of the people and the place (see next section).

The dispersal of population was one of the main tools of 20th-century urban policy and remains central to the governance of cities. It ranges from the British New Towns from the late 1940s, the 'Moving to Opportunity' programmes in the US from 1993 to 1998, to, more recently, the major, often forced, relocation of people from the inner areas of Chinese cities to new suburban housing (see Figure 2.4). The motivations for dispersal vary in each instance. In Chinese cities, the dispersal of residents is motivated, first and foremost, by land speculation, or supplying inner-city locations to global corporate investors as the basis for creating new competitive urban economies. Much of the British New Towns programme, particularly around London, was an attempt to manage the effects of escalating housing and labour costs by decanting people away from the major cities to more affordable locales. In doing so, dispersal was a tool of economic management, that is, seeking to create competitive, lower-cost urban labour markets, and an instrument to create new, affordable housing opportunities in the context of a growing population.

Figure 2.4: Moving to Opportunity

The Moving to Opportunity programme was a 10-year social experiment by the US Department for Housing and Development in the 1990s to help low-income families in poor neighbourhoods move from housing projects and public housing to private housing in low-poverty areas. It attempted to overcome the barriers to mobility by combining assistance with rents and the provision of housing counselling. At the same time, control groups were included to evaluate the effects of the programme: those receiving or about to receive rental assistance only. Five public housing authorities operated the scheme: Baltimore, Boston, Chicago, Los Angeles and New York. The final evaluation found that in comparison with the control groups, those families assisted with counselling, as well as rent vouchers, lived in better-quality housing in lower-crime areas. There were also health and well-being benefits, but there were no effects on their earnings or educational attainment.

The movement of people, particularly in the US, has been centrally concerned with the management and alleviation of poverty, often by breaking up major public housing projects. The popular belief expounded by liberal politicians and academic researchers is that concentrations of poverty are virulent and likely to create a context for different forms of social malaise (see, eg, Case and Katz, 1991). The 'neighbourhood effect' of concentrated poverty has been widely researched, and some findings indicate that people's life opportunities within poor places are constrained (see Brooks-Gunn et al, 1997; Van Ham et al, 2012). These constraints include the lack of job opportunities and social networks, which might otherwise provide support for people to gain access to employment, and exposure to criminality and social disorder, which does not provide 'positive role model behaviour' (Goetz and Chapple, 2010, p 210). Other research points to the socio-psychological effects of living among concentrated poverty, including lack of personal development and low self-esteem (Rosenbaum et al, 2002).

Policy programmes were premised on breaking cycles of deprivation and disadvantage by intervening in areas exhibiting higher-than-average levels of multiple deprivation, relating to indicators such as educational attainment, housing quality and unemployment rates. Donnison (1980, p 27) described approaches to multiple deprivation in cities as 'social policy goes spatial'. In the US, the pathological view of urban problems resulted in a variety of local-level initiatives aimed at 'problem' places, including the Community Action Programme. The remit of the Community Action Programme was to provide services to people in need, with the understanding that the role of public policy was to create opportunities for the urban poor to break their dependence on charity and welfare by acquiring the skills and competencies to compete in urban labour and housing markets (see Figure 2.5). The rationale of the policy intervention was to encourage poor people, and those at the margins of society, to take responsibility for their plight by changing their behaviour and attitudes. Only by doing so could the culture of poverty that held them back be eradicated.

Figure 2.5: Community Action Programme

Community Action Agencies have been running since the 1960s in the US to carry out the Community Action Program as part of the 'War on Poverty'. They are local not-for-profit organisations established under the US Economic Opportunity Act 1964 to provide support for those living in poverty, to help people to help themselves. There are now over 1,000 local agencies throughout the US. They can cover emergency assistance (such as food banks and homeless shelters), education (such as Head Start; the equivalent was the Sure Start pre-school programme in the UK), family development, employment and skills, transportation, housing, and health. The agencies depend on volunteer help, especially from low-income households, and are funded through grants from federal, state and local sources. There have been some issues concerning their governance and relationships with local government, but they remain a primary source of help for many who continue to live in poverty.

Imbroscio (2012a, 2013a) rejects the mobility paradigm, and the policies it encourages, as flawed. He suggests that a key problem is its encouragement of excessive mobility, creating residential instability by rupturing people's attachments to place. For Imbroscio (2013a), the consequence is the potential fragmentation of social bonds, the weakening of civil society and the creation of less neighbourly places. He notes that the 'placemaking efforts of Liberal Urban Policy in the postwar era usually have been more place-destroying than place-strengthening in nature' (Imbroscio, 2012a, p 11). Many studies serve to support Imbroscio's (2012b, p 35) view of the 'crippling popular discontent' of liberal urban policy programmes. For instance, Kleit and Manzo's (2006) study of dispersal policy in Seattle shows that many involuntarily displaced families were not willing to relocate because of social roots and attachment to their neighbourhood. As a policy tool, mobility is likely to have limited effects on people's material circumstances because moving people from one place to another is insufficient to overcome problems of low incomes, poverty and social disadvantage.

Place-based and people-based regeneration

Most urban policy is area-focused, or seeks to intervene in the problems associated with a specific place or territory. It is less likely to be people-based or focused on the needs of particular social groups. As Cochrane (2007, p 3) states, the problem with the definition of urban policy is that it 'starts from area rather than individual or even social group'. The implication here is that the problems of places, such as poverty and social deprivation, reside *within* the area, and are explicable with reference to the social and economic characteristics of the place. The problems of the place are thus explained as a problem of things contained within the place, including the values, attitudes and lifestyles of those who reside there. It is a small step from this conceptualisation of the urban problem, as place-based, to identifying the people contained within the place as the source of the problem. This conceptualisation is all too familiar a part of area-based approaches to urban policy, and it has been the dominant formulation in conceiving of the nature of the 'urban problem'.

The primary target of much post-1945 place-based urban policy was the emerging concentrations of people living in mass housing schemes or projects, often located in peripheral, semi-suburban or isolated parts of cities, far removed from ease of access to urban services. To cater for mass migration to the cities in the wake of a post-war economic boom, housing estates spawned in major cities, ranging from the infamous Robert Taylor Homes on the south side of Chicago to the Red Road Flats in Glasgow (see Figure 2.6). The British council estates, like their counterparts in the French *banlieues* and the US housing projects, became a target of negative stereotyping and, for Johnston and Mooney (2007, p 128), were 'seen as a residual locale of spatialised social problems'. They reflected new forms of residential segregation and the emergence of divided cities. These were characterised by stark spatial differentiations between working-class and middle-class neighbourhoods, and between places defined by their ethnic and racial mix, particularly in the US context, with sharp divisions between black and white areas of cities.

Figure 2.6: Red Road Flats, Glasgow

Source: http://en.wikipedia.org/wiki/Red_Road_Flats#/media/File:Red_Road_Flats,_Balornock_(from_Petershill_Road)_-_geograph.org.uk_-_1224863.jpg

The design and construction of the Red Road council estate by Glasgow Corporation in the 1960s was part of the city's rehousing programme following the tenement clearance and renewal that started in the 1950s. The first three towers in the new modernist Red Road estate were opened in 1966. The Red Road blocks were the tallest in Glasgow. In total, eight tower blocks were built by the local council to house 4,700 people who had previously lived in poor, overcrowded conditions in the city. The Red Road estate became known for crime and anti-social behaviour during the 1970s. There were also technical issues, including the extensive use of asbestos to fireproof the steel frame construction. By the 1980s, two blocks were no longer used for family housing, and were transferred for use by student and the YMCA. Improvements were made to the blocks. In 2003, Glasgow Housing Association took over the estate following a large-scale voluntary transfer process. It was later agreed that the costs of maintenance and improvement did not match the rental receipts and that phased demolition was the answer. By the end of 2014, two blocks had been demolished and tenants have moved out of the only occupied block.

The advent of modern urban policy in the 1960s was a response, in part, to the entwinement of race and poverty. Major demographic changes in the post-war period began to reshape the racial composition of Western cities, and in the US, the migration of black people from southern, predominantly rural areas to northern industrial cities was a feature of the period from the mid-1920s through to the early 1970s. In that period, the proportion of black people living in US cities increased significantly, and racism, manifest in segregated living, unequal access to jobs and services, and poverty, became a much more visible part of everyday life (see Logan et al, 2011). By the early 1960s, the northern cities were characterised by stark social inequalities, and by any measure, black people's material living conditions were significantly worse than those experienced by most of the white population. As Stobaugh (2012, p 248) notes, racial discrimination is 'a ubiquitous reality' and one of the main policy responses was the Model Cities Program set up in 1966 (see Figure 2.7). The programme's remit was to reduce poverty and to encourage alternative forms of municipal government, particularly the development of black urban leaders.

Figure 2.7: Model Cities Program

Set up by the US Demonstration Cities and Metropolitan Development Act of 1966, the Model Cities Program ran until 1974. Model Cities were set up following issues surrounding the initial War on Poverty programme and were aimed at improving the coordination of existing urban renewal programmes, providing additional federal funding and developing alternative governance with better citizen involvement. The programme included more than 150 areas, which received funding to develop five-year Model City projects. These were initially intended to be comprehensive social, as well as physical, renewal programmes. They later focused mainly on bricks-and-mortar renewal. Although Model Cities did have some success in developing a new generation of black urban leaders, there were also issues over governance arrangements, real participation and relationships with local administrations.

The racialisation of urban policy was one of the clear parallels between the US and the UK as concern was expressed by some British, primarily right-wing, politicians about the impact of immigration on the social and cultural traditions of the UK. The most infamous, and widely reported, episode was a speech by the Conservative politician Enoch Powell in 1968. This was the so-called 'Rivers of blood' speech, in which Powell predicted social unrest, including violence and rioting, in British cities if immigration was not curtailed. He conjured up an image of the future based on 'race wars' and the eradication of the 'majority culture'. In inflammatory style, Powell (1968, p 1) said that 'in this country in fifteen or twenty years' time the black man will have the whip hand over the white man'. While most people baulked at Powell's speech, the government responded by suggesting that 'immigrant settlement' was the paramount policy challenge. Thomas (2000, p 51) interprets such views as the product of 'the deep rooted racialisation of white popular and political opinion' that regarded 'black immigration as a territorial threat', requiring, as Marris and Rein (1972, p xvi) suggest, no less than 'the assimilation of the newcomer to the city'.

This understanding shaped the first formal urban policy in Britain in 1968, the Urban Programme (see Table 2.1). The Home Office, the government department initially responsible for the Urban Programme, defined the target areas as places in 'special social need'. These were:

Table 2.1: Area-based urban policy, UK: main initiatives, 1968–2010

Year	Urban policy
1965–76	
1965	Milner Holland Report on London housing
1967	Plowden Report on primary schools/Educational Priority Area (EPA) programme established
1968	Seebohm Report on social services
1968	Housing Act – General Improvement Areas (GIAs) established
1968	Urban Programme, Home Office-led
1968	Community Development Programme introduced 12 Community Development Projects (CDPs)
1974	Housing Act – Housing Action Areas (HAAs) established
1976	CDPs wound up
1977–79	
1977	White Paper on Policy for the Inner Cities
1978	Inner Urban Areas Act
1978	Department of Environment took on expanded Urban Programme
1978	Inner City Partnerships
1979–91	
1981	Urban Development Corporations
1980–81	Enterprise Zones introduced
1985	Estate Action
1988	Action for Cities consolidated entrepreneurial initiatives
1988	Housing Action Trusts
1991–97	
1991	City Challenge partnerships
1994	Single Regeneration Budget Challenge Fund
1994	English Partnerships formed
1995	Estate Renewal Challenge Fund
1997–2010	
1999	New Deal for Communities launched
2001	National Strategy for Urban Renewal launched

localised districts which bear the marks of multiple deprivation ... particularly housing; over crowding of houses; family sizes above the average; persistent unemployment; a high proportion of children in trouble or in need of care, or a combination of these. (Callaghan, 1968, col 1107)

The Urban Programme was modest and funded projects were small-scale and operated through local authorities, who applied to central government for grants to pay for up to 75% of costs. The range of funded initiatives was diverse, and Atkinson and Moon (1994, p 45) note that 'the prime criteria for approval seem to have been race'. Commentators suggest that the Urban Programme lacked any clarity of purpose, with Higgins et al (1983, p 58) describing it as lacking 'a precision of problem definition with no clearly formulated view of what urban deprivation was'. Edwards (1997, p 826) describes the allocation of Urban Programme funds as no better than 'intuitive judgements about, and glimpses from train windows of, pretty depressing places by itinerant civil servants'.

The spatial focus of the Urban Programme was criticised by many commentators for failing to recognise the structural nature of urban problems, or that the problems in places were not necessarily problems of places. This was the conclusion of participants in some of the Community Development Projects, an area initiative funded by the government that ran alongside the Urban Programme from 1970 to 1978. There were 12 projects in total in primarily urban areas, although Atkinson and Moon (1994, p 47) note that 'there were no clearly identifiable and agreed criteria underlying the selection process'. The Community Development Projects rejected social pathology as an interpretive framework and, instead, suggested that the problems of local areas were linked to the operations of national and international economic systems (see Green and Chapman, 1992). The prognosis identified by participants in the Community Development Projects was to reject spatial policies or localised interventions and to suggest the development of scaled policy programmes intervening in broader processes of social and economic change.

This observation was reflected, in part, in 1978, with the Inner Urban Areas Act focusing on the economic, as well as the social, aspects of decline in cities. The Urban Programme was retained and Inner City Partnerships were created in the six largest cities, joining national, local and community interests to encourage a collaborative approach and to bend mainstream resources to clearly defined areas. The term 'urban regeneration' was coined in the early 1980s, signalling the emergence of urban policy based on a property-led response to urban problems, with market-led strategies to lever in private property investment and a transfer of policymaking from the public to the private sector. Urban Programme priorities were changed as projects with a direct economic rather than a social focus were funded. Enterprise Zones relaxed land use controls and provided fiscal incentives in specific areas. Property-led regeneration was exemplified by policy instruments such as City Grants and the Urban Development Corporations, with the assumption that investment in buildings and infrastructure would generate new jobs and wealth and stimulate local economic growth. The objective was to tackle what were seen as market failures in land and property markets. By 1988, these initiatives were brought together under Action for Cities, focusing on physical renewal and the promotion of private sector investment, with resources focused on 57 Urban Priority Areas.[1]

This focus reinforced the place-based emphasis of urban policy, including a change in policy response in 1991 with City Challenge taking greater account of social, as well as economic and environmental, issues in disadvantaged urban areas. Local authorities took the lead in bids to government, although successful bids were required to take a partnership approach with business involvement and community support. Eleven areas were awarded City Challenge funding over five years, and the programme then informed the wider Single Regeneration Budget in 1994. The Single Regeneration Budget comprised two elements. First, English Partnerships was given its own ring-fenced funding within the Single Regeneration Budget. Its remit remained property-based: to undertake land clearance and reclamation and assist in providing premises in rundown areas. It brought together elements of previous property-led regeneration: Derelict Land Grant, City Grant and English Estates. The second element, the

Single Regeneration Budget Challenge Fund, operated for 10 years and combined 18 previously separate programmes. It was aimed at bringing about economic, social and environmental regeneration in local areas, leveraging in private sector funding, as well as 'bending' mainstream programmes.[2]

When the New Labour party came to power in 1997, policies to tackle social exclusion were introduced through a combination of programmes aimed at individuals, vulnerable groups and the most deprived neighbourhoods. The emphasis was on public service reinvestment and reform, tackling what were seen as spatial elements of deprivation by 'narrowing the gap' between the most deprived neighbourhoods and the rest. The New Deal for Communities was launched in 1999, with a Pathfinder programme targeted at the most deprived neighbourhoods, each area receiving £50 million for intensive regeneration in five thematic areas: health; housing and liveability; education; jobs; and crime. There was a strong emphasis on community control of budgets and the direct election of local people to local boards. Round Two in 2001 targeted 39 deprived neighbourhoods. The National Strategy for Neighbourhood Renewal, launched in 2001, targeted the 88 most deprived local authorities. The focus was on holistic intervention, local control, the coordination of services and community empowerment. Floor targets were introduced to measure departments' progress against their performance in the most deprived areas. The Neighbourhood Renewal Fund was also launched in 2001 and was distributed between the Local Strategic Partnerships in the 88 most deprived local authority areas.

These programmes have since been disbanded, and since 2010, UK urban policy, in the ways described earlier, has withered and central funding has all but disappeared. The onus is on local authorities to 'self-help' and to generate funding through partnerships with the private sector, while experimenting with decentralised forms of governance, backed up by strong local leadership. As we discuss in Chapter Eight, the onset of economic austerity in the UK, combined with the actions of the Coalition government elected in 2010, was the catalyst for change.

Urban policy, politics and governance

The form and content of urban policy is shaped by a mixture of both national and local politics, and by struggles between different interest groups seeking to shape urban political processes. To understand urban policy, one needs to situate it within the subdiscipline of urban politics, and to recognise that policy is a political object of government, as well as an active ingredient in shaping the nature of local political processes and outcomes. In other words, urban policy and politics are indissoluble, and there is complexity as to what policy is and what the socio-political forces are that shape and bring it into being. Any understanding of urban policy, therefore, has to pay attention to the nature of state or governmental interventions in urban systems. Such interventions are political in nature, and theories of urban politics seek to explain some of the socio-political processes that shape the substance of policy. Urban politics is the contestation between different social groups about the meaning and materiality of urban life, and it is illustrated by the actions of various protagonists, ranging from community groups to politicians and property developers, seeking to assert their vision and viewpoint of what the good city is or ought to be.

There are a host of theoretical positions seeking to explain the nature of urban policy. Foremost is the notion that we live in post-political times, or a socio-political context in which the dominant process is the search for consensus in crafting policy. Since the early 1980s, governments have encouraged partnerships between local governments and the private and non-governmental sectors, and the ideological landscape has changed to one whereby responding to the needs of urban citizens is, so is it alleged, less about political contestation, or debate about who gains or loses, and more about developing consensus around agreed and shared objectives. The understanding reflects a pluralist theory of urban politics, which conceives of policy as the outcome of competing interest groups (see Dahl, 1961). It is assumed that people know their interests and are able to collectively organise to pursue these. Pluralist theory notes that groups have more or less equal access to political institutions and that the government will represents their interests.

Any outcomes in terms of the shape of policy will reflect the diverse interests represented to government.

Here, the process of urban policymaking is bargaining between groups and the outcome is a 'best fit' that represents the broad cloth of opinions. What we see is the definition of policy as part of a rational, technical, problem-solving activity, in which the state is impartial and indifferent to lobby groups or specific, particular interests. The understanding is that whatever the urban problems are, they can be overcome by the application of appropriate procedure and process, underpinned by professional-bureaucratic support. Pluralist theory has been criticised as making unrealistic assumptions about the policymaking process, and failing to recognise that many people are prevented from involvement in policy, or may be unable to access groups to represent them (see Mills, 1956; Bachrach and Baratz, 1962). There is a failure of pluralist theory to recognise that urban policy processes are more likely to be characterised by the selective incorporation of opinions, depending on the relative powers held by, and vested in, different groups and individuals. For Mills (1956), society is characterised less by pluralism and more by power elites, such as corporate organisations, which shape the contexts in which urban policy seeks to intervene.

Alternative theories of urban policy and politics consider power to be a key concept and that the policy process does not necessarily entail consensus or equity of outcomes. Rather, urban policy is part of a contested political process that tends to favour some groups over others. The strongest version of this understanding is neo-Marxism, which regards urban policy as part of state activity to create conditions conducive to capital investment and accumulation. Here, government operates in the interests of corporate organisation by creating urban economies conducive to the realisation of profit. Where the politics arises is in the struggle between those propagating profit-seeking actions and those opposing them in favour of welfare. The notion of collective consumption has emerged to explain urban policy as a response to the welfare needs of citizens in those areas of life where goods and services are collectively consumed, and in which their provision is not necessarily guaranteed by either the state intent on minimising public spending or private sector organisations intent on maximising profit through high and often unaffordable prices. Collectively consumed goods include transport, education and health care, and the extent to which the state supports provision for them, either by direct provision or by subsiding costs, is part of a class struggle or political contestation between different groups.

For Castells (1978), urban social movements spring up to organise around issues of collective consumption, and are the basis of an urban politics that shapes urban policy processes. Urban policy as politics is the struggle to (re)produce the means for people to live, and the lives of many poor people in urban society are shaped by crises of collective consumption, or the unaffordable nature of many goods and services necessary for their sustenance. Such crises, including expensive transport and the lack of affordable housing, are a feature of most cities, and in places like London, they spawn a politics of periodic protests in which the high costs of urban living are to the forefront. A recent example is the New Era housing estate in East London, in which a threat to acquire its ownership by US investment company Westbrook Partners in November 2014 sparked protests by residents over fears that rents would triple. The Lever family owned the estate for more than 80 years, with rents as low as £163 a week for a three-bed flat. A resident said that they had been 'advised to sign 12-month contracts with a rent increase of 10%, after which the rent would be raised to "market value" of £2,000 a month' (quoted in Jessel, 2014, p 1).

The understanding of urban policy as a response to collective consumption issues is persuasive but also beset by some limitations. Cochrane (2007) notes that the focus on consumption issues as the driving force for shaping urban policy is too narrow and does not acknowledge the role of policy in shaping production and economic development. Theories of urban politics emanating from the US have sought to redress this by noting that urban political processes primarily revolve around economic development and, in particular, the realisation of profit through land and property development. The formative scholars are Logan and Molotch (1987, p xxvii), who note that 'local conflicts over growth are central to the organisation of cities'. This understanding led to the rise of growth coalition theory, which locates policy as part of the exercise of elite power, particularly around economic growth objectives. The objective of policy is urban growth, and the coalition operates to gain the support of local constituents to assure that growth is secured as the centrepiece of urban policy.

A later, more developed, version of growth coalition theory is urban regime theory (Stone, 1989), which argues that power is fragmented and regimes arise between local governments and private actors to enable policy to be constructed and implemented. While regimes are understood to be complex and outcomes indeterminate and never certain, Stone (1980, p 980) suggests that public officials are predisposed 'to favour some interests [primarily business elites] at the expense of others'. Given the significance of capturing growth, urban policy, as part of regime politics, is constructed around place-marketing and partnerships. This perspective, which some refer to as the New Urban Politics, notes that urban policy as politics is 'about local economic development, not least the competition between city governments for investments and infrastructural projects, downtown commercial revitalisation, and the conflicts surrounding development or redevelopment' (MacLeod, 2011, p 2632).

Growth coalition and regime theories are useful because they identify urban policy as a mechanism that seeks to unlock economic growth and boost urban competitiveness. This chimes with the period since the early 1980s in which urban policy shifted, politically, towards the Right in pursuit of the neoliberalisation of the city. By this, it is understood that policy was seeking to reduce public expenditure and direct state involvement in redressing the problems of cities, and, instead, to replace this with arm's length, even private, modes of governance. The growth logic is a new form of what Larner (2000, p 5) calls 'political-economic governance', premised upon 'the extension of market relations that privilege competition, efficiency, and economic success' (Dikeç, 2006, p 62). Here, the rise of the competitive city is simultaneously part of an allegedly new era of post-welfare, and urban policy is inextricably part of the governance of cities in ways whereby the primacy of the market, and private interests, are paramount.

An evaluation of urban policy

After decades of urban policy, the problems of cities have not gone away and, in many respects, they have worsened (see Shaw and Robinson, 1998; Gripaios, 2002; Katz, 2010). In a wide-ranging commentary on the failures of government policy in the US, Mead (2011, p 1) notes that after medical care policy, 'the single greatest policy failure of modern America is urban policy'. Despite the billions of dollars spent on programmes to alleviate poverty, crime and drugs use in the inner cities, Mead (2011, p 1) concludes that there is not much to show for the effort, concluding that 'the state of the American inner city is an unacceptable human tragedy'. Likewise, Shaw and Robinson (1998, p 52), in commenting on UK inner-city policy, note that 'disparate urban initiatives have been developed in a random and ad hoc manner, with little recourse to strategic or longer term thinking'. They note that most policies are developed 'to remedy the mistakes of a previous generation of urban initiatives', and that it has been difficult to detect much progress over the decades of different programme initiatives (Shaw and Robinson, 1998, p 61).

The possibilities of policy failure are linked to the short time frames for intervention; as Warwick (2012, p 4) observes, 'decision makers have notoriously short attention spans, looking for rapid policy effect rather than sustained long term improvement'. Coordinating policy in a fragmented system of governance also reduces the potency of policy because it can be unclear who has responsibilities for the different elements of policy development, delivery and implementation. Cochrane (2007) identifies the 'search for coordination' as one of the enduring themes of urban policy, a recognition that the problems of cities are not the single responsibility of any one government agency but are cross-cutting and require multi-agency interactions for their solution. For Cochrane (2007), opening up urban policy to a plethora of governance institutions is unlikely to lead to better policy or to solutions. This is because many of the problems are intractable and 'unmanageable'.

It is notoriously difficult to implement urban policy in ways whereby its objectives are met (Robson, 1988). Policy failure is more likely than not, and various commentators attribute this to a mixture of reasons, including the lack of funds. In 1988, Robson noted that the problem with UK urban policy was not that it lacked resources, but that policy programmes were piecemeal and ad hoc, and lacked long-term political backing. Urban policy has rarely been the highest priority of governments, and Atkinson and Moon (1994) suggest that political support for urban policy has been 'half-hearted' and the resourcing of programmes has been minimal and grudgingly provided. O'Connor (1999, p 79), in the US context, suggests that policy initiatives have 'been "small-scale," "modest," and "inadequate" in the form of a variety of tepid or short-lived community development programs'. Robson (1988) also points to the inefficiencies of targeting, in which policy usually targets the symptoms rather than causes of urban decline and disadvantage.

A debate about urban policy is how best to govern the problems of cities. Douglas Yates (1978) coined the term 'the ungovernable city' to highlight the more or less impossible nature of seeking to manage the problems of urban areas. For Yates (1978), the governance of urban policy is chaotic, and its practitioners are unable to make coherent decisions or develop effective policies and programmes. He suggests that 'city governments are at once too decentralized for overall policy making and too centralized to be truly responsive to its citizenry. By the same token they are both too independent of and too dependent on higher-level government' (Yates, 1978, p 49). This chimes with a popular view from the conservative right-wing that (urban) policy is restrictive of individual choices and competition in land and property markets, and may inhibit entrepreneurial activity. Glaeser (2011, p 250) notes that US state controls over inner-city development, including restrictions on land use, prevent economic growth, and that 'government does no good by propping up particular places'. He suggests that ineffective regulation and often chaotic, and contradictory, policies become the target of subsequent state intervention to ameliorate the problems that they have created.

Katz (2010, p 13) notes that these 'narratives of failure' about urban policy can be challenged by a 'counter narrative of limited successes, less dramatic but no less important'. Robson (1988, p 143) concurs by suggesting that in the 'diverse sets of policies there have indeed been some successes'. Robson (1988) highlights improvements to the physical environment, including the provision of new and improved facilities in inner areas. A recent example is the Olympic Park in London, in which, after the Olympic Games, people have access to an extensive park, including sporting facilities such as a velodrome and swimming pool. Most inner areas in the UK have seen major house-building programmes, including the refurbishment of older, existing stock, contributing to the stabilisation of the size of urban populations and, in some instances, a reversal of population decline. Environmental improvements are evident too, including the opening up of river frontages, such as the south bank of the river Thames in London, and the provision of new public spaces previously inaccessible. An example of the latter is the Granary Quarter in King's Cross, London, in which what was previously an industrial site, dominated by unused railways sidings, has been opened up to provide public meeting places and a range of residential, retail and leisure facilities (see Figure 2.8).

Despite the undoubted impacts, and benefits, of urban policy, there are some who claim it to be part of a process contributing to social disadvantage by widening inequalities in society (Mooney, 1999). The argument is that the plight and problems of poor people in cities are neglected, even exacerbated, by the administering of policy, while the demands of powerful corporate interests are prioritised. The evidence includes the privatisation of housing stock and the construction of new upscale dwellings in inner cities that are priced well beyond the means of many people and do not address the housing problems of people on low incomes. Commentators also note that urban policy has emphasised economic development at the expense of focusing on social and community concerns, and has provided private developers with powers to impose their visions of place-making (Imrie and Thomas,

Figure 2.8: Granary Square, King's Cross, London

1999). Here, urban policy is avowedly partisan and political and part of a system of corporate governance in which major private sector investors control access to resources, particularly land.

The punitive, disciplinary nature of urban policy, or policy as part of (re)moralising urban subjects, is also highlighted by authors who note that urban policy still tends to blame poor people for their poverty and lack of resources and skills. Crump (2002, p 581) rejects spatial metaphors such as the 'deconcentration of the poor' as unhelpful as they reduce the understanding of poverty to individual deficits and justify 'simplistic spatial solutions to complex social, economic, and political problems'. Such solutions tend to target poor areas for 'upgrading', and much urban policy in the US, UK and elsewhere continues to pour resources into uplifting places in which, as Newman and Ashton (2004, p 1151) suggest, 'the reality ... looks more like a new process of gentrification than ... community-controlled redevelopment'. This is, in Lefebvre's (2003) terms, part of an anti-democratic urbanism and the pursuit of policies that far from solving urban problems, are part of the problems themselves.

Conclusions

There is no simple way to understand urban policy partly because it is difficult to define or pinpoint precisely the objects or subjects of urban policy interventions. One difficulty is identifying urban policy as a discrete policy arena distinctive from other forms of government intervention. While it is possible to identify, at specific times and in specific places, the development of policy interventions aimed at problems located in urban settings, it is not clear that they are 'urban problems' per se, or problems that are ameliorated by recourse to specific area-based urban interventions. It is more helpful to regard urban policy as part of the totality of policies seeking to intervene in, and ameliorate, social and economic crises relating to people's welfare. Here, we also concur with Cochrane (2007, p 137), who suggests that because we live in an urban society, it is 'difficult to specify the boundaries between urban and other social policies'.

While there is complexity in the form and content of urban policy, including how to define it, much of it in the contemporary period is ideological in seeking to propagate neoliberal values. These relate to the promotion of self-help, minimal government and entrepreneurial, private sector-led governance as the basis of urban futures. Here, the focus of much contemporary policy is a new urban pathology in which, for Lindekilde (2012, p 113), 'the individuals' free choice is made the locus of change and regulation'. Urban policy is part of the vanguard in the recapitalisation of urban spaces, facilitating some of the means for global corporate investors to gain access to valuable land and property. Urban policy is also implicated in creating a 'certain spatial order' that, for Dikeç (2007), does not represent or respond to the needs of the many. In Chapter Three, we consider this aspect of policy and ask who the city is for and what the role of policy is in facilitating people's access to, and uses of, the goods, services and spaces of the city.

Notes

[1] There were also two area programmes that were housing estate-based. In 1985, Estate Action emphasised physical improvements to social housing

and estate-based management involving tenants and diversifying tenure. Housing Action Trusts, introduced in 1988, focused on the social and economic regeneration of communities, as well as the built environment, and were the first attempt by central government to transfer stock out of local authority control.

[2] In partnership with Regional Development Agencies and city councils, English Partnerships (EP), now superseded by the Homes and Communities Agency, had helped to establish 21 Urban Regeneration Companies (URCs) to drive forward regeneration in cities and subregions. Three pilots were set up in Liverpool, East Manchester and Sheffield to work with a range of private and public sector partners, including Local Strategic Partnerships, to redevelop and bring investment back into the city. Since 2000, a further 18 URCs were set up.

SUMMARY

There is no singular definition or understanding of urban policy, but, rather, a plethora of definitions that range from conceiving urban policy as policing people and social control, to seeing policy as seeking to globalise local economies by inserting cities into broader global flows of investment and economy. Urban policy is shaped by a moral imperative of government to encourage self-improvement among segments of the population. In recent years, the ascendency of neoliberalism, or the idea of minimal state intervention, coupled with facilitating freedom of choice, has become a powerful ideological orientation shaping public policy. Urban policy is increasingly a means to facilitate investment flows, and to create contexts for property-led development as the dominant way of place-making. An outcome appears to be the development of new socio-spatial inequalities in cities in which urban policy is not neutral or benign in its effects, but is a constituent element in shaping livelihood and habitability in cities.

RECOMMENDED READING

One of the best books on urban policy is Cochrane (2007). Readers should also consult Robson (1988), Johnstone and Whitehead (2004) and Dikeç (2007). In the US context, Imbroscio's (2013a) book *Urban America reconsidered* is excellent. For a longer historical overview of US urban policy, see Euchner and McGovern (1993).

WEB LINKS

The website of the Urban Institute, a Washington DC think tank, is informative and interesting (see: http://www.urban.org), so, too, is the website of the Center for an Urban Future, a New York-based organisation (see: https://nycfuture.org/about). In the UK, the Centre for Cities is a notable organisation (see: http://www.centreforcities. org), so, too, is The Policy Exchange (see: http://www.policyexchange. org.uk).

3

whose right to the city?

Introduction

One of the key objectives of urban policy is social control and the targeting of populations that contain risky subjects, or those that are a threat to the integrity of society and likely to engender social degeneration and moral collapse. From the English workhouses, originating in 1388, to the New Deal for Communities that started in England and Wales in 1998, social deprivation and people and places defined as 'deprived' have been a target of/for policy seeking to police the problems and tensions related to poverty and social disadvantage. In most cities, problems are described and defined by statistics, collected and interpreted by governments, which seek to show the differences between segments of the population relating to a range of social and economic indicators. Such indicators are a basis for the policing of the population and the formation and formalisation of policy interventions.

This chapter describes and evaluates the significance of policing the city and controlling the population as part of broader government objectives to create safe and ordered urban spaces. Such safety relates to individual health and well-being, and has moral overtones in relation to permissible behaviour and activities in public space. We outline the different ways in which issues of safety, security and control are intertwined with moral and political debates about 'the good city', and how these shape approaches to policing individuals' behaviour and the conduct of everyday life. We argue that discourses of urban order/ disorder and policy interventions, designed to manage the inhabitants of cities, raise broader questions about the acceptability of different social identities in urban life, and suggest that, all too often, such interventions reinforce dominant sociocultural norms along a range of axes, including gender, ethnicity, sexuality and disability.

We divide the chapter into three main parts. First, we outline the discourse of, and debates about, unruly places and urban disorder, which has been a dominant meta-narrative of the city over the last century (see Pile et al, 1999). We consider how particular spaces and groups of people living in the city have, in different contexts, come to be conceptualised as 'unruly' or 'undesirable', and show how such conceptualisations are embedded in stereotypical images that ascribe certain attributes and behaviours to particular groups. Second, we evaluate urban policy interventions to control so-called 'disorderly' places and people in the city. These include policies to redesign, secure and 'sanitise' urban public space(s) by marginalising and managing people and groups defined and labelled as 'undesirable' or 'uncivilised', and who are deemed by corporate actors and government officials not to fit into the (re-)imagining of what convivial public environments are or ought to be, that is, as spaces of consumption.

Third, we consider how far urban policy has sought to respond to the needs of diverse groups in the city, or whether, as some have suggested, policy does little to challenge the experiences of sexism, racism and homophobia that are often a feature of urban life. As we suggest, the city is experienced by certain categories of people and groups, such as children, minority ethnic groups, women and disabled people, in ways whereby their access to goods and services, including the occupation and usage of public space, may be compromised by a combination of thoughtless design and discriminatory attitudes and practices revolving around essentialised assumptions about identity. An important question, raised by Ray Pahl (1975 [1970]) 40 years ago, is how far urban policy is implicated in (re)producing social inequalities of access to resources in, and the opportunities of, urban areas. Who does the city belong to, and how is it fashioned in ways whereby some benefit and others do not?

Unruly cities and urban disorder

A key theme in urban studies is the unruly nature of cities characterised by social inequalities and the potential for conflict and disorder between different segments of urban society. A swathe of urban studies has documented the dangers in, and people's fears of, the city and threats to personal safety and private property (see Raban, 1974). Some of the earliest descriptions of the city conjure up its dangerous spaces, inhabited by unmanageable populations in places that are 'no go' areas for the respectable majority. Popular fictional accounts of the city describe dangerous spaces, such as Arthur Conan Doyle's (1891) short story 'The man with the twisted lip'. Here, Doyle's fictional character Sherlock Holmes is alluding to the criminality of the city:

> Between a slop-shop and a gin-shop, approached by a steep flight of steps leading down to a black gap like the mouth of a cave, I found the den of which I was in search ... I found the latch and made my way into a long, low room, thick and heavy with the brown opium smoke, and terraced with wooden berths. (Doyle, 1891, p 2)

The language of breakdown and disorder to describe urban society continues, as exemplified by newspaper headlines of riots in British cities in the summer of 2011, for example, 'Flaming morons: thugs and thieves terrorise Britain's streets' (*Daily Express*, 2011) and 'Mob rule' (*The Independent*, 2011).

These headlines, and associations of the city with disorder, are sensational and simplistic and fail to capture the systemic, structural nature of urban social relations. Some commentators suggest that cities are far more ordered than they seem, and that there are regularities in the social relations in urban spaces (Pile et al, 1999). Others note that how we are to define 'disorder/order' is not obvious, and Mooney (1999) suggests that to label something as 'disorder' is to know what 'order' is or ought to be. For Mooney (1999), both terms are ambiguous and reflect partial understandings of what urban life is and how broader structural forces shape it. Understanding how places and people in the city become known and differentiated as disorderly or orderly can be related to what Lefebvre (1991) refers to as the representations of space. These are the conceptualisations of space developed and deployed by spatial technicians, such as planners, architects and scientists, and represented through physical forms, such as maps, plans and models of the city form and process.

Representations of space, while only partial visions of the city, have been powerful in urban planning and policy. The ideal of conquering the disordered city, or imposing a new order from above, has been a key goal of urban planners since the 19th century. Visions of creating urban order are evident in the work of modernist architect Le Corbusier, for example, who developed grid-like patterns of high-rise buildings to address overcrowding and poor housing in cities (see Figure 3.1). Similarly, the creation of post-war 'new towns', such as Basildon and Milton Keynes in the UK, was a planned attempt at an antidote to the

Figure 3.1: Le Corbusier's Berlin Unité: a new urban order?

Source: http://en.wikipedia.org/wiki/Unité_d%27Habitation#mediaviewer/
File:Corbusierhaus_Berlin_B.jpg

pollution and overcrowding of many large urban areas and at addressing the housing needs of a growing population. What becomes clear is that imposing or creating particular spaces of order has not always led to a more ordered city, but quite the contrary. As Pile et al (1999) note of gated communities, while they have been built on the basis of insecurity and designed to shut out unruliness, they may have the effect of causing resentment from those outside them and serve to intensify social divisions in the city (see Chapter Four).

The unruly city thesis is related to the city as a place of strangers, comprising a collectivity of individuals, many of whom do not know each other. This presence of strangers signifies the modern city as a place characterised by the breakdown of sociability and the rise of fragmented, often socially distanced, communities. Raban (1974, p 15) described the city as comprising a 'community of people who are strangers to each other', while for Bauman (1995, p 126), 'city life is carried on by strangers amongst strangers'. These interpretations reflect the work of Georg Simmel (1921, p 322), who, in the 19th century, observed major rural to urban migration and conceived of the stranger as a newcomer or 'the person who comes today and stays tomorrow'. The stranger is the new immigrant or outsider or the person that may disrupt and challenge place-based social identities. Conversely, the good city is conceived by some as a place that welcomes the stranger, an environment of liberal values that offers refuge and hospitality (Mumford, 1961).

Unruliness is often attached to categories of people seen as not fitting into society, or individuals with physical and behavioural symptoms that do not accord with sociocultural norms. This discourse emerged in the 19th century as the state began to characterise and segregate people as the 'worthy' or 'unworthy' poor through legislation such as the 1834 Poor Law Amendment Act in England. While the association of the city with criminality was rife in the 19th century, other groups were also segregated based on their social and physical status and this had an imprint on cities. For example, disabled people have often seen their movement and presence in public spaces subject to legal constraints and informal social controls through discriminatory attitudes and practices (Imrie, 1996). State policy towards disability in urban areas is etched in social, welfare and planning policies that rarely recognise impairment as an important, or intrinsic, part of experience, and most of the urban environment is designed with little forethought as to how disabled people seek to move about and gain access to public spaces.

In some instances, legal controls relating to the occupation of urban environments were enacted, most notably, the notorious 'ugly laws' in a number of cities in the US (Schweik, 2009). These emerged in the late 19th century and were only repealed in many states in the 1970s. These laws, otherwise known as 'unsightly beggar ordinances', sought to control the use of impairment as a pretext for begging in public spaces and were designed to keep streets clear of individuals defined as 'diseased, maimed, mutilated, or in any way deformed, so as to be an unsightly or disgusting object' (quoted in Schweik, 2009, p 1). Anyone deemed to break the ordinance was likely to be arrested, fined and, in some instances, jailed or placed in an almshouse. Susan Schweik (2009, p 208) describes the ugly laws as part of a penal regime characterised by the systemic 'structural and institutional repulsion of disabled people'. The control of disabled people's presence in public space was also part of the rationale for asylums, and throughout the 19th century, there was a building boom of such environments. In 1892, *The Builder* magazine described the asylum in the following terms:

> a traveller will be sure to spy, in some comparatively secluded position, a great group of buildings, which by their modern air ... their tall chimney stacks and ... their bulky water tower, seem to belong rather to the busy towns than to country seclusion. (Quoted in Jarrett, 2012, p 28)

The segregation and exclusion of disabled people is just one example of how people's identity and their perceived characteristics, whether related to disability, class, race, gender or sexuality, have become the basis for divisions and exclusions in the city. Separating and differentiating groups has been a key part of explaining and tackling urban disorder. In the US, for example, the notion of an urban underclass became a pervasive trope in explanations of urban poverty in the 1960s and remains a current, if controversial, concept (see

Figure 3.2). US sociologist William Julius Wilson (1978, p 1) referred to the underclass as a 'massive population at the very bottom of the social class ladder plagued by poor education and low-paying, unstable jobs'. Wilson was particularly referring to the black population in US cities, and notions of an underclass have frequently had racial connotations associated with the existence of African-American 'ghettos' in cities struck by industrial decline. Policymakers associate the term with deviant forms of behaviour, such as crime, joblessness and a dependence on state welfare. Explanations for the underclass remain contested, but the core focus is who is to blame for poverty and people's living conditions.

Figure 3.2: The 'underclass': a contested concept

The idea of an 'underclass' has a long history but remains one of the most controversial concepts in the social science, as well as popular, lexicon. In the 19th century, commentators were alluding to a 'dangerous class' emerging in industrialised cities, whose members were united by their idleness and criminal behaviour. Recent definitions describe the underclass as a group of people who have become excluded and detached from the labour market and employment, or who are economically inactive. More contested are those definitions which suggest that members of this underclass share particular cultural characteristics and attributes, such as a reliance on state welfare, anti-social behaviour and an antipathy towards work.

A controversial influential figure in the underclass debate is the US commentator Charles Murray (1984). Murray suggests that the post-war welfare settlement created a class of people detached from the labour market and reliant on state welfare. His thesis is problematic for the way it associates the intrinsic characteristics and identities of people to the notions of moral decline and fecklessness. For example, in *The bell curve*, Hernstein and Murray (1994) hark back to eugenicist discourse to suggest that the poverty and marginalisation of African-Americans is partly connected to lower levels of intelligence.

Murray's notions of an 'underclass' have been criticised for applying a negative, derogatory term to a particular group of people, as well as failing to address the structural factors that have led to unemployment and poverty in urban areas (Wacquant, 2007). His ideas have had an influential effect on politicians, particularly in the US, and have partly contributed to the growing discourse of 'welfare scroungers', as well as the systematic withdrawal of benefits from certain groups, such as single mothers and the young unemployed, which has become a key part of neoliberal governance in recent years.

While debates about the existence of an 'underclass' have had less traction in the UK than the US, descriptions of the so-called 'feckless poor' are deeply rooted in British history, and, as Seabrook (2012) notes, have their roots in at least the Elizabethan Poor Law of 1601. The notion of the idle and the undeserving became particularly widespread from the 1960s, with young people, especially men, a key target of stereotyping as a cause of urban disorder (see Chapter Five). This can be seen most recently in relation to the riots that occurred in British cities in the summer of 2011. In a piece entitled 'London riots: the underclass lashes out' in the *Daily Telegraph*, journalist Mary Riddell (2011, p 1) describes the riots in the following terms: 'Feral kids ran amok.... Over a few days in which attacks became a contagion, the capital city of an advanced nation has reverted to a Hobbesian dystopia of chaos and brutality.'

In urban policy, 'disordered' people and places often become intertwined in a toxic mix. In France, Dikeç (2007, p 8) notes how the *banlieues*, or suburban social housing estates, have become associated in the popular and political imagination with 'alterity, insecurity and deprivation', with the ethnicity of their inhabitants increasingly cast as part of the problem, fuelling fears about immigration and 'Islamic fundamentalism' (Dikeç, 2006, p 161). Similarly, in the UK, certain areas have been deemed 'dysfunctional' by policymakers and politicians, with blame put on residents as the cause of this dysfunctionality. In 2010, Conservative minister Iain Duncan Smith caused controversy by noting that the workless inhabitants of Merthyr Tydfil, the town with the highest percentages of Incapacity Benefit claimants in Britain, should '"get on the bus to Cardiff"' to find work' (Adamson, 2010, p 1). His comments are typical of policy pronouncements that 'blame the victim' without acknowledging the structural factors (are there any jobs available?) that shape local employment and labour markets.

As Dave Adamson (2010), a local academic who contested Duncan Smith's comments, wrote at the time:

> The problems of Merthyr Tydfil are structural and not grounded in personal characteristics of the local population, which was responsible for much of the iron and steel production that built the British empire.... Rather, there has been an economic collapse of local employment opportunities and now more than 30 years of joblessness. If the local population is resigned to high levels of worklessness, it is because that is the reality of local economic opportunity.

Urban policy is frequently caught up in broader societal and moral debates about where responsibility lies for poverty and people's living conditions, and, as we show in the next section, it is concerned with 'ordering' those groups who fail to fit into government agendas about responsible forms of citizenship.

Managing places and people

The association of the city with disorder has led to an urban policy focus on managing the behaviour of urban inhabitants, as well as securing particular spaces in the city. An important part of urban regeneration since the early 1980s has been the rise of security and surveillance in public spaces and residential neighbourhoods to ensure safe and orderly conduct in the city. In this section, we consider some of the ways in which urban policy has sought to manage threats of disorder by seeking to safeguard urban spaces and to change or manage the behaviour of urban inhabitants.

Urban policy as the management of social disorder

Urban policy is concerned with managing spaces and people in the city deemed to be problematic. Those associated with disrupting the urban order are often constructed as from 'problem places', slum dwellers or those living in deprived housing estates or inner cities. These areas, and their inhabitants, may be labelled as a threat to the city and civilised society, and attempts to manage their populations have been, and remain, a significant part of urban policy. In the UK, for example, a background of deindustrialisation, high youth unemployment and political marginalisation of specific parts of the urban population, particularly black and minority ethnic groups, was the context for social unrest in the 1980s, as exemplified by major street riots in inner cities in 1981 and 1985. The prevailing political discourse of that time was a 'law and order' agenda, or the understanding that rioting was the expression of criminality to be dealt with by the policing and punishment of offenders. In 1981, Prime Minister Margaret Thatcher, in responding to riots in Brixton, London, rejected any sense of them being a response to poverty or social deprivation and said that 'No one should condone the events.... They were criminal, criminal' (quoted in Bateman, 2012, p 96).

Attempts to manage disorder by clamping down on crime and anti-social behaviour have become a key tenet of urban policy worldwide. One of the early initiatives in the UK was promoting environmental design to reduce crime, targeted at modernist housing estates associated with criminality, vandalism and anti-social behaviour. A genre of writings, from Jane Jacobs's (1961) *The death and life of American cities* to Alice Coleman's (1985) *Utopia on trial*, has associated environmental design with people's behaviour and notes that specific physical features are likely to foster crime and anti-social activities. Coleman (1985, p 177) outlined the understanding that 'human behaviour tends to deteriorate under the stress of inappropriate habitats'. The work of Oscar Newman

(1972) on defensible space has been important in drawing attention to the role of architecture and urban design in reducing opportunities for crime while creating places for positive social interactions. Such ideas have shaped the work of new urbanists (see Chapter Seven), and have been incorporated into government policies aimed at crime reduction and prevention (see Figure 3.3).

Figure 3.3: Secured By Design

Secured by Design (SBD) was inaugurated in 1989 to 'design out crime', in particular, to prevent burglary from dwellings. The scheme is operated by the Association of Chief Police Officers (Kane, 2011, p 4), which defines SBD as 'a police initiative to encourage the industry to adopt crime prevention measures in development design to assist in reducing the opportunity for crime and the fear of crime, creating a safer and more secure environment'. This pronouncement has primarily been aimed at commercial premises and residents seeking to secure their premises, and builders are able to sign up and become accredited in the construction of SBD buildings.

Cozens et al (2007, p 361) note that different evaluations of SBD indicate that it does 'reduce crime and the fear of crime'. A study by Teedon et al (2009) of Scottish properties where SBD-standard doors and windows were installed notes that housebreaking fell by 26% and attempted housebreaking by 59%. Tenants said that they felt much safer in their homes and less fearful of crime. Minton (2012) is sceptical about SBD and suggests that it is perverse for the police, and not architects, to be designing places. For Minton (2012, p 62), residential design based on SBD is producing 'bizarre places ... small windows ... security grills, electronic security, anti climbing paint'.

One of the most publicised, and copied, policy approaches to the perceived threats of urban social disorder was developed by Rudolph

Giuliani and his mayoral administration in New York City in the 1990s. Along with the police commissioner at that time, William Bratton, Mayor Giuliani developed a zero-tolerance approach to what was otherwise perceived as petty crime and low-level criminality. The thesis shaping zero-tolerance policies was outlined by Wilson and Kelling (1982) and labelled 'broken windows'. For Wilson and Kelling, the notion of a broken window was a metaphor for deviance and threats to the social order. Any neglect of the first signs of disorder in a neighbourhood, such as tolerating the breaking of windows, graffiti and other acts of vandalism, was likely to encourage further retrograde behaviour and create a downward spiral of neighbourhood decline into criminality. In a critique of the Giuliani approach, Harcourt (2001, p 23) suggests that policy based on broken windows reduces 'trust between the police and the community, and violates basic rights and scapegoats the homeless and other people we deem disorderly'. He argues that the broken windows approach does not reduce crime, but, rather, detracts from the more pressing issue of poverty, which is the context for so-called disorderly behaviour (see also Mitchell, 2003).

Several commentators have argued that urban policy has become ever-more associated with a repressive, penal state (Dikeç, 2006). Dikeç (2007), for example, argues that much of what was social and welfare policy in cities has been supplanted by the police state, and that urban policy is less about reformist measures to take people out of poverty and more about securing safe spaces for investment by reducing crime and disorder. Likewise, Cochrane (2007) refers to the emergence of a post-welfare policy discourse relating to safety and security in cities. This is characterised by policy seeking less to redress the causes of poverty and inequality that seem to be the basis of urban protest and more to police and punish those who engage in activities deemed to be a threat to the urban social order. For Goetz (1996, p 539), urban policy in the US is 'about controlling the dangerous classes' by pursuing policies that are implicated in the 'criminalisation of the poor'. This is witnessed by a rise in policing and community safety programmes that Goetz (1996, p 541) describes as top-down initiatives that focus on social deviance and appear to reflect a form of paranoia constructed around the fear of crime rather than its actuality (see Figure 3.4).

Figure 3.4: Securing the city?

There are numerous examples of the criminalisation of the poor and the use of repressive urban policy types shaped by the mentalities of policing. For instance, in advance of the 2014 soccer World Cup tournament, the Brazilian government attempted to secure safe spaces through a process known as 'pacification'. In the most high-profile cities, such as Rio de Janeiro, pacification involved the deployment of Police Units seeking to retake crime-ridden territories controlled by drugs dealers. This included the use of military weapon and tactics, and, subsequently, the creation of community-based policing in cooperation with local residents.

In France, Dikeç's (2006, 2007) work demonstrates how police have sought to quell social unrest in the *banlieues* by utilising repressive tactics. As President Hollande, quoted in Erlanger, 2012, p 1) declared, a core part of French urban policy is 'security, which means that the next budget will include additional resources for the gendarmerie and the police'. For Moran (2012, p 1), this approach is no more that pouring fuel on the fire of unrest; as he notes, 'it is no exaggeration to say that the police have been involved in the immediate causes of practically every episode of rioting in French suburbs since 1981'.

Since the early 2000s, a strand of urban policy has been the management and control of groups thought to pose threats to individual and national security. In the wake of the terror attacks of 11 September 2001 in the US and in the UK in London in July 2007, one response by governments has been assimilating groups that are deemed to be outsiders into the value set of the cultural majority as a prerequisite to assuring community cohesion and harmony. The task is to target populations that contain risky subjects, or those that are a threat to the integrity of society and likely to engender, or at least contribute to, social degeneration and moral collapse. The government's focus on societal integrity and the management of dissent in relation to core values is particularly targeted at Muslim people, who are often presented as a potential 'enemy within', characterised as not only resistant to learning about, and reproducing, the cultural values of the dominant culture, but also as sources of instability by, purportedly, propagating social practices antithetical to (Western) democracy and social integration.

Two of the more visible policies adopted by British governments are Community Cohesion, which purports to promote social integration, and Prevent, a programme aimed at counterterrorism. Husband and Alam's (2011) review of both policies notes that while Community Cohesion appears to promote social integration, albeit by requiring Muslim people to assimilate into, and accept, the dominant values of a non-Muslim society, Prevent is more likely to divide Muslim and non-Muslim communities, and to work against the integrationist ethos embedded into the Community Cohesion programme. This is because Prevent is based on the assumption that terrorism is more likely than not to be nurtured in Muslim communities, and this makes them 'legitimate targets of suspicion' (Husband and Alam, 2011, p 4). Prevent can be seen as an erosion of human rights principles, while Community Cohesion offers no more than 'a political nurturing of toleration' and assimilation into the dominant sociocultural value system. The former constructs minority groups, such as Muslim people, as 'deviant others', while the latter panders to nationalist feelings and views of what constitutes 'proper citizenship'.

One solution proffered by state officials to challenge and overturn such pernicious discourses is a universalist politics of recognition. Yet, as the authors rightly argue, this does not recognise distinctiveness or 'individuals' and communities' quite different needs and priorities' (Husband and Alam, 2011, p 219). Community Cohesion and Prevent may be regarded as examples of degenerate policy design, or programmes that create new tensions and problems of social order rather than the amelioration of them. For Husband and Alam (2011, p 208), they contribute to the stigmatisation of Muslim communities, while failing to address 'the fundamental causes of radicalisation or intergroup tensions and political disinterest'. Husband and Alam suggest that such causes are rooted in systemic poverty and social marginalisation relating to class inequality. The important message here is that the understanding of people's social exclusion ought not to be reduced to categories of race, religion, cultural type or identity per se. Rather, a focus on class, and its intersections with ethnicity and other social bases, provides a basis for a more coherent understanding of multiple deprivation and its social manifestations, which is a topic we return to in the penultimate part of the chapter.

Creating safe spaces in the city: managing the public realm and securing investment spaces

One of the most important urban policy interventions by governments in terms of managing the city is providing and maintaining public space, and responding to the competing claims of groups to gain access to, and usage of, the public realm. The vision statements and strategy documents of many city councils refer to the need to maintain effective public space(s). This is often defined as the (re)production of highly controlled environments in which people's behaviour is based on the discharge of tightly defined, prescriptive rules and quasi-legal regulations. Consider Dublin City Council's (2011, p 11) argument for a public realm strategy; it states that:

> How public spaces are planned, designed and built, how clean they are, and how safe we feel while using them influence both the quality of our experience of the city and how we feel about it as the place in which we live, socialize, visit or work.

It also notes that the 'quality' of the public realm 'affects the city's competitiveness and ability to attract investment' (Dublin City Council, 2011, p 8). Here, the paramount concern for the City Council is the (re)creation of the public realm as a safe space for consumption.

The existence of, and ideas about, public spaces in the city that are accessible and usable by all has often been associated with the notion of democratic rights. Public space was not just something to be occupied and used by all inhabitants of the city, but a meeting place for expressions of democracy: a place of free speech, or where people could come together to protest or express their views. One of the perennial themes in urban policy literature is the erosion of the public realm, or at least the subsuming of public space to the goals of safety and economic competitiveness. Mitchell (2003) and Minton (2006) document the decline of the public ownership of space and the rise of the private sector's acquisition of public environments. Their work suggests that the process of privatisation of the public sphere is akin to the creation and perpetuation of exclusive spatial enclaves in which city spaces are primarily transformed into sites of commodification, seeking to promote corporate capital accumulation and wealth generation. Part of the rationale of the 'renewed' public sphere is to ensure people's access to, and involvement in, the new spaces of consumption.

Such access is also premised upon creating safe and secure public spaces to enable consumption to occur without threat or hindrance. A number of strategies have been deployed in order to secure urban investment spaces, and these include creating privately managed zones off-limits to 'socially undesirable' behaviour. Business Improvement Districts (BIDs) (described in more detail in Chapter Four) illustrate the increasing securitisation of urban space. The privatisation of urban policy (outlined in Chapter Four) is intensifying in a context whereby major redevelopment projects incorporate significant private ownership of, and control over, what were previously publicly owned sites. This is most evident with retail-led regeneration, and some of the biggest schemes, such as Liverpool One and Westfield Stratford City in London, are described by Minton (2012, p 1) as 'privately owned and privately controlled places, policed by security guards and round the clock surveillance' (see Figure 3.5). Minton (2012) regards such spaces as private estates and a step back to the late 18th and early 19th centuries, in which, prior to the coming of local government, urban areas, including the streets and 'public' spaces, were owned and controlled by private landlords.

These environments, while ostensibly public places, operate by virtue of a complexity of private legal rules and regulations that define who has the right to be there. It is not clear how such rules are set, or what

Figure 3.5: Liverpool One

Source: http://en.wikipedia.org/wiki/Liverpool_One#mediaviewer/File:Wall_
Street,_Liverpool_ONE

the permissible limits on behaviour are. Minton (2009) highlights this
by recalling how the developer of Liverpool One, Grosvenor, ignored
her request for information about their rules regarding people's access
to, and use of, the public realm. She had more luck gaining access to
the Estates Management Strategy for Stratford City, which states that
'the public will generally have access to the site except where there are
good reasons for restricting access' (quoted in Minton, 2009, p 31). The
statement is vague and it provides scope for a broad interpretation of
what access is or should be. It is not subject to democratic scrutiny
or control, and it reflects the values of the private managers, who do
not need to account for the rules that they invent to govern what are,
purportedly, public environments.

Such rules are related to securitisation strategies that range from the
(re-)aestheticisation of urban space to the public presence of private
security police forces. It has become commonplace to secure public

spaces, particularly high-profile public buildings, by use of a defensive aesthetic or architecture, characterised by bollards, fences, gates and other elements to restrict access and movement. Coaffee (2004, p 201) refers to such architecture as a 'ring of steel' and provides a description of the central shopping area in Belfast in the 1970s: 'where access to the centre was barred, first by concrete blockers and barbed wire, and then later by a series of high metal gates'. Designing counterterrorism features into public spaces has become an official part of both US and UK (urban) policy, referred to by Németh and Hollander (2010, p 20) as 'the fortification of the built environment'. They cite Marcuse (2006), who suggests that much high-profile public space in New York City has become off-limits to the public due to security restrictions, and that 'the city has been secured *from* the public rather than *for* it' (quoted in Németh and Hollander, 2010, p 22; emphasis in original).

Governments and policymakers, then, have become ever-more preoccupied with managing public spaces, which means controlling behaviours and maintaining order within these spaces. While one element of this involves a 'law and order agenda', the other side of this coin involves initiatives to engender 'responsible' behaviour more generally among city residents. The making of the (self-)responsible and active citizen is also the subject matter of nudge theory, or what some refer to as libertarian paternalism (Jones et al, 2011). Nudge theory chimes with liberal government agendas that seek to dismantle centralist, prescriptive directives in favour of freeing up individuals to act in ways commensurate with attaining self-directed goals relating to lifestyle, employment and well-being, and it has become increasingly visible in shaping urban policy or specific interventions in cities to improve health and well-being.

An example of nudge theory in practice is Figure 3.6, which shows a sign at Waterloo railway station in London encouraging people to walk to work as part of a perceived health benefit. The message is designed less to coerce people into particular ways of behaving and more to highlight options or choices by outlining the relative benefits of behaving in one way as against another. Bovens (2008, p 208) describes this 'as a manipulation of people's choices via the choice architecture, i.e. the

Figure 3.6: Seeking to shape people's behaviour: a 'nudge' directory board

Source: Rob Imrie

way in which the choices are presented to them'. Another example is shared space or the redesign of streets to create calmer, more convivial, spaces. Shared space has sprung up all around Europe and North America and the objective is to calm traffic by eradicating a formal street order, including traffic signs, crossing points and pavements (see Figure 3.7). The understanding is that by merging pavements and roads into single surfaces, and by removing direction signs and instructions to users about conduct in space, uncertainty about people's behaviour will be induced in those using shared spaces. A consequence is that users, particularly motor vehicle drivers, will proceed with caution and their responsiveness to others in shared spaces will be enhanced.

Research suggests that shared space does not necessarily create the behaviour that it is supposed to engender, that is, users proceeding with caution due to the lack of signs and a formal street order. Rather, it appears that the street order, dominated by motor vehicles, is barely changed, and that shared space is not effective in changing the way people behave (see Imrie, 2012, 2013). For some categories of users,

Figure 3.7: Shared space, Brighton

Source: Rob Imrie

such as vision-impaired people, research shows that shared space may endanger their lives because there is no longer a pavement as an exclusive, protected space (Imrie, 2012). Vision-impaired people navigate by following boundaries between the pavement and road or identifying physical fixtures that enable them to orientate themselves. By ignoring the significance of pavements and demarcated or edged boundaries in facilitating vision-impaired people's ease of mobility, shared space environments are illustrative of a broader problem in which the bodily needs of specific people are not necessarily considered to be an important constituent element of (urban) policy formulation and implementation.

Social identities and the rights to the city

An important, if underdeveloped, observation about urban policy is its potential contribution to reinforcing value systems that do not challenge the dominance of sociocultural norms relating to how bodies are labelled and, consequentially, how people may be assigned specific bodily identities. The labelling of people, marked out by the colour of their skin, their gender or a perceived bodily impairment, is a powerful process in society that may render it difficult for them to gain access to different goods, services and resources in cities. A plethora of research documents the manifold ways in which sociocultural processes are implicated in creating unequal urban geographies based on the essentialisation of people's bodily identities (Mitchell, 2007; Dyck, 2010). Examples range widely from homophobic attacks against gay and lesbian communities, which may force them to relinquish rights to be in certain public spaces, to the construction of thoughtless design that prevents disabled people gaining ease of access to housing, workplaces and everyday environments. In both instances, different groups' rights to occupy space are withheld and/or not recognised by society.

One claim is that urban policy seeks to reproduce the efficient city or places dominated by the mobile, productive, masculine body and ways of being. In the context of gender, for example, urban geographers have sought to draw out the interrelationship between patriarchy and urban forms and processes. Feminist geographers have shown how the city 'confines women to traditional roles within the family' (Peake, 1993, p 416), how their assumed responsibility for domestic labour creates barriers to mobility and how inequalities between men and women, including the threat of violence, manifest themselves in how urban space is designed, such that women are excluded from or are 'ill at ease' with particular spaces (Peake, 1993). Chant (2013) notes that women are more likely than men to be disadvantaged in relation to access to decent work, the acquisition of skills, financial and physical assets, intra-urban mobility, personal safety, and security, and are underrepresented in urban governance, particularly in the global South. Similarly, a recent United Nations report on the *State of women in cities 2012–13* noted that women are failing to gain from the economic growth and prosperity of urban areas (UN-HABITAT, 2013).

Women are only one group marginalised in terms of their everyday experience of urban labour markets and environments. The same could be said for children, for whom the designed environment is not scaled to their body sizes and in which they are endangered, disproportionately to the population as a whole, by poorly designed roads and traffic systems. Data show that children are particularly at risk in relation to urban road systems, and in 2012, 2,272 children under the age of 16 were killed or seriously injured on the roads in the UK (Department for Transport, 2013). Some research indicates that the space for children's play and recreation has been transformed by a mixture of public policy and parental controls; as Karsten (2005, p 275) suggests, the 'space of the street used to be a child space, but … it has been transformed into an adult space'. Others note that the content of most (urban) public policy is impervious to children, and rarely identifies them as a specific part of the population or a group whose needs may differ from adults (Brooks-Gunn et al, 1997).

This is revealing of policy exclusions, silences and absences, and is particularly to the fore in relation to issues of sexuality. Commentators have highlighted the latent homophobia that shapes the experiences of lesbian, gay and transgender people in the city (Hubbard, 2008). City spaces tend to reflect heteronormative values, and public policy rarely departs from, or challenges, this value system. Hubbard (2008) refers to the design of 'straight spaces' in cities, such as male and female public toilets, and notes that these revolve around traditional sex stereotypes or heterosexual bodily ideals. These are spaces that are insensitive to bodies that do not conform to the 'standards' of heteronormativity, and, as Hubbard (2008) suggests, reinforce in a very public sense the 'not normality' of bodies that cross established sex/gender boundaries. Figure 3.8 sets out a recent blog posted by an Irish student, which was published in the US newspaper *The Huffington Post* and went viral on social media, describing the effects of such experiences in very personal terms.

Figure 3.8: Homophobia in the city

As part of a university anti-homophobia campaign, Irish student Olan Harrington wrote a letter entitled 'The Day I Held My Boyfriend's Hand' describing his experience of homophobia in Cork city.

> "I held my boyfriend's hand the other day. I caught it and held it until we reached the main gates of University College Cork, as I usually do on campus, only this time I didn't let go after we'd passed through. We moved along the Western Road, toward Washington Street, and as we reached the innards of Cork City, something strange lingered over me. I had become anxious, and soon I wasn't speaking. I was afraid. In my silence, I shot glances around, searching for anyone who might do us harm. I felt an unease as cars slowed down next to us.
>
> I wondered whether they would shout 'Faggot!' or 'Queer!' at us, as they had done before when I had been in previous relationships or had otherwise felt like showing my love and affection through the simple act of hand holding.... That day I felt so scared that I became angry at the homophobia that I had ignored since my teens, and I felt so angry that I couldn't let go. I held my boyfriend's hand all the way to Paul Street in the centre of the city."

Source: http://www.huffingtonpost.com/olan-harrington/the-day-i-held-my-boyfriends-hand_b_6271910.html

While such design exclusions may be described as thoughtless, they reveal deep-rooted prejudices against particular cultural variations and lifestyle choices. Weisman (1994), in a powerful critique of 'man-made' places, coins the term 'discrimination by design' to describe the exclusion and marginalisation of particular groups in the city. She refers to the ways in which the physical environment is planned, designed and built on the basis of entrenched power relations, which render some groups oppressed and excluded from public space at the expense of others. Weisman (1994) argues that for inequalities manifest in, and generated by, the built environment to be addressed, changes in who has the power to plan and design these environments are required. The same point might be made of urban policy given its role in the planning and functioning of cities, and over the past few years, there have been calls for urban planners and practitioners to recognise the needs of diverse groups and to involve them in decision-making about policy (see Chapter Five).

Discussing the relationship between urban policy and gender in the UK, Grimshaw (2011) argues that prior to 1997, there was little emphasis on addressing gender inequality in terms of the processes or outcomes of regeneration programmes. This is despite the fact that most single parents are women and that they 'are amongst the poorest in society but the most active in communities' (Grimshaw, 2011, p 329). While the New Labour government's emphasis on community involvement in regeneration partnerships brought more of a focus, she argues that the results have been uneven. For example, a national evaluation of the New Deal for Communities concluded that men were more likely to take up formal positions of power in regeneration partnerships than women. Women, she argues, participate in different ways to men, through informal community organising, and often in ways that go unrecognised by formal regeneration structures.

Research into the involvement of disabled people in urban regeneration programmes has shown that they fare little better. Imrie (1996) has demonstrated how disabled people are excluded from decision-making forums in the context of access to the built environment. This has often led to building initiatives (public and commercial buildings, as well as housing) failing to meet access requirements for wheelchair users and other groups. Similarly, in exploring the Single Regeneration Budget, Edwards (2003) found that disabled people were often not recognised as part of the community to be involved in regeneration partnerships. There was an assumption among regeneration practitioners involved in the Single Regeneration Budget that disabled people should be associated with particular types of initiatives, particularly those focused at getting the unemployed into training or the labour market, and not necessarily seen as people with the capacity to participate in decision-making processes. We discuss these dynamics, or the politics of community involvement, further in Chapter Five and note that they have a very real impact on how different groups come to experience the urban arena.

Conclusions

The notion of the disorderly and unruly city is difficult to dispel and it is reinforced by media reports that conjure up images that project an ongoing urban crisis. From sensational reports about the negative climatic effects of urban lifestyles to the reporting of crime, violence and poverty in cities, the impression conveyed is of urbanisation at a tipping point, and that in order to sustain a civilised life, significant changes in people's behaviour and patterns of sociability will be required. The question of 'Whose city?', and who has the rights to inhabit and occupy urban space, is embedded into the socio-political values that shape urban policy. Urban policy is an active intervention in shaping the rights to public space. In many cities, urban order is characterised by what Mitchell (2003) describes as a street order marked by racism, sexism and homophobia. Such order has rarely, if at all, been challenged by urban policy, and there is evidence that, like other forms of public policy, it reinforces values and practices that do not encourage public expressions of difference that depart from sociocultural norms and practices.

SUMMARY

The chapter outlined how urban policy is concerned with the management of disorder and unruly activities and policing city spaces to ensure that an urban order is maintained. Securing people's safety is a paramount part of urban policy, and this ranges widely from creating safe streets and neighbourhoods, free from crime, to providing defensive architecture to thwart possible terrorism against public and corporate spaces. The concern with disorder reflects a moral stance embedded into urban policy about what the good city is or entails, who has the right to occupy space, and what constitutes right and appropriate behaviour. The chapter suggested that the moral nature of urban policy is problematical because there is evidence that certain people, and their lifestyles, are categorised as immoral and become a target of policing and social control in ways whereby they may be excluded from public space.

RECOMMENDED READING

The edited book by Pile et al (1999) provides an excellent overview of themes embedded into this chapter. On urban policy and the penal city, see also Cochrane (2007, ch 5) and the various writings of Louis Wacquant and Mustafa Dikeç.

WEB LINKS

It is worthwhile looking at the Secured by Design website (see: http://www.securedbydesign.com) and the site of the European Forum for Urban Security (see: http://efus.eu/en/). The site Neighbourhood Scout shows how places in the US are rated by safety (see: http://www.neighborhoodscout.com/neighborhoods/crime-rates/top100safest/). There are many 'safer cities' initiatives and one of the informative sites is UN HABITAT (United Nations Human Settlements Programme) (see: http://unhabitat.org/safer-cities/).

4

privatisation and entrepreneurial urban policy

Introduction

While much urban policy addresses issues of social reproduction and consumption, economic regeneration has always been a feature of policy programmes. Seeking to boost local economies became the paramount theme of urban policy in many Western countries in the wake of deindustrialisation and the breakdown of Keynesian social and welfare policy in the 1980s. The dismantling of state-centred expenditures and the shift towards market solutions placed the emphasis on 'self-help' in directing local politicians towards cultivating and capturing economic growth as the means to boost incomes and consumption and to enhance the livelihoods of urban citizens. Growth coalitions and property-based interests attained centre stage, and urban policy revolved around major property-led regeneration (PLR), characterised by the provision of urban infrastructure, such as roads, office parks, retail centres, new dwellings and telecommunications.

Infrastructure provision provides cities with the potential to capture flows of global investment, engage in place-marketing and diversify local labour and housing markets. This chapter outlines and evaluates the importance of PLR, noting that while it has always been part of urban policy programmes, it became the dominant aspect of city building worldwide throughout the 1980s and 1990s, and still retains an important place in policy today. It is particularly associated with privatism and the understanding that urban policy has, in different periods, encouraged the privatisation of places and the erosion of the public realm. The more extreme examples are gated communities or urban enclaves characterised by elites living in luxury separated from the poor. This chapter explores the manifestations of privatism in different contexts, and draws on examples from different parts of the Western world, including the US, Australia and the UK.

The chapter is divided into four parts. In the first section, we define 'privatism' and chart its emergence in urban policy since the 1970s. The emergence of 'privatised' urban policy was part of a broader critique of the Keynesian social and economic welfare settlement, a critique that precipitated privatisation in various forms in many areas of public policy. The second section discusses the impact of privatism on urban politics and mechanisms of governing, most particularly through the 'rolling back' of state control of urban policy and the emergence of public–private partnerships. These changing modes of governance imply not just different relationships between the state and private sector organisations, but also different ways of 'doing' urban policy, described by Harvey (1989) as a shift from 'urban managerialism' to 'urban entrepreneurialism'.

In the third section we outline the key manifestation of privatised urban policy in the form of PLR, in which governments have sought to encourage major, often speculative, investments by global property companies in land and real estate development. In the fourth section, we note that entrepreneurial forms of urban policy have, if anything, increased in scale and popularity since the 2000s. As we argue, one of the key criticisms of property-led, entrepreneurial forms of urban policy is that it is creating increasingly privatised spaces within the city that serve to deepen social divisions, as the emergence of Business Improvement Districts (BIDs) and gated residential communities bear witness to. We conclude by reflecting on some of the understandings of, and dilemmas presented by, privatism in urban policy, which shows little sign of abating today.

The emergence of privatism in urban policy

The notion of privatism, defined by Barnekov et al (1989, p 1) as 'a reliance on the private sector as the principal agent of urban change', emerged as part of urban policy discourse in the early 1980s. It was part of a critique of the perceived ineffectiveness and inefficiency of the welfare state stemming from so-called New Right, neoliberal politicians and governments (see Figure 4.1). In the UK, following the fiscal crisis and economic depression of the 1970s, Prime Minister Margaret Thatcher's Conservative government came to view the welfare state as stymieing economic development as a consequence of over-regulation and over-bureaucratisation. New Right commentators argued that a rolling back of state influence was required to allow the market free reign in stimulating economic growth (Friedman, 1962). Such an ideology was to change both the way in which the 'urban problem' was understood, and the governance arrangements through which urban initiatives were delivered.

Figure 4.1: What is privatism?

'Privatism' is support for the private sector and the market as effective ways to deliver services, generate wealth and promote individual freedom. It is connected with the ideology of neoliberalism, associated with individuals such as Adam Smith (1776) and Friedrich Hayek (1944). Hayek's concern was how individuals could maximise their personal freedom and autonomy. He suggested that state intervention worked against individual choice and liberty. Neoliberal schools of thought emphasise the market as a way of distributing wealth and resources, and favour minimal state intervention.

These principles reflect how neoliberal, or New Right, governments engage the private sector and develop privatising strategies in economic and social policy premised on assumptions about the benefits of the market. These include:

> that the private sector is inherently dynamic, productive
> and dependable ... that private institutions are intrinsically
> superior to public institutions for the delivery of goods and
> services ... that market efficiency is the appropriate criterion
> of social performance in virtually all spheres of community
> activity. (Barnekov et al, 1989, p 1)

In the 1980s, privatisation in economic and public policy
included: the sale of public assets and services to the private
sector, such as water, electricity and public housing; the
contracting out of state services to private providers and the
creation of a pseudo-market within state agencies, for example,
the creation of the purchaser–provider split in the National
Health Service; and cutting state regulations and bureaucracy,
such as planning controls or taxes on businesses, in order to
encourage private sector innovation and development. The
objective was to foreground the private sphere in the context
of the 'individual' and the 'family', and to promote the self-
reliance and entrepreneurialism of individuals as a counter to the
dependency claimed to be part of distributive welfare regimes.

In dealing with the consequences of deindustrialisation that many
cities in the developed Western world were experiencing, including
high unemployment, poverty and growing socio-spatial inequality,
there was a growing conceptualisation from the late 1970s that
urban decline would only be reversed by addressing cities' economic
fortunes. The New Right's solution put emphasis on cities as engines
of economic growth. In the UK context at least, the construction of
the urban problem as one of economic decline had begun prior to
the Conservative government's election to power in 1979. The 1977
White Paper 'Policy for the inner cities', produced by the then Labour
administration, noted that a lack of private sector investment due to
broader economic changes was a significant factor in the decline of
inner-city areas, and recommended a significant role for the state in
addressing the urban challenge (Imrie and Thomas, 1999). With the
election of the Conservative government in 1979, this interpretation of

the urban problem continued, but with a difference: local government and the public sector were to be pushed back, allowing the emergence of governance arrangements that placed the private sector in a partnership, or sometimes leadership, role in economic development.

Privatism was associated with an interpretation of the urban problem as economic decline, in which the fortunes of cities were intimately intertwined with their national economies. The response in terms of urban policy was a supply-side one, with governments expected to provide the infrastructure and create the political-economic conditions conducive to attracting private businesses and enterprises, thereby facilitating local economic development and, in turn, national economic growth. It was suggested by government ministers in the 1980s that economic development would create 'trickle-down' effects for local communities, with private sector investment leading to job and wealth creation and social benefits. The private sector was perceived as the answer to cities' social, as well as economic, ills, albeit indirectly. A persistent theme and criticism running through much literature on privatism in urban policy is that 'trickle down' either fails to occur or occurs very unevenly across communities and spaces within the city (Imrie and Thomas, 1999; MacLeod, 2011).

The New Right's conceptualisation of, and response to, the urban problem manifested itself in ways that are still readily visible in contemporary urban policy. Foremost were the new urban governance arrangements that it ushered in. In common with the directions taken by governments in relation to all spheres of policy, that is, seeking to contract out policy development to non-governmental and private sector organisations, the state was to have a reduced role in managing and funding urban regeneration. Partnerships between the private and public sector were to become commonplace, and new types of relationships were to be formed between the private sector and local government. The substance of urban regeneration also became focused around physical, property-led regeneration, with deregulation of land-use planning tools and other incentives providing a means through which to attract and foster private development.

Urban entrepreneurialism and the changing nature of urban governance

One of the biggest shifts created by the New Right's free market ideology was a reorientation of the role of the state in delivering social and economic policy. No longer was the state to have a direct redistributive role in providing welfare or managing the economy and wealth creation; rather, it was to facilitate, and enter into, partnership with the private sector. The Conservative government in the UK saw local government as representing the worst excesses of the interventionist welfare state, and throughout the 1980s, it sought to alter and ultimately reduce the financial and political powers of local authorities (Atkinson and Moon, 1994; Imrie and Thomas, 1999). Government policy during this time became more centralised, leading to tensions in central–local government relations.

The reconfiguration of the role of the state, and local government in particular, had impacts on urban governance and the management of urban regeneration strategies, described by Harvey (1989) as a shift from urban managerialism to urban entrepreneurialism (see Figure 4.2). Urban entrepreneurialism implies not only new institutional arrangements, for example, the emergence of public–private partnerships as the drivers of urban growth, but also that local governance bodies engage in entrepreneurial activities and 'ways of doing' in order to attract investment and facilitate job creation.

Figure 4.2: Understanding urban entrepreneurialism

Harvey (1989) describes the shift from 'urban managerialism' to 'urban entrepreneurialism' to denote changes to how cities in deindustrialised nations are being governed. The term 'urban entrepreneurialism' has become a core part of the vocabulary used by urban policy analysts, and it describes the following:

- ■ A shift to public–private partnerships or other networks and alliances in urban governance.
- ■ Refocusing public sector resources on attracting investment and the deregulation of planning controls.
- ■ Strengthening inter-urban competition as cities compete with one another to attract global flows of investment and workers.
- ■ Repackaging cities as sites of consumption and spectacle by exploiting and selling the unique characteristics of 'place'.
- ■ The public sector often assuming the risks of urban development, while the private sector reaps the benefits.

These characteristics are not exhaustive, and how they become manifest is tied up with the local socio-political relations of particular cities. The 'entrepreneurial city' implies a substantive shift in both the nature of institutional governance arrangements and the actions that are needed to enable cities to attract capital and to compete on a world stage.

Shifting institutional relationships: public–private partnerships

Public–private partnerships, or growth coalitions, became part of the institutional landscape of cities in the 1980s as cities saw the emergence of business elites who became increasingly involved in leading local economic development (Cochrane et al, 1996; Tickell and Peck, 1996). The emphasis on public–private partnerships in the UK borrowed from the US approach to urban redevelopment that had been in place since the post-war period. From the 1950s in the US, increased federal expenditure on urban renewal led to an arrangement in which state subsidies were provided to enable the private sector to redevelop rundown inner-city areas (Barnekov et al, 1989). In this context, the government created the conditions for private redevelopment by acquiring parcels of land that needed development and selling them at a reduced rate to developers. The business sector in the US became increasingly influential in urban development at this time, characterised by the setting up of business-led development committees in many US cities.

While it is debatable how far the influence of the business community extended in the same way in the UK, the 1980s saw a growing influence of business elites engaging in partnerships with local authorities. Tickell and Peck (1996), for example, document the growth of business elites in Manchester as part of a reorientation of local governance towards state entrepreneurialism. The zeal with which Manchester's local authority sought to engage in different types of partnership arrangement with the private sector led to the involvement of businessmen (and Tickell and Peck stress the focus on business*men* rather than business*women*) in some of the most powerful positions in the city's institutions. This, in turn, created new hierarchies of influence, as well as different ways of doing urban politics, in which 'business relationships, personal friendships and other "informal" links' became far more significant (Tickell and Peck, 1996, p 597).

The 1980s were marked by the emergence of unelected bodies appointed by central government to steer urban regeneration, thereby displacing powers from local government. These bodies were led by business or private sector leaders, and the most high-profile in the context of British urban policy were the Urban Development Corporations (UDCs). These were appointed by central government between 1981 and 1993 to take charge of economic development and regeneration in 13 designated areas, many of which included inner-city brownfield sites. The UDCs were the example *par excellence* of the privatisation of urban policy. They sought to reorient the governance of urban regeneration from locally elected governments to single, private sector agencies, and to change the substance of regeneration activities by creating conditions conducive to a strong business climate. While their aims included the development of housing and social facilities, their main focus was land reclamation and physical redevelopment. To carry out these tasks, the UDCs were accorded special powers to acquire land and bypass local governance arrangements (see Imrie and Thomas, 1999).

The power of the UDCs as a mode of urban governance was their single agency status, directly accountable to central government, and their ability to 'leapfrog' the politics and perceived intransigence of local government. The then Secretary of State for the Environment had a direct role in appointing the Board of the UDC, which included locally elected councillors but, perhaps more importantly, also business people and those sympathetic to the political sensibilities of the Conservative Party (Imrie and Thomas, 1999). UDCs operated with a small number of staff, contracting tasks to consultants, in a marked departure from the bureaucracy of local government. Some UDCs, such as the Cardiff Bay Development Corporation, appeared to intentionally not recruit staff from local agencies and organisations. A key debate about the UDCs is their lack of local democratic accountability as they were able to bypass local democratic structures, and in certain locations they developed conflictual relationships with local authorities. This led to suggestions that they were handmaidens of central government (see Brownill, 2013). Studies show that the relationships that UDCs developed in and across their designated areas were subject to variation, pointing to the need to be aware of the 'locality' in exploring institutional linkages and modes of governance (see Imrie and Thomas, 1999).

The establishment of such bodies is not confined to UK urban policy processes. For example, in the context of the Sydney Olympics in Australia in 2000, Owen (2002) notes how two new bodies – the Olympic Co-ordination Authority (OCA) and Sydney Organising Committee for the Olympic Games (SOCOG) – were established by the New South Wales government to coordinate the Games. Specific legislation was enacted by the state to centralise planning regulations in order to clear the way for the development of local sites and to circumvent local planning powers. As Owen (2002) notes, the relationships between the OCA/SOCOG and three local councils that had been earmarked for development sites differed significantly. While one embraced the entrepreneurial zeal of the OCA and involvement of private developers, another raised objections to the siting of a stadium in their locality and railed at the lack of community consultation in the process. As with the UDCs, this example demonstrates how the politics of locality matter in terms of understanding the dynamics of urban entrepreneurialism.

Property-led regeneration and economic development

As urban governance arrangements shifted in the 1980s, so, too, did the substance of urban regeneration, which became focused predominantly on property-led regeneration. Inner-city sites were seen as spaces with the potential to attract global flows of investment and to generate capital through increased land value or rents. Rather than attracting manufacturing industry, the emphasis was about developing post-industrial cities based around service sector activities. The property industry, as a key player within the service sector, was to have a major role in the regeneration of derelict areas (Atkinson and Moon, 1994).

PLR became widely visible across the cities of advanced industrialised nations, as evident in the growth of office blocks, retail developments and high-end housing. In London, the development of London's docklands, and particularly Canary Wharf, became a potent symbol of the property-led regeneration (see Figure 4.3). Under the auspices of the London Docklands Development Corporation, the derelict docklands area of East London became transformed, 'with 25 million sq. ft. (2.3m sq. m.) of commercial space built, a new office centre to promote London as a World City at Canary Wharf, 24,000 homes and a level of owner occupation up from 5% to 43%' (Brownill, 1999, p 43). This combination of developments, the creation of high-end office complexes, luxury housing and entertainment venues, has become commonplace in cities across the globe.

Figure 4.3: Property-led regeneration, London's docklands

Source: Rob Imrie

This photograph shows high-cost residential apartments built in the 1990s as part of the major redevelopment of London's docklands. Many of these apartments were part of a first wave of global investment in London's regeneration and have never been occupied. The apartments are primarily a shelter for investment finance, not people, and are a means of making money.

There was, and still is, an international diffusion of ideas and practices shaping such initiatives. For example, many cities in the UK have looked to the US for examples of waterfront regeneration, while it is acknowledged that the development of Dublin docklands, Ireland, including its International Financial Services Centre (IFSC), was heavily influenced by developments in London docklands. Part of the aim of such property-led regeneration was place-marketing, as flagship developments were used to boost cities on a world stage and to act as an impetus to further investment. Increasingly, this boosterism has taken on a cultural focus, as flagship cultural or sporting developments, for example, high-profile museums, concert or sporting venues, are used to attract investment (see Chapter Six).

In seeking to facilitate PLR, governments became involved in a number of measures designed to attract the private sector in an increasingly competitive inter-urban environment. These included:

- *Tax incentives and allowances* that sought to attract businesses and property developers to key locations (see Figure 4.4).
- *Grant provision to businesses*, providing subsidies to attract and stimulate local economic development. For example, in the UK, grant programmes such as the Urban Development Grant and Derelict Land Grant, payable for the reclamation of land, were established as a way of deploying public monies to attract private investment. The UDCs were similarly engaged in significant grant-giving to the development industry.
- *Relaxation or streamlining of planning regulations* was another facilitative action. For example, in the case of the Sydney Olympics, legislation was enacted that provided for 'fast-tracking' developments. The usual planning procedures, such as the submission of an environmental impact statement or consultation with the community, were bypassed.
- *Acquisition and preparation of property and land* – in some cases, government agencies were provided with powers to acquire, consolidate and prepare land in order to sell or rent it to private developers. For example, the UDCs' remit particularly focused on acquiring derelict land and improving local infrastructure to increase inner-city land-use values. Land acquisition was achieved through Compulsory Purchase Orders and the divesting of land from local authorities.

Figure 4.4: Developing Dublin docklands through tax incentives

Source: http://en.wikipedia.org/wiki/Dublin_Docklands#/media/File:Grand_Canal_Square.jpg

The regeneration of Dublin's inner city illustrates the use of tax incentives to stimulate PLR. Dublin's inner city and docklands experienced a significant loss of population and employment during the 1970s and 1980s as part of a broader national economic decline. In response, the government introduced the Urban Renewal Act and Finance Act in 1986, which put in place measures to fuel property investment in Designated Areas in the city. The aim was to revitalise key urban areas, including initiatives to stimulate job creation and economic development. Given the parlous state of public finances at the time, tax concessions focusing on property development became the key strategy. These measures, described by Williams and Boyle (2011, p 8), included:

■   tax allowances in respect of capital expenditures for the construction or reconstruction of commercial buildings, to be set off against income or corporation taxes;

- a double rent allowance, which occupiers could set off against trading income for a period of 10 years for new leases on commercial buildings;
- the remission of rates for a 10-year period;
- income tax relief for owner-occupiers of newly built or refurbished residential units;
- tax relief for investors in rented residential property within specified size limits; and
- a reduced corporation tax rate of 10% for licensed companies involved in international financial services locating in the IFSC.

The incentives appeared initially successful, as residential development mushroomed within two of the city's most high-profile Designated Areas: the Custom House Docks, the focus of a large-scale waterfront development overseen by a single authority, the Dublin Docklands Development Authority; and Temple Bar, which was rejuvenated as a 'cultural quarter'.

The tax relief approach has been criticised, not least for the imbalance in the type of residential accommodation it created, mainly high-end apartments aimed at young professionals, and the failure to operate within statutory planning frameworks or processes (McGuirk, 2000). It has also been suggested that the incentives contributed to the overheating of the property market, which played a role in the country's economic crash from 2008 (Williams and Boyle, 2011).

In some cases, combinations of incentives were used in areas of persistent economic decline. In the UK, Enterprise Zones (EZs) were designated across the country in the early 1980s in areas deemed to be experiencing severe economic decay. They introduced a number of incentives designed to attract businesses, including streamlined planning procedures and tax concessions. The impacts of the EZs have been much debated, and some have argued that they had the effect of displacing companies from one part of a city region to another (see Hall,

1982; Sissons, 2011). Here, local companies moved to take advantage of the incentives but few new jobs were created, nor was there a diversification of local economies (Cochrane, 2007; Tallon, 2010).

The focus on PLR has been subject to critique (Turok, 1992; Imrie and Thomas, 1993). It has been suggested that the notion that property can stimulate economic growth is flawed, particularly where other factors that are necessary for growth are missing. Relatedly, PLR may exclude other strategies or foci for regeneration, not least those that have a greater social dividend, such as education and training. PLR also creates uneven effects across communities in terms of the distribution of benefits. For example, the development of London's docklands was criticised for displacing local communities and failing to create employment for local people (Brownill, 1999, 2013). This was also the case in the regeneration of Dublin's docklands, where the development did little to address the needs of the area's pre-existing communities. Unemployment in inner-city Dublin increased during the time of the development, and there were few trickle-down or 'spread' effects to local people already living in the area (McGuirk, 2000).

Urban entrepreneurialism in the 2000s: new privatised spaces and forms of governance

Since its emergence in the 1980s, urban entrepreneurialism has become embedded as a dynamic element and strategy of contemporary urban policy. It has been argued that trends towards PLR and networked forms of urban governance have intensified in a context of increasing neoliberal globalisation. Swyngedouw et al's (2002) discussion of large-scale urban development projects (UDPs) in 13 European cities, including Dublin, Athens, Bilbao, London, Lisbon and Vienna, shows that they are shaped by, and, in turn, shape, processes of global economic restructuring. They are 'the material expression of a developmental logic that views megaprojects and place-marketing as means for generating future growth and for waging a competitive struggle to attract investment capital' (Swyngedouw et al, 2002, p 551). These cases highlight a number of features that tie entrepreneurial urban policy projects together: they focus on speculative rent extraction as a way of generating capital and on pump-priming land-use values to extract higher levels of rent than would have existed previously; they are managed by 'quasi-autonomous bodies', albeit ones in which the state plays a key role (often absorbing the risk of such speculative projects); and they operate through 'exceptionalities' in terms of statutory planning regulations, through special measures that often apply to designated areas or zones.

Swyngedouw et al's (2002) research raises a number of questions about the outcomes of entrepreneurial development projects and their mechanisms of accountability. The conclusion from Swyngedouw et al (2002) in relation to these large-scale European UDPs was that they had led to greater fragmentation of the social and physical environment of their respective cities. This is a recurring criticism of PLR: whether by overinflating rent prices so that local residents are unable to buy in redeveloped areas of the city, or by creating segmented labour markets in which highly paid professionals are marked out from an unskilled, lower-paid workforce, such developments lead to fragmented, polarised spaces in which luxury apartments and wealthy professionals often coexist alongside rundown public housing and areas of deprivation. Meanwhile, accountability measures on such projects are minimal. Thus, the unelected nature of many of those appointed to the bodies overseeing UDPs, and the unregulated nature of the way they do business, means that there are few openings for local communities to influence decision-making processes.

These criticisms of the impacts of entrepreneurial urban policy, the increasing fragmentation of city spaces and the privatisation of governance mechanisms are persistent themes in recent urban policy literature (MacLeod, 2002, 2011). It is argued that we are seeing the emergence of ever-more privatised spaces within the city that segment different areas and communities. The emergence of glamorous, consumer-led city centre or waterfront developments has, in many cases, displaced certain sections of the community who previously had a foothold there: low-income families, indigenous small businesses and those whose housing status is precarious. The creation of these environments is also bound up with active governance strategies to keep out those who are seen as undesirable, or whose 'faces do not fit', by increasing surveillance over urban space. MacLeod (2002), for example, discusses how the regeneration of Glasgow's downtown, through the creation of high-end consumer spaces and the staging of hallmark events, has been accompanied by a revanchist politics in which homeless people have been targeted and removed from the city centre amid concerns that they were damaging business and the city's image (see Figure 4.5).

These urban dynamics also indicate a new relationship between public and private space. The creation of exclusive spaces, such as gated residential communities, shopping malls and now even whole town centres, are often built upon privatised, or semi-privatised, modes of governance and management. For example, gated residential

Figure 4.5: Consumer spaces, Riverside Museum, Glasgow

Source: http://en.wikipedia.org/wiki/Riverside_ Museum#mediaviewer/File:Riverside_museum_from_front

communities or high-end retail developments are run and managed by semi-private governance agencies or organisations, with the effect of closing down, or colonising, notions of the 'public' in urban space. An oft-cited example is the privatisation of shopping malls in which property companies have acquired public space from local authorities (Minton, 2006). These privatised geographies, and their associated governance mechanisms, can be exemplified in two different types of urban space: BIDs and gated residential communities.

Managing and developing town centres: Business Improvement Districts

One of the ways in which the privatisation of public space manifests itself is in the creation of new institutional arrangements to manage town centres, or 'downtowns'. BIDs have been established across the cities of many industrialised nations, and have their origins in Canada and the US (see Ward, 2007). BIDs are described as 'public–private partnerships in which property and business owners in a defined geographic area elect to make a collective contribution to the maintenance, development, and marketing and promotion of their commercial district' (Ward, 2010, p 1178), although they operate slightly differently in different localities. In the US, property-owners in a specific geographical area make a contribution. In the UK, businesses have to make the contribution. In both countries, the contribution is compulsory, although this is not the case in certain countries, such as Australia (Ward, 2007).

BIDs are widely cited as an example of policy transfer in urban governance. For example, it was the apparent success of BIDs in the US, and in a few specific cities, most notably, New York, Philadelphia and Washington DC, which influenced the UK government to introduce legislation to facilitate the establishment of BIDs in 2003 and 2004.

Since then, BID schemes have mushroomed (Ward, 2006; Cook, 2008, 2009). The process of developing a BID involves establishing a consensus among local businesses and other stakeholders regarding the need for such a scheme, holding a vote on the establishment of the BID and the amount to be levied, and establishing a partnership structure that becomes responsible for the BID's activities (see Figure 4.6). Here, key actors with a stake in the local economy of the area come together, including members of the local authority and the local business community (Ward, 2007).

The functions that BIDs perform vary across countries and cities, but they usually engage in a number of core activities: improving the appearance of the physical environment through initiatives such as lighting, street cleaning and the planting of shrubs; producing promotional material and lobbying local politicians regarding issues in

Figure 4.6: Union Square Business Improvement District, San Francisco

Source: http://en.wikipedia.org/wiki/Union_Square,_San_
Francisco#mediaviewer/File:Union_Square,_SF_from_Macy%27s_1.JPG

their area; and engaging in the securitisation of their areas through the use of CCTV and other surveillance strategies. The latter is achieved by employing security guards or 'ambassadors', who meet and greet the public but also monitor any 'civil disobedience' that may disrupt the ambience and environment of the area. The rationale for BIDs feeds into a wider discourse about re-imagining the liveability of urban spaces and creating attractive work and leisure environments. Ward (2010) notes how the driver for BIDs in a number of towns in Wisconsin, US, was the perceived need to reorient the mix of local businesses in order to attract a particular cosmopolitan class of people, in Richard Florida's (2002) terms, the 'creative class' (see Chapter Six), into downtown areas through the development of cafes, bars, entertainment venues and new apartments. This aspirational discourse is a common feature of BIDs as areas compete in 'quality of life' stakes.

There has been significant debate about the success of BIDs, and, more controversially, how they should be interpreted as a form of governance (Ward, 2010). BIDs represent many of the features of entrepreneurial urbanism as they embody the neoliberal idea that a private sector-led response, seemingly unfettered by the politics and bureaucracy of local government, is the most effective way to revitalise downtown areas. Proponents of BIDs associate them with a range of benefits, including lower crime rates and greater cleanliness (Cook, 2009). BIDs raise significant questions about the nature of public space and who the 'public' is. While it is clear that certain segments of society, particularly well-heeled consumers, are welcomed, those who might behave in less civilised ways are not. BIDs have self-appointed powers to remove those who might disrupt the 'civic order' of their areas, whether they are street performers, informal market traders, political activists or homeless people. It seems that they are increasingly blurring the boundary between the public and private by operating 'as a mode of publicly regulated private government' (MacLeod, 2011, p 2644) in which democratic accountability has little role to play and urban spaces become sanitised, both visually and politically.

Gated communities: the privatisation of residential space

Another example of the privatisation and corporatisation of urban space is the growth of private residential estates, or gated communities, which have become common across cities in the US, the UK and Australia (see Figure 4.7). In broad terms, gated communities imply private residential developments, separated from public space to varying degrees by boundary mechanisms, such as gates, fences and security guards, and within which private governance arrangements exist (Atkinson and Flint, 2004; McGuirk and Dowling, 2007, 2009a). The management of such developments or communities often occurs through residents contracting out to private companies, or residents' committees managing the physical and environmental infrastructure of the sites themselves through restrictive covenants. These covenants, as Kenna (2010, p 441) describes in the Australian context, 'represent a communal tactic to ensure that the private structure of the neighbourhood works to maintain property values and maintain a certain standard and appeal to the residential development'. They may comprise rules about the nature of housing and landscaping, including the colours of paint and the size of driveways, as well as appropriate social conduct.

Gated communities represent a growing segregation of spaces and communities within the city in which those with the resources have the freedom to choose a particular type of lifestyle and, in some cases, 'opt out' of public facilities and spaces within the city. Most privatised residential developments are occupied by middle- or upper-class property-owners, although, as Pow (2007) notes, in some countries, those on lower incomes also inhabit such spaces, often by leasing properties in these areas. Residents buy into a lifestyle that brings them together with people with similar incomes and social mores but, perhaps more significantly, separates them from those segments of society perceived as undesirable. Fear of crime is often cited as a reason for the existence of such communities. The erection of gates, fences, security systems and CCTV that characterises such developments are all-powerful architectural and geographical indicators of the separation of one class of people from others.

Figure 4.7: A gated community, Brickell Key, Florida

Source: http://upload.wikimedia.org/wikipedia/commons/9/9d/Brickell_Key_
from_north_20100211.jpg

Brickell Key is an artificially created island off the shore of Miami,
and a unique type of gated community. Effectively, it is 'gated'
by the water surrounding it, and it caters for super-rich people
and their families.

While there is consensus that gated communities increase spatial
segregation in the city, a number of authors point to the diversity of
types. Blakeley and Snyder (1997) propose three types of privatised
residential developments in the US: lifestyle communities, which focus
on a shared appeal to a particular lifestyle or type of leisure (retirement
communities might be one example of this); prestige communities,
with a concern for privacy and exclusivity and few shared amenities;
and security zone communities, which emerge largely out of people's
concerns to protect themselves from the fear of crime. Their typology
draws attention to other features, including the amenities of such
developments, the types of residents who inhabit them, the extent of
security features and the rationale behind the enclosure. These are

not the only characteristics considered, and McGuirk and Dowling's (2009b) analysis of Master Planned Estates (MPEs) in Australia reveals the need to explore a range of other dimensions. They include the nature of different governance arrangements within and around MPEs, the lived experience of life within such estates, and the impact of local housing market conditions in determining outcomes of MPEs (see Figure 4.8).

Figure 4.8: Living in Master Planned Estates in Sydney, Australia

Kenna's (2010) research with the residents of one MPE, Macquarie Links in the city of Sydney, Australia, provides insights into the rationales and perceptions that shape people's decisions to move to such communities. In a questionnaire administered to residents, she found that:

- 80% cited the presence of gates and security as a reason for buying a property in the development, and that the estate had 24-hour security and a concierge on the gate;
- many of the residents had moved into the estate from relatively local areas, a decision shaped by some direct experiences of crime or social disorder, as well as 'talk of crime'; and
- residents appreciated the private governance structures that provided them with control over the estate environment and lifestyle.

Residents spoke about the deterioration of the local neighbourhoods that they lived in prior to moving to Macquarie Links, whether in terms of vandalism, rubbish on the streets or anti-social behaviour. Kenna (2010, p 438) argues that residents' decisions to move are due to fragmentation in urban living, which 'gives some urban residents a sense of disorder and a lack of control over their residential environments'.

In the context of urban entrepreneurialism and growing urban privatism, gated communities raise particular points of debate. Private residential developments, like BIDs, can be understood to be exemplars of neoliberal urbanism insofar as they create private spaces focused on profit and maintaining property values. They also institute private governing mechanisms in which property developers and self-created private communities have a key role to play. The boundary between public and private can be more complex. For example, in discussing the emergence of MPEs in Sydney, Australia, McGuirk and Dowling (2009b) challenge the notion that such estates are privately produced entities devoid of public regulation. Rather, they note how planning policies and practices in the state of New South Wales have encouraged the development of MPEs, and how public–private partnerships have often been the mode of operation in such developments.

Insofar as the governance of the estates themselves is concerned, they also identify a spectrum of arrangements, from those in which amenities are held under Community Title (a legislative arrangement that facilitates the provision of the private infrastructure of such estates, in which the residents, rather than the local council, are responsible for managing the estates through a locally formed community association) to ones in which public access to amenities is allowed. As they highlight, it is important to note the contingencies of local places and contexts that shape such relationships. In this example, privatism is not an all-or-nothing process, or a one-way trajectory.

Conclusions

The trend towards urban entrepreneurialism and privatism that came to prominence in the 1980s has become a defining feature of cities across industrialised nations. The impact on cities of global economic restructuring and the need for cities to compete on a world stage has led to a reorientation of urban governance in which faith in the private sector and market has become all-embracing. Yet, questions about what privatism is and how it is manifested are a significant source of debate. Privatism can be witnessed in the creation of specific types of spaces, and of particular forms of urban governance bodies and institutions, and in ways of doing business, for example, contracting out services or running things in a business-like manner.

Privatism does not mean the complete erosion or sidelining of the state and public sector in urban development (McGuirk and Dowling, 2009a; MacLeod, 2011). Rather than a full-scale takeover of urban governance and policy by the private sector, what we see are complex relationships between the public and private sectors in the management and development of urban space. Thus, the state may not be retreating, but entering into different types of roles with the private sector and other agencies, whether in the context of BIDs or the management of private residential communities. Meanwhile, government grants and other forms of finance remain a significant part of regeneration funding in many countries, despite the entrepreneurial idea that the state should act as a lever to private sector capital (Cochrane, 2007).

Privatism has the potential to create significant fragmentation and differentiation in the urban realm. Some people, and communities, can be left with little access to resources or decision-making and excluded from urban space and the politics that surrounds it. This is apparent not just in the growth of privatised spaces such as gated communities and high-end shopping malls, but also in what Atkinson and Flint (2004, p 875) refer to as 'time–space trajectories of segregation'. These are 'private network spaces', such as private toll roads and other infrastructures to convey the affluent from their private residential estates to high-end spaces of consumption without the need to engage in or with the broader public or social groups or areas that may be seen as risky. This is the creation of 'secessionary' urban environments in which a particular segment of society withdraws from public space (MacLeod, 2011). Insofar as these dynamics show signs of intensifying, questions about the outcomes of such trends remain a significant source of debate, not least in terms of trying to reclaim some notion of public or civic space within the city.

SUMMARY

Privatism is interlinked with neoliberalism and the assertion that deploying the skills of the private sector is an effective way to allocate resources and create wealth. Notions of privatism in urban policy came to the fore in the 1980s in the UK and the US as part of a critique of the interventionist welfare state and local government. Privatism is linked to the idea of urban entrepreneurialism, suggesting that cities need to compete on a world stage for private sector capital and investment. Urban entrepreneurialism implies a shift to public–private partnerships in urban governance, the use of public sector resources to attract investment and the marketing of cities for cultural and economic capital. Privatism in urban policy is dominated by PLR and the creation of different types of privatised spaces, including high-end city centre developments and gated residential communities. Privatism appears to contribute to greater socio-spatial fragmentation in the city, and privatised governance is associated with a democratic deficit in terms of its accountability to the public and local communities.

RECOMMENDED READING

The literature on urban entrepreneurialism and PLR is vast. On privatism in urban policy from the 1980s, see Barnekov et al (1989) and Harvey (1989). On PLR, see Imrie and Thomas (1999). A good critique of PLR is Turok (1992). On urban entrepreneurialism in the context of neoliberal globalisation, see the special issue of *Antipode* (2002, vol 34, no 3). For a review of current debates regarding privatism in urban governance, see MacLeod (2011).

WEB LINKS

A useful source of information about privatisation and privatism is 'Corporate Watch' (see: http://www.corporatewatch.org/magazine/50/autumnwinter-2011/neoliberal-project-privatisation-and-housing-crisis). On the privatisation of the public sphere, Anna Minton's website is a useful source of information (see: http://annaminton.com).

5

community planning and partnership

Introduction

Urban policy, as a process, is developed and delivered through a range of governance mechanisms, including neighbourhood and community planning and partnerships. Some of the most significant terms associated with urban policy are 'community' and 'partnership' (see Imrie and Raco, 2003). The former has been particularly extolled in the World Bank's *World development report* (2003, p 2), which declared that 'what is most clear is that the quality of urban governance and management is critical to gaining the benefits and reducing the negative aspects of cities of any size'. This observation reflects the World Bank's promotion of sustainable urban strategies, which are based on an understanding that the renewal of cities is dependent on governance through the context of community, or where there is a focus on rebuilding places through utilising the capacities of diverse associations, movements and groups.

In this chapter, we explore approaches to rebuilding people and places through recourse to community planning and policy. The chapter is divided into four parts. First, we discuss the various ways in which 'community' is defined and the ambiguities contained in such definitions. Second, we explore how the term is put to work in shaping policy interventions. Referring to examples from cities in Western countries, we show contrasts and continuities in approaches to community urban policy and highlight the popularisation of key concepts, such as social capital. Third, the role of partnership in the development and delivery of urban policy is discussed, and we outline its different manifestations and issues relating to partnership working and modes of implementation. Fourth, we develop a critique of community involvement in regeneration, evaluating how far, and in what ways, it has become embedded into urban policy processes.

Defining community

'Community' is one of the most complex and ambiguous terms in the English language. It has multiple meanings and is applied in many different contexts. While community is often invoked to refer to something concrete, such as a specific group of people, or a particular neighbourhood or organisation, the term is, as Anderson (1983) suggests, constructed and imagined. Anderson shows how nations are imagined as communities based around collective images and symbols, such as national anthems and national sporting events. These build affinity across a nation's members. At a different scale, media or newspaper reports often represent particular communities in different ways, either as lawless or dysfunctional neighbourhoods, or as idealised places to live. The language of community can be infused with nostalgia and has moral overtones. Community is commonly represented as a 'good thing', and politicians often bemoan the demise of community and associate community decline with societal breakdown. This association looms large in urban policy discourse, making community a key site for policy interventions.

Before exploring how community has shaped urban policy, it is helpful to identify the different ways in which the term community has been understood. Four definitions in particular are noteworthy:

1. *Community as a place or bounded geographical area*: community is usually associated with a particular place or neighbourhood, related to a group of people who coexist within geographical boundaries. This does not necessarily mean that these people have shared interests, but merely that they inhabit the same area.
2. *Community as an interest group*: communities are said to exist around particular interests and/or shared identities. For example, we might

talk about the 'gay community' or the 'Irish community'. Again, these groupings, based around 'a set of common characteristics, social practices, values and beliefs' (Latham et al, 2009, p 149), are not mutually exclusive as people occupy multiple subject positions in which their sexuality or ethnicity may be just one element.

3. *Community organisations and the community sector*: community can be defined as community organisations or 'the community sector'. Inhabitants of a neighbourhood may form a residents' association or community group to represent shared concerns about their area. Community groups organised around shared beliefs and identities are also commonplace, ranging widely from sports clubs to political associations. Organisations may be more or less established and some may receive funding from the state to undertake their work and have paid staff, while volunteers run others. Such organisations comprise civil society, or the third sector, representing institutions that are neither part of the state nor part of the market, nor seen by governments as a key part of the institutional infrastructure for the provision of welfare services.

4. *Community as a process*: definitions of community may be underpinned by an understanding of how individuals come together and interact, and the processes that lead communities to develop. The practice of community development refers to 'working with people in communities to achieve greater levels of social justice' through the identification of shared goals and cooperation between different community members (Gilchrist and Taylor, 2011, p 9). The way in which individuals within a community are perceived to interact differs considerably depending on one's political and epistemological perspective. For example, it has been suggested that recent interpretations of community in urban policy assume that communities represent, and operate through, processes of consensus-forming and shared values, but they may instead be shaped by conflicts and multiple overlapping interests and networks (Wallace, 2010).

This list of definitions is not exhaustive, but indicates some of the common understandings of community. Connections between people have changed significantly over the past century and the term 'community' traditionally assumed interactions between people based on face-to-face encounters in relatively small geographical areas. The emergence of new technologies is creating communities based on virtual interactions. Expanded population migration has also led to the creation of transnational or diasporic communities that stretch across geographical areas. The understanding of what a community is needs to reflect these changing forms of sociality and interconnection (Amin and Thrift, 2002).

Community and the urban problem

The discourse of community has a long history in relation to urbanisation. Reflecting on the moral values associated with community, sociologists such as Ferdinand Tonnies and Emile Durkheim, writing in the late 19th century, viewed urbanisation as the antithesis of community. In the shift from pre-modern, feudal societies to industrialised, urbanised societies, they saw the dissolution of social bonds, such as the family and religious institutions. As outlined in Chapter One, urban commentators in the late 19th and early 20th century, including Patrick Geddes, Ebenezer Howard and Lewis Mumford, saw cities as places that were disorderly, dirty and immoral, associated with criminality, poverty and poor health. This was in contrast to the representation of the rural idyll, in which the environment was safe and unpolluted, and where bonds of 'neighbourliness' still existed. Howard (1902 [1898], p 11) quotes from Lord Rosebury, stating:

> There is no thought of pride associated in my mind with the idea of London. I am always haunted by the awfulness of London: by the great appalling fact of these millions cast down as it would appear by hazard ... working each in their own groove and in their own cell, without regard or knowledge of each other, without heeding each other.

Howard's (1902 [1898]) analysis of the city as a site of community and societal breakdown, sucking the life out of rural areas, is questionable. Despite politicians referring to the 'rural' as an idealised image, or nostalgically linking it to a time or way of being that has been lost, a number of studies conducted in US and UK cities in the late 1950s and 1960s, including Young and Willmott's (1962) *Family and kinship in East London*, suggested that community did exist in urban environments but in different forms to those idealised by Howard and others. Studies such as Young and Willmott's sought to demonstrate that the 'dualistic split between traditional community and the impersonal ties of modern society is not one that holds up to scrutiny' (Latham et al, 2009, p 152). Yet, despite the historical discourse surrounding community in relation to urbanism having moved on from the 19th-century thinkers, the remnants remain in terms of how the 'urban problem' is conceptualised and how urban policy responses refer to, and target, something called 'the community'.

Communities, and the characteristics associated with them, have often been problematised as contributing to social and/or economic breakdown, an analysis frequently infused by a racial dimension. For example, the riots in US cities in the 1960s, and those in Britain in the 1980s, were linked by some politicians and commentators to characteristics of the black community and concerns about the threats of ghettoisation based around immigration (Cochrane, 2007). The construction of problematic communities has a strongly moral dimension and associates community breakdown with a decline in family values or 'fecklessness'. That said, communities have also been seen by urban policymakers as the solution to urban problems, as well as the source of them. Thus, urban policies have sought to identify or bring into being particular communities as the targets of, or conduits for, urban funding and regeneration programmes by mobilising people to become active citizens in their local areas.

Imrie and Raco's (2003) work is helpful in understanding how urban policy has invoked the notion of community. They suggest that policy has engaged with community in three different ways:

1. *Community as an object of urban policy*: communities are identified as entities 'to be worked on' (Imrie and Raco, 2003, p 6). This suggests that governments have to identify or constitute communities by, for example, defining a community as a particular

area or neighbourhood. This is a contentious issue as studies show that policymakers' definitions of boundaries may differ from the perceptions of those who live in these particular areas (Atkinson, 1999; Wallace, 2010). *How* communities are worked on once they are identified will also reflect the diagnosis of the 'problem' and its solutions.

2. *Community as a policy instrument*: in this context, communities are seen as part and parcel of the making and implementation of urban policy. Such an approach is evident in the shift towards community-based regeneration since the 1990s: that community groups and local residents should be active participants in, and take responsibility for, regenerating their communities. The notion of the community as a policy instrument raises questions about the ideology behind it. Is it about giving power to local communities or about the management of these communities and the legitimation of government programmes?

3. *Community as an outcome of policy*: certain urban policies seek the creation of 'community' as a policy outcome. In other words, community, or at least a certain version of it, is seen as a desired end in itself, often for its perceived potential to generate social and economic stability. For example, the communitarian vision that underpinned much of New Labour's urban policy assumes that strong social ties contribute to social integration and stability.

These understandings are not mutually exclusive, and policies may include all three elements. It could be suggested that community has always been part of the urban policy agenda, but the responses to, and understandings of, the term have taken different forms at different times. For example, as we suggested in Chapter Two, urban policy in the 1960s in the UK was dominated by the social pathology approach to defining urban problems (Atkinson, 2000). We noted that the Urban Programme, introduced in 1968, was concerned with addressing problems of particular populations and communities living in relatively discrete areas, and was deemed to require an 'intensively targeted social work approach which would change the behaviour of the relevant groups/individuals' (Atkinson, 2000, p 217). Communities were constituted as the scale at which initiatives were targeted, with Urban Programme projects focused on encouraging deprived populations to 'help themselves' through initiatives targeted at improving education, health and the local environment. Community was an object of government, as well as a conduit through which social change was to happen.

This understanding of community waned from the late 1970s and early 1980s as the shift to physical and economic regeneration took place, and economic development was prioritised over the needs of specific groups and communities. Local communities were marginalised from urban policy initiatives, and there was an assumption that communities would benefit from wider private sector investment in urban areas in a process of 'trickle down'. From the late 1980s, there was recognition that 'trickle down' had failed to materialise and that disparities in urban areas had, if anything, become greater (Imrie and Raco, 2003). Since the 1990s, there has been a recognition of the need to involve communities in urban regeneration programmes. After the election of the New Labour government in 1997, urban policy became infused with the language of community empowerment and partnership. In the period since 2010, the Coalition government has carried this forward with their notion of the 'Big Society' and their aspirations to de-concentrate 'big government' and to hand power to people to take greater responsibility for (their) self-government (for a fuller account, see Chapter Eight).

In the remainder of the chapter, we consider the resurgence of 'community' as an object of policy, not least in thinking about some of the broader dilemmas presented by the notion of community in urban policy. This involves addressing questions such as: 'Who has the right to define who or what a community is?'; 'What political agendas or ideologies lie behind the activation of communities as a policy instrument?'; and 'How far are policy pronouncements about creating (idealised) communities realised in practice "on the ground"?' We primarily refer to the period up to 2010, and revisit the period since in Chapter Eight.

Reinvigorating community in the 1990s: communitarianism, social capital and community 'activation'

While community-based programmes and interventions have always been a part of urban policy, in the 1990s, there emerged a reassertion of the role of the community as both a target of, and conduit for, urban regeneration, particularly in the UK. This move should not be viewed as a clean break with the property-led regeneration focus that dominated the 1980s. By the early 1990s, the then Conservative government was recognising the need to involve communities in programmes such as City Challenge and the Single Regeneration Budget (SRB), which brought the public, private and community sectors together in partnerships to bid for money for different projects in specific geographical areas. Nevertheless, the advent of the New Labour administration led by Tony Blair in 1997 introduced a specific set of ideas about how the community should be conceptualised and mobilised in the context of urban regeneration.

New Labour's approach to urban policy, which sought to make communities central targets and instruments of urban renewal, cannot be understood without a broader contextualisation of their political ideas. The New Labour government was associated with the idea of 'Third Way' politics. This refers to the idea that neither states nor markets are the best distributors of wealth or the most effective means of governance. Giddens (1998, p 70) states that 'the neoliberals want to shrink the state; the social democrats, historically, have been keen to expand it. The third way argues that what is necessary is to reconstruct it'. Steering a way between the political Left and Right, Blair and others argued that this reconstruction should involve new partnerships between the state and civil society in a context where governments did not direct, but rather took on a 'steering' function among a range of different organisations and networks. Here, communities were to become key sites and mechanisms of governance, particularly at the local level.

Blair's ideas about the role of community in society were influenced by ideas emanating from the political philosophy known as communitarianism. While not necessarily reflecting a coherent set of ideas or thinkers, communitarianism mourns the loss of collective endeavours and behaviours in society, and stresses the significance of collective bonds that bind individuals together. It views communities as a means of overcoming social fragmentation and instability in society (Etzioni, 1994; Putnam, 2000). Its key proponent, Amitai Etzioni (1994, p 15), argues that communitarianism reflects the need to rebalance individual rights with wider societal responsibilities. As he states in his key missive *The spirit of community*, 'We suggest that *free individuals require a community*, which backs them up against encroachment by the state and sustains morality by the gentle prodding of kin, friends, neighbors and other community members' (Etzioni, 1994, p 15, emphasis in original). For some, the communitarian vision is a romanticised, nostalgic one, and does not account for the political or structural divisions shaping social relations (DeFilippis et al, 2006).

Communitarian ideas shaped New Labour's redefinition of urban decline as a consequence and symptom of social exclusion. Rather than focusing purely on structural factors (eg poverty and economic deprivation) as a cause of urban decline, social exclusion suggests that those living in deprived neighbourhoods are marginalised in many different ways from the social, economic and political opportunities presented to those who are part of 'mainstream' society. As Kearns (2003, p 38; emphasis in original) describes it, social exclusion is 'about *disconnection* from mainstream society in terms of distance, experience and aspiration'. While these ideas might have had appeal in terms of recognising deprivation as a multifaceted phenomenon, commentators such as Levitas (2005) have been critical of the concept, not least for its apparent integrationist agenda, that is, its focus on creating cohesive communities into which those deemed to be socially excluded have a responsibility to integrate, and its sidelining of poverty in explaining the experiences of those living in deprived neighbourhoods.

Explanations of urban disadvantage based on social exclusion and the decline of cohesive communities followed a natural trajectory in terms of New Labour's policy response. Following the communitarian agenda, building social capital was a key goal of urban policy (see Figure 5.1). Social capital has been defined in many different ways but broadly refers to the networks, linkages and social norms that connect individuals and communities together. These can range from networks between families, friends and neighbours to those between local organisations and institutions. New Labour's diagnosis was that many deprived neighbourhoods were suffering from low levels of social capital due to high rates of family breakdown or crime and anti-social behaviour, which challenged local trust relations among residents. To develop greater social capital and, hence, it was envisioned, more cohesive communities, local residents were to be key conduits for urban renewal. As New Labour's keystone document on urban renewal, *A new commitment to neighbourhood renewal, national strategy action plan*, stated: 'Communities need to be consulted and listened to, and the most effective interventions are often those where communities are actively involved in their design and delivery, and where possible in the driving seat' (Social Exclusion Unit, 2001, p 19).

Figure 5.1: Understanding social capital

The concept of social capital has developed from a number of different quarters, including French social theorist Pierre Bourdieu and US sociologist James Coleman. It has most recently become associated with communitarian ideas and the US political scientist Robert Putnam (2000), who popularised the term in his book *Bowling alone: the collapse and revival of American community*. Putnam mourns the loss of social capital in US society, which he sees as detrimental in terms of promoting strong democratic government and economic growth and stability.

For Putnam (2000, p 19), social capital is defined as the 'connections among individuals – social networks and the norms of reciprocity and trustworthiness that arise from them'. He draws a distinction between different types of capital: *bonding capital*, which refers to strong personal ties or relationships between individuals often living in the same area (such as family, friends and others), 'which enable people to "get by"' (Kearns, 2003, p 43); and *bridging capital*, which refers to dispersed linkages across individuals and organisations.

A number of studies have used Putnam's ideas by assessing levels of social capital among residents of deprived neighbourhoods and how it might matter in the context of urban renewal (Stanley et al, 2012). Others are sceptical of the concept and DeFilippis (2001) challenges Putnam's assertion that low-income neighbourhoods are bereft of social networks and reciprocal relations, and that more social capital is naturally a 'good thing'. He suggests that Putnam's interpretation fails to recognise the context of power relations or *economic* capital that shapes the lives and networks of people living in such neighbourhoods.

The notion of putting communities 'in the driving seat' was, from New Labour's perspective, a reflection of the need to build the capacity of, and activate, communities in deprived areas by building up the skills, self-esteem and reciprocal relations of those living in disadvantaged communities. This vision to redress what had become something of a lacuna during the years of property-led regeneration could, on the surface, be seen as a welcome development in providing local residents with a stronger role in the governance of their areas. There was a strongly moral tone underpinning much of the discourse about community involvement. Third Way politics introduced a particular set of ideas about citizenship and the relationship between individuals, communities and the state. This relationship can be broadly summed up in the phrase 'no rights without responsibilities', which implies that individuals' rights, such as the right to claim welfare benefits and entitlements, are dependent upon the discharge of particular obligations.

Thus, members of communities living in deprived neighbourhoods were expected to 'help themselves' rather than be dependent on the government or institutions of the (welfare) state, as access to certain entitlements, such as income support provided to those out of work, became increasingly predicated on fulfilling certain obligations, including attending work-focused interviews or engaging in various job-seeking initiatives. In the context of urban policy, this has led some to conclude that New Labour's focus on social capital and community activation was about 'transferring the responsibility for solutions to deprivation to communities in deprived areas' (Dillon and Fanning, 2011, p 28).

Putting 'community activation' into practice: regeneration partnerships and the politics of participation

The emergence of community-based regeneration strategies is tied up with the idea that communities, however defined, are best placed to make decisions about the direction and development of the areas where they live. To this end, community-based urban policy ushered in new forms of governance arrangements, most notably, urban regeneration partnerships, in which the community has a seat at the table, along with private and public sector institutions, in terms of decision-making. It should be acknowledged, again, that partnership arrangements in urban policy are not new. Since the late 1990s, there has been a burgeoning of institutional forms in which partnership working has become the accepted *modus operandi*. As outlined in Chapter Two, City Challenge and the SRB, operating in England and Wales in the mid-1990s, were two of the first schemes in which communities, along with the private and public sector, had to come together to bid for pots of money to regenerate tightly defined geographical areas. It was the launch of the New Deal for Communities (NDC) and multiple other initiatives, including Local Strategic Partnerships, which led to partnership working becoming embedded in the tapestry of urban governance.

The NDC, as the New Labour government's flagship regeneration programme, illustrates many of the features of the 'community turn' in urban regeneration. The NDC was launched in 1998 with the aim of addressing disadvantage in England's 88 most deprived neighbourhoods. Between 1998 and 2011, 39 NDC Partnerships were established across a range of cities in England, with each allocated a budget of around £50 million. As an area-based initiative (ABI) based around partnership principles, the NDC took its lead from its predecessor, the SRB, which, in its latter years, sought to promote a holistic approach to tackling disadvantage by focusing on issues such as joblessness, crime and the lack of educational opportunities, as well as physical and environmental issues. The NDC carried on this holistic approach, with each partnership 'expected to achieve change for three place-based outcomes: crime, community and housing and the physical environment (HPE); and three people-based outcomes: health, education and worklessness' (Lawless and Beatty, 2013, p 944).

Where the NDC differed from the SRB was in its stated claim to have learnt the lessons of some of the shortcomings of previous partnership-based ABIs. One of these was the relative short-termism of previous approaches, in which the sustainability of initiatives and change was threatened by short timescales for funding. The NDC sought to rectify this by working to a 10-year timescale, with the intention of allowing initiatives to 'bed down' in local areas. Perhaps more significant was its claim to have learnt from previous mistakes regarding community involvement. The SRB was frequently criticised for involving communities only as an 'add on', or at the latter stages of the bid process. In contrast, the NDC sought to place local residents and communities at the centre of the programme, as key partners. Bids for the scheme had to demonstrate that communities had been involved at every stage of the decision-making process, and community members were expected to be representatives on NDC partnership boards, along with the public, private and voluntary sector (Beebeejaun and Grimshaw, 2011).

While the NDC was associated in government discourse with notions of community participation and empowerment, numerous studies have problematised the way in which 'the community' was represented and realised in the initiative (MacLeavy, 2009; Wallace, 2010). Drawing on the experience of the NDC in Bristol, for example, MacLeavy (2009) suggests that the NDC can be read as an instance of the rolling back of state infrastructures, aiming at a reconfigured relationship between the state and citizen in which 'the community' takes personal responsibility for change in their local area through a process of self-government. Beebeejaun and Grimshaw (2011, p 2001) similarly note that 'evaluation of the NDC has questioned the possibility of deprived communities to engage in area-based regeneration given their lack of power in the face of a government-led agenda', not least in the context of competing forms of knowledge between regeneration professionals and local people about deprived neighbourhoods. These issues apply in relation to not only the NDC, but also community involvement in regeneration more broadly, and we consider some of these in more detail in the next section.

Critiquing community involvement in regeneration: some dilemmas

Community involvement in regeneration partnerships has come under scrutiny from a range of commentators (Atkinson, 1999; Pollock and Sharp, 2012). Partnership working seems to represent a 'good thing': it is associated with collaborative ways of working in which consensus-seeking is sought; it appears to address the democratic deficit that has shut local residents and communities out of policymaking processes in the past; and it has the potential to contribute to the empowerment of local communities by giving them a voice in decisions that are made about their local areas. Case studies of such partnership arrangements indicate that the picture is far more complicated than this, with some critics suggesting that there is a 'tyranny' of participation in which the involvement of communities in partnerships is merely a tokenistic act designed to legitimate government policy (Pollock and Sharp, 2012). There is, then, significant debate about the motivations and intentions that lie behind government pronouncements about partnership and participation, and about how far pronouncements on paper become translated into participatory practices on the ground.

Constituting the 'community' and the politics of representation

One key issue that shapes debate about community involvement and partnership working in regeneration concerns how the community is constructed in the first place, and who has the legitimacy to represent the community. This is closely linked to Imrie and Raco's (2003) notion of the community as both an object to be worked on and a policy instrument. Government policies have frequently constituted communities in particular ways to fit policy goals and agendas. In initiatives such as the NDC, there are a number of ways in which this constitution becomes apparent. First, the prominence put upon ABIs has assumed a stable community living within particular geographical boundaries. Second, neighbourhoods and/or communities are often constituted in government statements as having particular norms or 'politics of behaviour' (see Wallace, 2010). For example, Wallace (2010, pp 814–15) explores how New Labour's discourse around poor neighbourhoods assumes 'a perceived behavioural fault line that exists ... between the decent, responsible majority and a deviant antisocial minority', a line that is used by the government to try and engage the 'responsible majority' in actions that tackle the 'deviant minority'. The difficulty with this, as Wallace suggests, is that it locates both the problem and its solution within the community in an act of self-responsibilisation that removes the emphasis from broader state infrastructures or interventions.

Understandings of community set out in urban policy initiatives frequently draw on assumptions and even stereotypes about communities that ignore the complexity of their social relations and divisions. The construction of urban communities by policymakers and regeneration practitioners can differ markedly from those of the inhabitants of these areas themselves (see Figure 5.2). Yet, particular conceptualisations or definitions of the community set out in policy pronouncements have real consequences for the practices of community involvement in regeneration partnerships, determining who can be involved and in what capacity. Certain constituencies have been marginalised in regeneration partnerships, as exemplified by Edwards'

(2008) documentation of the marginalisation of disabled people in the SRB, and Beebeejaun and Grimshaw's (2011) study of integrating gender and ethnicity into the NDC. Even where particular constituencies are identified as part of communities, there are tensions in how they are represented. MacLeavy's (2009, p 866) study of the Bristol NDC programme highlights tensions associated with the failure to reflect and represent the heterogeneity of the minority ethnic 'community' within the area, such that 'different ethnic groups frequently perceive themselves as in competition with one another' for receipt of NDC funds. Such tensions serve to reflect the complexity of the social and political relations of communities that are frequently ignored or sidelined by policymakers.

Figure 5.2: Contestations in representations of the community in the Kent coalfields

In her ethnographic study of the regeneration of the former Kent coalfields in South-East England, Doering (2014) explores how different actors in the regeneration process, from regeneration officials to local community activists, constructed different versions of the community and 'communityness', with significant implications for the process of partnership and community participation. The historical context to the coalfields formed an important backdrop to these constructions. As an ex-mining community, the locality was bound up with a very particular set of social and political relations based around the organisation of largely male employment and trade union involvement.

For local community activists, many of whom had been former trade union officials or local councillors, a narrative of community based around perceived strong trust relations and social networks was seen as a positive thing. Key events, such as the Miners' Strike of 1984/85, were seen to have reinforced community solidarity. Regeneration officials interpreted this history rather differently. They constructed the mining villages as 'traditional, backward-looking and obsolete, diametrically opposite to contemporary, modern society' (Doering, 2014, p 6), and viewed the community's perception of the strike as problematic rather than positive.

Doering demonstrates how these competing versions of the community had consequences for the structures and practices of community engagement in the regeneration process, including decisions about who to recruit to community liaison groups established by the Regional Development Agency (RDA) in each colliery site. In one site where the former mining community was fragmented, the RDA bypassed former members of the 'past' community in favour of 'future users' of the site, made up largely of middle-class professionals living nearby.

The concern of officials was to move away from those who represented the village's problematic past, who they perceived as not holding a consensual vision of the regeneration process. In another site, following criticism of this approach, public meetings led to the election of 'traditional' community representatives, bringing mining concerns to the fore.

Top-down participation?

The move towards community involvement in partnership working in the 1990s and 2000s was part of a broader reorientation in governance arrangements. This was to replace top-down, centralised government with multiple networks characterised by civic organisations entering into institutional arrangements with public and private sector bodies. For New Labour governments, this reorientation was supposed to have a distinctly local flavour. The 'local' was the scale at which new partnerships and networks were to come together, seemingly unfettered by the control of central government. The reality has been different; while there are more dispersed forms of governance in and across localities, central government, particularly since 2010 and the Coalition government, has maintained tight control over the parameters and extent of partnerships' actions, often through policy prescriptions and guidelines or financial controls.

This 'control at a distance' has been a feature of urban regeneration partnerships and modes of partnership working (MacLeavy, 2009). With the emergence of initiatives such as City Challenge and the SRB, schemes were issued with a set of policy prescriptions and guidelines by central government about how partnerships should work, who should be involved and who the community should comprise (Edwards, 2003, 2008). While definitions of what the government understood by the term 'partnership' were often vague, they set the terms of how participation as a process would proceed. Like the construction of 'community' itself, this top-down prescription came under fire for failing to understand the unequal relationship that exists between different local partners in terms of their political and financial resources and capacity to participate (Foley and Martin, 2000; Robinson et al, 2005).

For example, a common criticism of City Challenge and the SRB was that despite extolling the need for community organisations to be involved, such groups rarely took the lead in partnerships and were often engaged at the last minute of the bid process (Foley and Martin, 2000). More significantly, this top-down approach to participation raises questions about the agendas and motivations that lie behind exhortations of partnership working. It is suggested that partnership, as prescribed in urban policy, does not represent a process in which local communities are in control or empowered, but, rather, is an imposed and often partial process in which community organisations and representatives have to play by the 'rules of the game' set by central government.

Negotiating the structures and processes of partnership

Finally, an issue of heated debate in studies of community involvement in partnership is the practicalities for groups engaging in partnership forums and processes. Partnership suggests a process in which all partners are equal, but studies show this to be far from the case. Fraser

(1997) highlights that groups have different resources in terms of getting a 'seat at the table', and even when they do so, certain voices carry more legitimacy and weight than others and shape the deliberative realm. In the context of regeneration partnerships and their management boards, community representatives are often baffled by the jargon and process, particularly relating to the parameters of funding and meeting milestones (Robinson et al, 2005). For some groups, such as those representing disabled people, the practicalities of where board meetings are held, whether at locations and venues accessible to people with different impairments, or the format of documentation for meetings can prove to be significant barriers (Edwards, 2002).

The structuring of the participative sphere in regeneration partnerships highlights the boundaries and hierarchies that exist between different forms of knowledge. A key concern is the tension between regeneration professionals, with their 'expert knowledge', and residents of targeted areas, who bring with them localised knowledges and their embodied experience of living in particular neighbourhoods. As Beebeenjaun and Grimshaw (2011, p 2007) note, the focus placed on community capacity-building in initiatives such as the NDC assumes a deficit in knowledge, or in a particular type of knowledge, on the part of local residents and groups: it 'does not challenge the hierarchy which places professional knowledge as more valuable than local knowledge, and this patronization is further reflected in how community representatives are sometimes treated'. These epistemic tensions, which become reflected in specific practices of partnership working, do little to facilitate participative agendas that are supposed to put the community in the 'driving seat' of urban renewal.

Conclusions

Having read this chapter, one could be forgiven for thinking that the notion of 'community' in urban policy has been thoroughly captured by the state as a way of legitimising a set of governmental practices. Much of the recent literature on New Labour's use and interpretation of community in urban policy stresses how the term has been co-opted as a way of promoting a moral, self-responsibilising agenda. It is important to note that in both theoretical and empirical terms, there is potential for alternative spaces and practices to exist that may challenge dominant discourses of community as they have been deployed in urban policy over the last 15 years. Case studies such as Doering's (2014) shed light on the micro-contexts in which community groups seek to reassert, however minimally, their own articulations of community and community needs.

Acts of resistance are double-edged for community groups, and particularly for those organisations that rely on state funding. Building consensual relationships with the state risks incorporation and depoliticisation; speaking out or engaging in conflictual tactics risks being shut out of debate and may ultimately undermine the survival of community groups and interests. Part of the difficulty, as DeFilippis et al (2006) outline, is that the communitarian vision of social relations propagates a romanticised, consensual view that fails to recognise communities as shaped by particular social and political relations and tensions; it minimises the complexity of communities and the structural contexts in which they exist and are produced. For DeFilippis et al (2006, p 686), there is a need to reassert a vision of community that neither romanticises it nor sees it as an empty concept. This calls for a more nuanced and complex understanding from the state of who and what the community is, but also a recognition that community organisation needs to 'maintain conflict at the core of its activity' for progressive change to occur (DeFilippis et al, 2006, p 130).

SUMMARY

The chapter highlighted 'community' as a contested term, related to particular social and moral values. Urban policy often fails to recognise the complexities and multiplicities of the social relations that make up communities 'on the ground'. Policy initiatives conceptualise urban communities in different ways, simultaneously envisioning them as a root cause of urban problems, through a pathologisation of particular characteristics of communities, as well as the policy solution. Since the 1990s, there has been a renewed emphasis on the participation of local communities in regeneration, particularly under New Labour governments in the UK and reiterated by the Coalition government. Community-led regeneration has been associated with the growth of partnership-based governance in urban renewal. Such governance has been criticised for assuming the existence of communities in particular areas, or for constructing top-down definitions of who or what the community is. There is often a failure for community representatives to be equal participants in partnership processes.

RECOMMENDED READING

On the resurgence of 'community' in urban policy under New Labour, see Imrie and Raco (2003). Putnam's (2000) book is a classic statement of the decline of sociability and community, and an important book. A good critique of the concept of community is DeFilippis et al (2006) and Wallace (2010).

WEB LINKS

A good source of information about community and regeneration is the British Library (see: http://socialwelfare.bl.uk/subject-areas/services-activity/community-development/).

6

culture and the creative city

Introduction

One of the key components of contemporary urban policy is the promotion of culture and creativity as the basis for transforming the social and economic fortunes of cities. While cities have always been regarded as places of intense sociocultural activities, networks and exchanges, in recent times, culture has been (re-)appropriated as a category of/for social and economic policy development. International cultural networks have expanded significantly since the early 1990s as part of place-marketing and branding exercises. Mega-projects have become essential features of major cities, including flagship cultural projects, festivals and sporting events, such as Formula 1 motor racing. Seeking to 'get onto the map', so it is claimed, requires cities to develop a distinctive cultural economy portfolio. Supranational organisations have become involved in orchestrating cultural policy, and the United Nations Educational, Scientific and Cultural Organization (UNESCO) has promoted a creative cities movement, with 25 member cities from 17 countries. Likewise, the European Union's (EU's) Capital of Culture programme is indicative of place promotion, and is a model copied around the world as places seek to cultivate creativity as the basis of urban renewal.

In this chapter, we explore the rise of culture-led urban policy and regeneration and the ways in which it manifests itself in cities across developed world nations. We examine the influences that have led to culture and 'creativity' being seen as a solution to urban problems, and the multiple initiatives spawned by such influences. We discuss debates about the impact and efficacy of culture as a means of promoting socially just forms of urban development. Critics have pointed to a number of problems with culture-based initiatives, not least the lack of clarity about how cultural initiatives contribute to sustainable economic strategies, and who has 'cultural ownership' over representations of the city. In observing some of the many regeneration initiatives replete with cultural venues or quarters, it has been argued that the promotion of the creative city is little more than property-led regeneration, designed to attract a particular (cappuccino-drinking) class of people to consume a specific articulation of culture.

This raises a number of fundamental questions about how we define culture, why certain articulations of culture get promoted in visions of the city and others do not, and who benefits from these representations. A key message of this chapter is that cities are shaped by contestations between groups about how culture should be articulated, and we consider how these contestations are played out through specific examples and case studies. We divide the chapter into three parts. First, we outline the origins of culture-led urban policy and note that it has historical roots. Second, we describe and evaluate the development and deployment of different cultural strategies in cities. Third, we discuss the contributions of culture-led urban policy and how far it represents a means to redress deep-rooted problems of systemic social inequality and poverty in cities.

The origins of culture-led urban policy and regeneration

Historically, cities have looked to display their social and cultural wares, ranging from the holding of festivals in ancient Greek towns and cities to the rise of museums in the 19th century and the emergence of international fairs (see Figure 6.1). However, since the late 20th century, there has been a growing trend for cities to draw on and market their cultural resources as a means of promoting urban development and competitiveness. One of the key influences in this trend has been the perceived need of cities to reinvent themselves in the wake of deindustrialisation and the decline of manufacturing industry. In the 'post-industrial' era, cities and city regions have sought to restructure their economies around service sector and knowledge-based enterprises as they compete for labour and capital in the global urban order. Culture has played several important roles in the reorientation of city economies as a consequence of capitalist restructuring.

Figure 6.1: The Great Exhibition, London, 1851, and the Crystal Palace

Source: http://upload.wikimedia.org/wikipedia/commons/9/92/Crystal_Palace_
from_the_northeast_from_Dickinson%27s_Comprehensive_Pictures_of_the_
Great_Exhibition_of_1851._1854.jpg

One of the formative cultural events of the industrial era was the Great Exhibition of 1851, held in Hyde Park, London. There were 100,000 objects exhibited from over 15,000 contributors, with exhibits from Britain and the Empire. The structure to house the exhibition, 'the Crystal Palace', was reconstructed at Penge Park (later renamed the Crystal Palace Park) in 1854, and it operated as the world's first theme park for over half a century, attracting over two million visitors a year to a variety of sporting and cultural events. The building was destroyed by fire in November 1936.

Cultural industries, in the form of fashion, design, music and film, and sites of cultural consumption, such as art galleries, museums and sports venues, contribute to the city's economy and labour market, particularly by generating high-waged work. Culture is also used to place cities on the world stage to attract investment and labour. Place-marketing initiatives such as 'Glasgow's Miles Better' campaign is an example of the latter (see Figure 6.2). These two roles are far from mutually exclusive. The creation of cultural venues and industries can form part of strategies to emplace cities on a world stage. There has been significant debate about how far cultural strategies lead to economic development, and whether this *should* be the role of 'culture' in the city (Belfiore, 2002; Evans, 2005). While we will return to these debates later in the chapter, there is little question that urban planners see culture as a key resource in fostering urban renewal and development.

Figure 6.2: Glasgow's Miles Better

Source: http://upload.wikimedia.org/wikipedia/en/b/be/Glasgows_Miles_Better.png

One of the first branding or place-marketing slogans to try to attract people back to deindustrialising cities took place in Glasgow from June 1983, symbolised in the 'Mr Happy' motif. It was part of the city's campaign to challenge entrenched negative views of Glasgow as a place of crime and violence and instead to promote a positive image of the people and the place.

The push towards culture-led urban policy has been shaped by influential academics, including Charles Landry and Franco Bianchini (1995) and their notion of the 'creative city'. They understand 'creativity' as promoting innovation to challenge the instrumental rationality of static urban planning systems, characterised by inertia and prescriptive processes (Landry and Bianchini, 1995). Such ideas have been developed by Richard Florida (2002), and his notion of a 'creative class' has been influential in reorienting the agendas of cities towards a 'creative turn'. Florida argued that if cities are to flourish, they need to attract a new class of highly educated professionals based in the knowledge and/ or creative industries, including engineers, architects, designers and artists, as well as those working in the legal and management fields. Florida proposed that members of the 'creative class' have particular cultural and lifestyle preferences, described as 'bohemian and urban in outlook' (Zimmerman, 2008, p 232). To attract them, cities need to offer the three T's: technology, talent and tolerance. His argument suggested that if cities attract this relatively mobile and footloose group of people, hi-tech industry, seeking their specialist labour, will follow. For urban planners, creating the right kind of cultural environment, a trendy, hip, culturally diverse environment, is key to luring the creative class and, ultimately, creating economic growth.

Florida's thesis has popular appeal among city planners and policymakers across the US and beyond. His publication of a 'creativity index', setting out a ranking of the most creative cities in the US, with San Francisco and Austin, Texas, topping the bill, has been mimicked in other countries, not least in the UK, where the think-tank DEMOS developed a Bohemian Britain Index in 2003. Based on a composite scoring system of three indicators derived from Florida's index (ethnic diversity, the proportion of gay residents and the number of patents per head), Manchester emerged as the UK's most bohemian city, followed jointly by London and Leicester (see: http://www.demos.co.uk/ press_releases/bohobritain). Numerous studies of cities, ranging from Copenhagen to Milwaukee, Kristiansand to Brisbane, document how creative strategies have been developed and implemented, and with what effects (Zimmerman, 2008; Lysgård, 2012; see also Figure 6.3).

Figure 6.3: 'From brew town to cool town': the reinvention of Milwaukee

Source: http://upload.wikimedia.org/wikipedia/commons/7/79/Milwaukee_Art_Museum_1_%28Mulad%29.jpg

Florida's ideas about revitalising cities by attracting the creative class have been applied in Milwaukee, Wisconsin (see Zimmerman, 2008). Milwaukee is a 'rust-belt' city that has suffered economic and population losses over the past 30 years. Zimmerman documents how the city's civic leaders, following consultation with Florida, developed a creative city strategy, which included:

- Renewing the image of Milwaukee through place-marketing: the city revised its official logo, which 'was a vaguely-industrial, gear-like symbol underscored with the slogan "Milwaukee: the Genuine American City"' (Zimmerman, 2008, p 233). It was replaced by representing the city through a new iconic building, the Calatrava-designed extension to the Milwaukee Art Museum.

- Using web-based marketing to reinvent the city as a 'cool' destination, highlighting the city's status as a college town and its music scene.
- Creating a social network entitled Young Professionals of Milwaukee as part of marketing to attract new young talent to the city.
- Redeveloping Milwaukee's downtown, centred on the Calatrava building as a cultural spectacle. Environmental improvements were made and 3,000 new residential units were built with the intention of attracting professionals to live and work in the city centre.

The results have been far from egalitarian. Poverty has increased and there have been net job losses, and the city is increasingly divided by social class and ethnic status (see Zimmerman, 2008).

Florida's thesis has been subject to numerous evaluations and criticisms (Comunian, 2011). Some commentators, such as Malanga (2004, p 1), have criticised his economic analysis, suggesting that 'A look at even the most simple economic indicators, in fact, shows that, far from being economic powerhouses, many of Florida's favored cities are chronic underperformers'. Perhaps more potent are criticisms that question the political assumptions and value judgements embodied in Florida's ideas. Peck (2005) points out that Florida's thesis has little to say about urban inequality and those who sit outside the creative class. It ignores the structure and divisions of urban labour markets in which a low-paid, flexible workforce may be servicing the needs of young, upwardly mobile professionals, or the gentrification and rising house prices that may accompany the arrival of 'creatives'.

Peck (2005) argues that the creativity thesis is built around the commodification and consumption of culture, and the selling of an urban 'experience'. As Peck (2005, p 763) writes: 'rather than civilising urban economic development by "bringing in culture", creativity strategies do the opposite: they commodify the arts and cultural resources, even social tolerance itself, suturing them as putative economic assets to evolving regimes of urban competition'. Notions of the creative class therefore reproduce and reinforce neoliberal agendas that utilise place-marketing to promote certain stylised ways of living at the expense of addressing structural problems and inequalities in cities. Such criticisms have not dampened the attraction of creative strategies for city managers, and in the next section, we consider some of the diverse ways in which 'culture' has been deployed by policy makers.

Deploying culture: strategies and practices

The deployment of culture as part of the toolkit of urban planners and policymakers takes many forms. From place-marketing campaigns to flagship development projects and sporting events, cultural strategies have become part of the development agenda of cities of all sizes across the globe. In this section, we explore the different ways in which culture has manifested itself in the creation of urban environments, but before doing so, it is necessary to identify a couple of issues regarding understandings of cultural intervention as they impact upon debates in urban policy.

The first of these relates to the way in which we define 'culture'. Raymond Williams (1985) wrote about the complexity of the term 'culture', and proposed that a distinction could be drawn between culture as it is expressed in society to reflect particular practices or ways of life of different social groups, and culture as artistic or intellectual activity, that is, art, film, theatre, music and so on. This distinction, between culture in terms of *society* and culture *as art*, is significant as the two have been invoked in different, and sometimes overlapping, ways in culture-led urban policy. For example, while developments such as art galleries, museums or theatres reflect the promotion of culture as art, certain visions in the marketing of cities have drawn on representations of cultural practices associated with specific groups. Bolognani (2012) notes how the culture of Bradford's South Asian community has been variously invoked and latterly rendered invisible in the city's urban regeneration strategies and place-marketing.

There is a second, and related, debate in the literature regarding culture-based urban development, and this concerns the notion of culture as an activity of consumption, and culture as production, through the cultural and/or creative industries. Culture, as it contributes to urban development, is often perceived to revolve around consumption. Sites such as art galleries, restaurants and designer coffee bars have become key designations of urban space. Place-marketing campaigns frequently seek to turn whole cities, or particular cultural quarters within them, into consumption experiences, whether marketed for their nightlife or retail experience. It has been argued that notions of culture as consumption have eclipsed debates about the productive capacity of culture and cultural industries to contribute to urban economic development and labour markets as enterprises in their own right (Pratt, 2008).

There is some dispute regarding definitions of cultural and/or creative industries (see Figure 6.4). Broadly, cultural industries have been defined as 'those industries that produce and circulate texts which contribute to create and disseminate meaning in society' (Lysgård, 2012, p 1289). This may include enterprises based around music, film, architecture, fashion and design. In some cities, clusters have built up around specific cultural industries, such as the music industry in Sheffield (Cochrane, 2007), advertising in Lisbon and fashion and design in Milan (Foord, 2008). The point here is that cultural industries can contribute to the productive potential of the city, and this is increasingly picked up on by urban policymakers. Numerous cities now have strategies to develop creative industries, as exemplified by publications such as Dublin City Council's (2010) *Defining and valuing Dublin's creative industries.*

Figure 6.4: Cultural and/or creative industries: definitional issues

The cultural industries are concerned with the production of some kind of 'symbolic content', including advertising, literature, publishing, theatres and art galleries. The concept of culture has become confused in recent years since the term 'creative industries' was coined. Foord (2008) suggests that the term 'creative industries' initially emerged in Australia, but it has become more widespread since the UK's Department for Culture, Media and Sport (DCMS) started using the term instead of 'cultural industries' to reflect 'those industries which have their origin in individual creativity, skill and talent and which have the potential for wealth and job creation through the generation and exploitation of intellectual property' (DCMS, 2001, p 5).

This definition, along with its categorisation of 13 types of activity, including software and information technology (IT) development, television, and radio, links creative industries to notions of entrepreneurialism and the 'smart economy'. While, for some, this definition marked little more than political posturing by Tony Blair's New Labour government, it rapidly gained traction around the world, and is widely used as a basis for classification today. There have been moves to reclaim the meaning of the cultural industries as distinct from the creative industries. For example, the United Nations (UN) Conference on Trade and Development in 2004 distinguished between creative industries that copyrighted and distributed creative content and cultural industries that directly produced cultural outputs through the arts in local contexts (Foord, 2008).

Cultural industries have therefore become associated with 'those wishing to prioritize the *social* meaning of cultural production, distribution and participation, including ideas of collective ownership of culture and the significance of not-for-profit production' (Foord, 2008, p 95; emphasis in original).

Situating the city in a global market, Dublin City Council's (2010) document recommends developing the skills and competencies of the workforce to participate in the creative industries, and building global connections that are seen as crucial to the sector. It notes: 'a policy priority must be to develop the communications and broadband infrastructure within the Dublin region to surpass that of other global hubs of innovation such as Seoul in South Korea ... the city region must deepen its international links with a number of key cities recognised as world centres of excellence in the creative industries' (Dublin City Council, 2010, p 3). Such documents represent faith in the creative industries to foster the development of 'smart economies'. Other commentators recognise the limits of the sector, not least the risks attached to creative industries in terms of their sustainability and the limited employment opportunities that may stem from them (Lysgård, 2012).

With these debates in mind, we now explore some of the different ways in which culture has been deployed within cities. Some of these follow an urban boosterism model in which flagship, property-based developments seek to promote the potential of cities on a world stage. Others are more concerned with utilising culture as a tool for promoting social inclusion. We discuss these different approaches and consider some of the contentious aspects of creating the 'cultural' or 'creative' city.

Flagship urban developments and architectural spectacles

One of the most powerful material and representational elements of culture-based urban strategies is the use of flagship developments and buildings to promote the city and create new arenas for consumption. The revitalisation of urban centres and derelict inner-city areas has frequently focused around the development of large-scale cultural initiatives, such as the building of the BALTIC art gallery in Tyneside and/or associated retail developments aimed at attracting consumers to the city centre. For instance, Liverpool One, a major retail development in the centre of Liverpool launched as part of the city's year as European Capital of Culture in 2008, has been a central component of the city's regeneration, while the development of the London Olympics site in East London has included the Westfield Stratford City shopping centre as an integral element (see Figure 6.5).

Figure 6.5: Westfield Shopping Centre, Stratford, London

Source: http://upload.wikimedia.org/wikipedia/commons/d/d2/Westfield_
stratford_city.jpg

These developments are about more than their function. Physical redevelopment is often used to promote spectacles of urban design and architecture. Celebrated architects, such as Norman Foster, Daniel Libeskind and Frank Gehry, have been used around the world to create iconic structures that transform cities' skylines and raise their visibility on the world stage as centres of urban design. Examples include the Sage concert hall in Gateshead and 'The Gherkin' in the City of London, both designed by Foster and Partners, or the Guggenheim Opera House in Los Angeles, designed by Gehry (see Figure 6.6). These buildings are not just material entities, but also symbolic and designed to imbue cities with cultural prestige (Jones and Evans, 2008).

The development of flagship projects is about not just one-off initiatives, but also the development of cultural quarters in cities. Historically, many cities were associated with particular quarters where artists

Figure 6.6: Guggenheim Museum, Los Angeles

Copyright: Rob Imrie

or writers congregated, such as the Left Bank in Paris or Soho in London. Since the 1980s, cities have been (re)discovering, inventing and seeking to promote cultural quarters as a means of spurring inner-city redevelopment. The meaning of 'cultural quarter' in this context is somewhat different to its historical origins. Proponents of the concept suggest that cultural quarters can be created as a result of a range of interlinking factors, including the presence of cultural activity revolving around production and consumption, a prominent 'public realm' (including streetscapes that encourage people to meet), and a strong evening economy (see Figure 6.7; see also Montgomery, 2004a, 2004b). Examples of 'invented' cultural quarters include Dublin's Temple Bar, the Sheffield Cultural Industries Quarter, Hindley Street in Adelaide and Manchester's Northern Quarter (Montgomery, 2004b).

Figure 6.7: Cultural quarters: necessary conditions and success factors

Activity

- Diversity of primary and secondary land uses.
- Extent and variety of cultural venues.
- Presence of an evening economy, including cafe culture.
- Strength of small-firm economy, including creative businesses.
- Access to education providers.
- Presence of festivals and events.
- Availability of workspaces for artists and low-cost cultural producers.
- Small-firm economic development in the cultural sectors.
- Managed workspaces for office and studio users.
- Location of arts development agencies and companies.
- Arts and media training and education.
- Complementary daytime and evening uses.

Built form

- Fine-grained urban morphology.
- Variety and adaptability of building stock.
- Permeability of streetscape.
- Legibility.
- Amount and quality of public space.
- Active street frontages.
- People attractors.

Meaning

- Important meeting and gathering spaces.
- Sense of history and progress.
- Area identity and imagery.
- Knowledgeability.
- Environmental signifiers.

Source: Montgomery, 2004a.

A criticism of cultural quarters is that rather than promoting the development of spaces that artists or writers can inhabit, they lead to them being pushed out through gentrification and rising property prices (Mathews, 2010). Cultural quarters can also end up focused around consumption rather than production and the fostering of cultural industries. In the mid-1990s, Dublin's Temple Bar become better known as the hen and stag party capital of Europe than a centre of cultural creativity. There is a repetitive and circuitous nature to much inner-city regeneration based around the development of cultural quarters and similar initiatives. Pointing to the redevelopment of old industrial docklands areas, Cochrane (2007, p 113) suggests that 'the fashions of recent years have been clear: even the most landlocked cities have done their best to find some sort of waterfront'. From London Docklands to Baltimore, Darling Harbour, Sydney to Cardiff Bay, the redevelopment of industrial waterfronts into apartments, hotels and entertainment complexes has become perhaps the most common, and now clichéd, strategy of physical regeneration in the inner city. Such trends persist as cities seek to emulate each other in the race for cultural and economic capital.

Place-marketing

Associated with the development of urban spectacles and flagship developments are strategies used by urban policymakers to promote cities on a world stage. In the game of inter-urban one-upmanship, officials are trying to market the cities they represent on the basis of their distinctive cultural offering as a means of attracting inward investment, new residents and tourists. Place-marketing has become important in cities that have experienced the effects of deindustrialisation and are seeking to reinvent themselves materially and symbolically. Milwaukee, cited in Figure 6.3, is an example of this. In the process of place-marketing, culture is used to brand a city to reflect a unique identifier or selling point designed to attract investors and visitors. Cities look to their heritage or key cultural figures as a source of inspiration. In Glasgow, the work of Art Nouveau architect and designer Charles Rennie Mackintosh became central to the city's marketing in the 1990s, and was deployed in city logos, souvenirs and jewellery and was celebrated through some of his key architectural achievements in the city (see Figure 6.8). In similar contexts, Barcelona has become known for its associations with Gaudi, and Bilbao with Guggenheim after the building of the flagship Guggenheim Museum in 1997 (Evans, 2003).

Figure 6.8: The Lighthouse, Glasgow

Source: http://en.wikipedia.org /wiki /The_Lighthouse,_Glasgow#mediaviewer/ File:Wfm_mackintosh_lighthouse.jpg

The Glasgow Herald Building, designed by Mackintosh, was converted into 'The Lighthouse', Scotland's Centre for Design and Architecture, as part of Glasgow's status as UK City of Architecture and Design in 1999.

One of the difficulties with place-marketing is 'brand decay'. As soon as city marketers devise a particular brand based around an iconic symbol or activity, such as nightlife, retail or art, it quickly becomes passé as ideas and cultural mores move on. Similarly problematic is ownership of iconic city representations. How far do the images created of a place resonate with the local population, or take meaning from local communities' understanding(s) of the city? As with the flagship developments discussed in the previous section, city marketing or branding exercises can serve to present a glamorous image that is somewhat at odds with the reality of living in particular places and local identities. Questions have therefore been raised about the 'democratic legitimacy' of branding exercises, and an important task in assessing the efficacy of place-marketing exercises as part of culture-led regeneration is to ask how far they have meaning for, or affect, the identities of city inhabitants (Garcia, 2005; Miles, 2005; Eshuis and Edwards, 2012).

Key events and festivals

Culture is also deployed in the city through the staging of large-scale, often short-term, events or festivals. The fierce competition that has become part of the bidding process for sporting events such as the Olympic Games bears witness to the prize(s) that can be gained for cities if they are successful: increased inward investment; a raised profile on the world stage; and greater levels of tourism. One only has to look at the London Olympics to see the huge, and, some might say, potentially unrealistic, aspirations vested in the event, which range from the physical regeneration of a huge area of East London, including transport and infrastructural developments and new housing, through to employment creation and longer-term visions aimed at improving young people's participation in sport (Gold and Gold, 2011). Large-scale sporting events and festivals are valued as levers for the economic and cultural revitalisation of cities and an opportunity to rebrand urban environments.

Supranational cultural and political institutions have become well-aware of the potential benefits of cultural events in promoting and renewing cities, and have put in place initiatives that are well-known in the repertoire of urban cultural spectacles. One well-documented programme is the European Capital of Culture (formerly European City of Culture), devised in 1983 by the European Community (EC) (now EU). Designed with the goal of adding culture to the EC portfolio, and as a means for creating cohesion between the countries of the EC, the initial designation focused on promoting the cultural assets of well-known European cities, such as Athens, Florence and Paris. The designation of Glasgow as City of Culture in 1990 marked a break in the focus of the initiative, which became more attached to regeneration goals. For example, while the aims of the European Capital of Culture are to 'highlight the richness and diversity of European cultures' and to 'celebrate the cultural ties that link Europeans together', it is also stated that 'studies have shown that the event is a valuable opportunity to regenerate cities', 'raise their international profile, boost tourism and enhance their image in the eyes of their own inhabitants' (see: http://ec.europa.eu/culture/our-programmes-and-actions/capitals/european-capitals-of-culture_en.htm).

Since the 1990s, the designation has been awarded to smaller and medium-sized cities, and to promote various regeneration projects. Cities including Cork, Lille, Porto, Graz and Maribor have all received the European Capital of Culture mantle. Assessments of its success have varied. Glasgow's year was celebrated by many as a success, but commentators, such as Garcia (2005), point to continuing problems with the programme, including the low level of funding provided by the EU and the lack of robust monitoring.

Utilising culture as a means of promoting social inclusion

As outlined, culture has come to be associated with the revitalisation of cities through highly visible developments, often centred on retail or consumption-led cultural events and facilities. Questions have been raised about the social dividends of such projects and who they benefit. A different way in which the role of culture has been understood in cities is as a tool for tackling social exclusion in deprived urban communities and neighbourhoods, sometimes in conjunction with, or as part of, large-scale cultural events. In the UK, there has long been recognition that the arts has a role to play in urban regeneration and engaging communities, but the potential for culture and sport to contribute to social inclusion and neighbourhood renewal was highlighted when New Labour came to power in 1997, as evidenced in the National Strategy for Neighbourhood Renewal (DCMS, 1999). The report (DCMS, 1999, p 8) stated that 'arts and sport, culture and recreational activity can contribute to neighbourhood renewal and make a real difference to health, crime, employment and education in deprived communities'.

Since that time, there has been an increasing focus on the potential of sport and culture to contribute to social cohesion and engage particularly 'hard-to-reach' groups. For example, Coaffee (2008) notes how local councils, such as Sunderland, have implemented schemes aimed at engaging teenagers in sports and other cultural activities, with the aim of reducing 'risky' behaviours. Such developments, in terms of community-based arts and sports programmes, are not limited to the UK, but have been used around the world (Evans, 2005). There are questions to be asked about such initiatives and their role. It has been suggested that the benefits are often overstated and that there is little evidence about their social impacts. Others raise concerns about the strategy of using arts to pursue instrumental ends in which culture becomes just another mechanism of social policy. This is expressed by Belfiore (2002, p 104), who states that 'culture is not a means to an end. It is an end in itself'.

Debating culture-led urban policy

Strategies for urban development in which culture plays a role have been subject to considerable debate and contention. Many of these debates relate to the outcomes of cultural initiatives. To what extent are they contributing to the longer-term sustainable economic and social development of cities, and what kind of city environments are they creating? What representations of culture are articulated, and who benefits from these articulations? The next sections address some of the issues raised by these questions.

The legacy of cultural developments: economic, physical, social and cultural benefits?

A key question in relation to culture-based urban policies relates to the social and economic additionalities they bring, or their impacts and benefits. It has been suggested that there are significant gaps in knowledge about the impacts of culture where it is included as a component of regeneration strategies, and that it is often assumed that cultural regeneration initiatives, particularly flagship developments, will have guaranteed benefits, not least through a trickle-down effect (Evans, 2005). While recognising that cultural initiatives are initiated for both economic and social reasons, that is, to increase economic competitiveness and promote social inclusion, commentators suggest that there needs to be a much greater engagement of those who are affected by cultural developments in cities in devising criteria for evaluation, not least local communities, and a broadening of evaluative criteria to include the social and cultural, as well as the economic and physical, impacts of culture-based regeneration (Garcia, 2005).

Part of the issue relates to the *type* of regeneration initiative or development put in place in culture-based strategies. Headline-grabbing flagship developments based around the renewal of city centres have been seen to leave city residents on the fringes in terms of participation, both socially and spatially. Boland (2010), for example, notes how many of Liverpool's local communities felt socially and culturally excluded from the city's European Capital of Culture initiative in 2008, which involved a significant rebranding exercise and the development of the city centre as a 'showcase' through cultural and retail developments. The designation and its effects were criticised for prioritising consumer-led culture aimed at the middle classes and visitors from outside the city at the expense of addressing disadvantage in many of the city's communities. Socio-economic inequalities in Liverpool have persisted during and since the period of the European Capital of Culture.

Such observations point to the importance of 'legacy' in the wake of events in terms of sustaining long-term benefits for the inhabitants of host cities that go beyond short-term cultural spectacle. The notion of 'legacy' has received attention in the context of the London 2012 Olympics and formed a central part of the London 2012 bid. Part of the Olympics' long-term agenda has been the redevelopment of Stratford, East London, which had previously included a swathe of derelict industrial land, to bring social and economic benefits to the local community. Sites including the Olympic and Paralympic Village were to be turned into new homes, replete, so it is alleged, with affordable housing, educational facilities and a new health centre (see Figure 6.9). As negotiations continue regarding the future of the main

Figure 6.9: The Olympic Village, London

Source: Mike Dolton

Olympic stadium, questions have been raised in the media about the legacy goals and their outcomes. As a recent newspaper article asked: 'Will the park benefit the boroughs that border it or become an oasis amid continued deprivation? Will it become another Canary Wharf, attracting upwardly mobile City workers but failing to cater for families from Newham?' (Gibson, 2012, p 1).

There are real questions to be asked about high-profile developments and the distribution of benefits that come with them. The evidence that exists in relation to such developments suggests that they are underachieving with regards to their 'distributive effects' (Evans, 2005). The evidence shows that community-based participatory cultural projects are likely to be far more beneficial in sustaining urban regeneration, but in the eyes of city marketers and managers, such projects are less glamorous and unlikely to project a city onto the world stage. The preference for high-visibility spectacle over a more profane, community-based form of arts programming points to a hierarchy of cultural phenomena, but in a context of fierce inter-urban competition, it is a hierarchy that becomes increasingly difficult to contest.

Culture for whom, by whom?

Debates about the social and economic impacts of cultural development and regeneration are closely tied to whose representations of culture get promoted, and for what audience. In discussing the 'ambiguities' of the cultural turn in urban policy, Cochrane (2007, p 118) suggests that 'there is continuing tension between approaches to culture which see it as something to be mobilized for promotion or marketing and those which are aimed at supporting, improving or reflecting communities and their shared (or contested) understandings' (see also Miles and Paddison, 2005). Evidence of these complexities can be seen in the ways in which some groups have resisted 'official' articulations of culture to brand the city, but also how and why particular representations of the city are deployed to the exclusion of others.

Representations of culture in place-marketing aim to attract a certain class of people: highly educated professionals with an appreciation of art and fine dining, or well-heeled tourists with money in their pockets to spend on consumption experiences. To do so, they invoke images and representations of culture that may be far removed from those that the city's inhabitants, or a significant proportion, recognise. For example, in discussing the reinvention of Milwaukee as a 'cool town', Zimmerman (2008) notes that representations of the city's working-class and African-American population were all but absent. The city's newspapers published articles calling upon residents to change their working-class identity and stop resisting the city's future, which lay in embracing creative infrastructures and imaginaries.

Even when place-marketing and urban regeneration strategies draw on, and deploy, local cultural practices and representations, they may be subject to manipulation and the fickleness of political realities. This is evident in Bolognani's (2012) work on place-marketing and urban regeneration strategies in Bradford. Noting how the culture of the city's South Asian community has variously been seen as 'good culture, bad culture, no culture' in regeneration strategies, she charts how representations of culture are shaped by, and reflect, local, national and international political realities. Notions of a multicultural Bradford, represented in initiatives such as the creation of a Museum of Spices and the Mela (a festival drawing on influences from the Indian subcontinent), were promoted as part of urban regeneration strategies up until 2002, but following 9/11 and riots between Muslim youths and police in the city during the summer of 2001, these cultural articulations became seen as negative. Since that time, multicultural representations have become invisible in the city's regeneration strategies, being replaced by culturally neutral city centre office and retail developments (Bolognani, 2012).

In some cities, there is evidence of the ways in which official articulations of culture have been disrupted by alternative, or unofficial, versions put forward by different groups in the city. O'Callaghan (2012), for example, considers alternative conceptions of culture in Cork, Ireland, when the city was accorded the status of European Capital of Culture in 2005 (see Figure 6.10). Unhappy with the way in which the 'official' body, known as Cork 2005, was developing events for the year, a group called 'Where's Me Culture?' established itself with an alternative programme of events. What was at stake here was a tension between those practitioners who saw the European Capital of Culture initiative 'as an opportunity for Cork to stage an international arts event, and those who saw it as an opportunity to stage Cork's culture for an international audience' (O'Callaghan, 2012, p 186). These two understandings of culture in the city, O'Callaghan argues, are indicative of tensions in the European Capital of Culture agenda itself, which is overly ambitious given its multiple objectives to combine cultural and economic imperatives, promote both local and European cultural identities, and stage large-scale international events, while also seeking to build the local, smaller-scale cultural sectors of host cities.

Figure 6.10: Cultural consumption: the English market, Cork

Source: Claire Edwards

O'Callaghan (2012) documents how, with a budget of €21 million, the Cork European Capital of Culture initiative sought to combine the staging of cultural events with a broader regeneration agenda. To administer the year, the city council established an independent company, Cork 2005, comprising representatives from the council, the arts and the private sector. In 2004, a number of individuals active in the city's arts sector created a group called 'Where's Me Culture?' to stage a series of alternative events to the official programme and open up the cultural terrain to people beyond the Cork 2005 organisers. While Cork 2005 was concerned with situating Cork in an international cultural scene, 'Where's Me Culture?' was a 'home-grown' initiative that drew on local symbols and representations to promote its agenda.

The differences between the 'official' and 'unofficial' versions of Cork as European Capital of Culture were articulated in the images and identities promoted by each. The official logo of Cork 2005 was a generic image of fireworks. 'Where's Me Culture?' identified with an explicitly Cork identity by drawing on the long-running People's Republic of Cork initiative, which hosts a website and produces T-shirts based on socialist-style propaganda to promote, in a humorous fashion, Cork's status as the 'rebel county'. 'Where's Me Culture?' organised a number of counterposing events throughout the year, including Big Party and Big Picnic events and a weekly Speaker's Corner. Their website was also used to promote events hosted by different groups.

'Where's Me Culture?' did not intend to be strictly oppositional to Cork 2005's official programme and agenda, but, rather, as O'Callaghan (2012, p 196) notes, 'questioned the notion that it was the "right" of any one group to mobilise a place-based representation of culture'. It cannot be said, either, that their articulation of culture was any more real, or valid, than the official version. What such examples point to is the messy and politicised nature of 'culture', which far from being neatly packaged to be sold around the world, is subject to continuous contestation and conflict in local contexts.

Creating cultures of urban 'sameness'?

An important issue relates to the creation of urban cultures in a context of globalisation in the race to become part of the urban global hierarchy. Somewhat ironically in a situation where highlighting the distinctiveness of cities has become part of urban policy agendas, some commentators have argued that creating urban spectacles and place-marketing is only serving to homogenise urban environments in a commodified cultural landscape (Miles and Paddison, 2005). As mentioned earlier in the chapter, one only has to look at the multiple waterfront developments that have spread across the globe aimed at revitalising derelict inner-city industrial sites to witness the global circulation and borrowing of urban visions. This spreading of sameness can, in part, be put down to what authors such as Peck (2005) and McCann (2004) have referred to as 'fast policy transfer': a situation in which policy ideas are taken up in one location and applied in other (urban) contexts with little recognition of the specificities of different locales. In this context, certain cities are held up as visionary examples, or guiding lights, of urban development, which other cities subsequently seek to emulate in their quest for economic revitalisation.

We can see evidence of fast policy transfer in many instances of culture-based regeneration and development, and the ideas promoted by proponents of creative city strategies, or the creative class, actively foster these modes of policy circulation. Florida's (2002) creative class thesis suggests that all cities have it within themselves to create a cultural context that will be attractive to the creative class if they follow his prescriptions. Ranking cities as centres of creativity, or 'best places', serves to perpetuate the notion that if cities implement policy lessons from those topping the ranks, they will be on an upward trajectory (McCann, 2004). This assumes that ideas can be picked up and dropped into different environments without taking account of the economic, political and institutional relations that frame contrasting urban contexts. As studies show, local contexts *do* matter. Discussing the role of iconic buildings or flagship developments in culture-led regeneration, Evans (2005) suggests that there is a growing realisation that not all cities may be in a position to sustain such ventures, with projects becoming redundant due to a lack of visitor numbers or sustained revenue funding. The notion that 'every city must have one' is a fallacy that fails to reflect the different economic and institutional contexts of cities across the globe.

Conclusions

As this chapter shows, the promotion of 'culture', however defined, is a key strategy deployed by city managers to regenerate urban areas and emplace cities on a world stage. Such strategies are fraught with dilemmas that are often overlooked in place-marketing visions which suggest that culture is something apolitical or value-neutral. The fast policy transfer of ideas about the creative city, and the types of environments and social relations that such ideas engender, such as shiny retail complexes or bohemian arts quarters designed to attract an upwardly mobile segment of society, suggest a universality that ignores or is ill-equipped to deal with the specificities of particular places or the multiple identities or forms of culture that make up cities. In other words, there is often a marked disparity between how city promoters and place-makers would like to portray their cities and how the people who actually live there perceive and understand them. It is clear that the use of culture as a regeneration tool is often associated with forms of consumption and capital accumulation. The motivation behind using culture as a strategy in urban regeneration foregrounds broader tensions that require greater attention from urban planners: what are the social and economic dividends of policy initiatives based around cities as 'sites of culture', and how are these to be distributed among those who inhabit cities?

SUMMARY

'Culture' is a complex term with multiple definitions. Two key understandings relate to culture as art or intellectual activity and culture as the practices of everyday life. Urban policy literature draws attention to the distinction between culture as consumption, through retail and restaurants, and culture as production, through creative and cultural industries. Cultural strategies have emerged to enable cities to reinvent themselves and their economies in the wake of deindustrialisation. The influence of ideas about the emergence of a 'creative class' in fostering urban entrepreneurialism has also been important. Cultural strategies in the city take many forms, including architecture-led flagship developments, cultural quarters, place-marketing, key events and festivals, and using sports and cultural policy to promote social inclusion in deprived areas. Some of the key dilemmas about culture-based urban policy concern the long-term socio-economic effects of cultural developments, and about cultural ownership of the city and which representations of culture are promoted.

RECOMMENDED READING

A good starting point to learn about culture-led regeneration is the special issue of *Urban Studies* (2005), 'The rise and rise of culture-led regeneration' (vol 42, nos 5/6). Other issues of *Urban Studies*, the *International Journal of Cultural Policy* and the *International Journal of Urban and Regional Research* are fertile hunting grounds. On the impact of sporting events, see the edited collection by Gold and Gold (2011). Those interested in notions of the creative city should read Florida (2002) *The rise of the creative class*.

Web links

One of the most comprehensive sources of information about culture, creativity and cities is the Comedia-Charles Landry website (see: http://www.charleslandry.com). It lists a range of relevant and up-to-date publications.

7

urban renaissance and sustainable urban development

Introduction

In the late 1980s, cities were (re)discovered by a number of political and academic commentators, and the emergence of a new phase of policy ensued seeking to (re)create urban areas as good places to live. The Congress for the New Urbanism in the US in the 1990s highlighted the many benefits of city living, predicated on changing urban design to ensure people's ease of access to goods and services, and creating places to encourage social interaction and a greater public presence. A heightened understanding of the social and economic costs of urban sprawl has led some commentators to call for the creation of compact cities, or repopulated places where scarce urban land is used to its maximum potential (Barton et al, 2003). There was also recognition of the socio-ecological consequences of urbanisation, and the need to restrain consumption in cities as part of wider endeavours to enhance the quality of ecology and the environment. The renaissance of cities thus became a major theme of the 1990s and continues to shape urban policy, particularly in addressing sustainable development and ensuring that cities are able to sustain urban living and lifestyles.

This chapter charts the rise of the sustainable city agenda, and describes and evaluates its various manifestations in shaping urban policy. These include measures to reduce car use, to encourage the development of public transportation (including walking and cycling), to 'green' the environment and to develop brownfield sites over greenfield locations. In older, deindustrialised cities, such as Cleveland, Ohio, policy is encouraging neighbours to use vacant sites as a means to boost property values and community spirit in neighbourhoods characterised by derelict land and condemned buildings. In other places, self-sufficiency is encouraged as a means for urban populations to be less dependent on global flows and supplies of resources. Thus, in Amsterdam and Birmingham (UK), urban farms are encouraged to enhance food security, and cities such as Austin, Texas, are seeking to secure energy by developing local sources of supply owned by the community. In many cities, the recycling of waste is commonplace and there is heightened awareness of the need, if limited actions, to reduce air and waterborne pollution to enhance the health of citizens.

Amid the plethora of policies and programmes under the banner of sustainable development is the underlying tension of how far city governments can reduce consumption and manage its socio-ecological effects, while simultaneously seeking to ensure the livelihoods of citizens by promoting economic growth. It is our contention that much of what is labelled sustainable development is no more than the pursuit of economic development as the basis of wealth creation and human betterment and well-being. The adoption of sustainable development by policymakers is part of the rediscovery of cities as places that provide potential for not only renewing deindustrialised environments, but also using renewal programmes as the basis for the growth of new economic sectors, such as financial services and cultural and creative industries. Such sectors are seen as the basis for the renewal of economic growth in declining urban areas and (self-) sustaining economic recovery. We argue that sustainability, how it is defined and put into practice, is closely aligned with 'the notion of continued quantitative growth' (Fry, 2011, p 23).

We divide the rest of the chapter into four parts. First, we situate the rise of sustainability in shaping urban policy within historical debates about what the good city is or ought to be. As we suggest, discourses about sustainability and the city are not new and are part of a long-standing consciousness about the deleterious effects of city living. Second, we extend these observations to discuss the rise in popularity of sustainable development as an organising principle of urban policy, particularly since the early 1990s. The chapter then turns to a critique of urban policy shaped by sustainable development discourse, and suggests that it may be understood as supportive of, and seeking to propagate, the market as the main mechanism of city revitalisation. This takes different forms, including state-sponsored projects to repopulate city centres and encourage gentrification, and the promotion of smart city policies that place faith in technology to deliver the good city. We conclude by outlining alternative visions of creating cities that resist market-oriented forms of sustainable development policy.

The 'good city' and urban environmentalism

In Chapter One, we highlighted how many commentators at different times in history have drawn attention to the negative consequences of urbanisation, from health problems related to air and water pollution, to the wastefulness of urban sprawl consuming scarce land and encouraging car-dependent journeys. The early part of the 20th century was characterised by policy ideas and experiments in urban form and city building, and brought forth different conceptions of what the good city is or ought to be. Ebenezer Howard (1902 [1898]), the inspiration behind the Garden City movement, regarded the modern, industrial city as perpetuating social divisions and inequalities antithetical to people's pursuit of good and healthy living. The French architect Le Corbusier (1929, p 166) envisaged the contemporary city as a high-rise environment, the Ville Contemporaine, which, in his words, was 'an organ that is compact, rapid, lively and concentrated'. Other, competing models of the good city included Frank Lloyd Wright's (1932, pp 1–2) Broadacre City, the antithesis to Le Corbusier's compact city form (see Figure 7.1): 'We will spread out, and in so doing will transform our human habitation sites into those allowing beauty of design and landscaping, sanitation and fresh air, privacy and playgrounds, and a plot whereon to raise things'.

Figure 7.1: Broadacre City

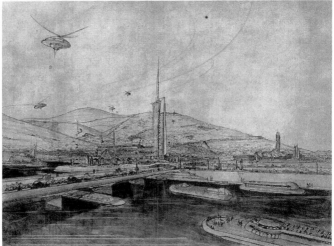

Source: http://upload.wikimedia.org/wikipedia/commons/9/95/Wright_
Sketches_for_Broadacre_City.jpg

Frank Lloyd Wright's plan for Broadacre City was a decentralised
settlement with homes separated by open space. It was a vision

of the symbiosis of agrarian and urban societies to ensure that people's enduring relationship with nature was maintained despite the coming of an urbanised society. As Frank Lloyd Wright (1932, p 62) said: 'of all the underlying forces working toward emancipation of the city dweller, most important is the gradual reawakening of the primitive instincts of the agrarian'. Frank Lloyd Wright (1932) outlined his plan for Broadacre City in his book *The disappearing city*.

What these visions had in common was the concern to improve the conditions of human habitation by designing cities to enhance people's welfare and to protect, and to nurture, non-human, ecological environments. Such concerns were heightened with urban growth after 1950 and a significant rise in people's consciousness of the impact of human activities on the environment. As Jamison (2008, p 281) notes: 'a wide range of urban environmentalist ideas and practices began to circulate' in countries across the Western world. This consciousness was stirred not only by people's daily observations, but also by a range of publications that highlighted the environmental impacts of industrialisation and urbanisation (Jacobs, 1961; Carson, 1962). Foremost was Rachael Carson's (1962) powerful book *Silent Spring*, which drew attention to the hazards of the pesticide DDT and questioned the raison d'être of the industrial world shaping technological interventions in nature. Her publication, along with others, drew attention to the widespread environmental damage caused by rapid, often unregulated, industrial processes and both the visible and invisible effects of polluting industries (Burton, 1968). Jamison (2008, p 285) describes petrochemical smogs above the major cities in the US in the 1950s and 'the toxic waste sites that had spread like a plague across the urban landscape'.

One of the most infamous toxic sites that became a focal point for environmental action and legislation was Love Canal near Niagara Falls, a site acquired by Hooker Chemical in 1947 (see Gibbs, 1982). They used it for chemical disposal, and by the early 1950s, it was filled with 21,000 tons of toxic waste. The site was covered with clay and soil, and after Hooker Chemical deemed it safe for urban development, it was sold back to the city of Niagara Falls in 1953. By the late 1950s, housing construction occurred directly adjacent to the Love Canal landfill, and over the next few years, more than 100 homes were built and a primary school was opened. Over the years, chemicals and toxic waste seeped into the canal and local waterways, and oil and other pollutants appeared. There was inaction until 1978, when highly toxic dioxins were identified, leading the Federal Disaster Assistance Agency to intervene. Clean-up projects were started and over 800 families were relocated from the site, which, to this day, remains largely abandoned.

Urbanisation is characterised by many episodes like this. David Harvey (1999) refers to them as the political economy of waste, or seeking to offload the costs of urban-industrial processes into areas where resistance is weak and protest is unlikely to be effective. This has tended to be in poorer communities and, in the US context, predominantly in places where black and minority ethnic groups live. The growth of environmental justice movements, campaigning to reduce the costs of urban pollution and eradicate environmental inequalities, has been a feature of the policy landscape since the mid-1960s. This was a period of heightened consciousness of urban environmental pollution, and the recognition that there was a lack of legal regulation to force polluters to pay for or ameliorate their practices. Governments readily accepted externalities, such as air and water pollution, as a price to pay for wealth creation. The first Earth Summit in 1970 was symptomatic of people being disaffected by a socio-economic and political system that appeared to propagate an urban policy that placed few constraints on industry and did little to check or control polluters and what many regarded as excessive consumption.

The deleterious environmental effects of urbanisation were not the only cause for concern. The publication of Jane Jacobs' (1961) influential book *The death and life of great American cities* drew attention to the human failures of post-war US urban renewal, and, in particular, the problems of modernist urban policy and planning. For Jacobs (1961), one of the major issues was the impact of urban sprawl and mass transit systems, leading to the loss of rural habitat and creating dependence on polluting motor vehicles, with consequences for air quality. Jacobs' main focus was the social consequences of modern urbanism and the critical role of purposive policy in shaping the urban habitat. For Jacobs, the modern city was a joyless, often dehumanising, experience crafted around monotonous places bereft of character or any sense of place. The city was anti-social and had become a place that did not encourage people to linger or interact; it lacked vitality and a diversity of buildings, residences, businesses and other uses. Commenting on the development of intra-urban motorways, Jacobs (1961, p 6) observed that they were 'Promenades that go from no place to nowhere and have no promenaders. Expressways that eviscerate great cities. This is not the rebuilding of cities. It is the sacking of cities'.

The observations of Jacobs and other urban-environmental commentators had little impact on urban development throughout the 1970s and early 1980s, and, as outlined in previous chapters, the pursuit of economic growth continued to trump any other policy agenda. By the mid-1980s, urban policies were seeking to enhance the economic competitiveness of cities by encouraging new knowledge-intensive industrial sectors, and pursuing property-led regeneration as a means to stimulate land values to attract inward investment. While the pursuit of economic competitiveness as the basis for urban revitalisation focused policymakers' attention on unblocking constraints to growth, the process came under increasing scrutiny by environmental groups and others concerned with its social and environmental costs. Not only was a growth agenda for cities seen as harmful to people forced to breathe poor air quality due to the escalating numbers of motor vehicles, but the impact of economic growth on the environment was also presented as likely to inhibit the potential of future growth (see Imrie, 1994).

In 1987, the World Commission on Development (Brundtland Commission) (1987, p 12) drew attention to the broader issue of environmental degradation, noting that 'it is impossible to separate economic development issues from environmental issues ... and environmental degradation can undermine economic development'. This was not a break with an economic logic or policy driven by a growth agenda, but it did warn that people's livelihoods and the state of local economies depended on nurturing, and caring for, the planet's fragile ecological resources. It reflected a discourse of ecological modernisation, or eco-modernisation, which has become pre-eminent in influencing sustainable development policies and is premised on shaping economic development in environmentally sensitive ways (see Figure 7.2). The Brundtland Commission was not an attack on the wastefulness of capitalism, but, rather, argued that economic growth was reconcilable with overcoming environmental problems.

Figure 7.2: Eco-modernisation

Mol and Spaargaren (2000) note that the idea of eco-modernisation dates to the early 1980s. It was derived from debates about how far capitalism was ever likely to be ecologically sensitive, and was an attempt to head off arguments that the maintenance of the prevailing urban-industrial order was tantamount to the destruction of the earth. Instead, eco-modernisation proclaims that the existing economic and social system, that is, capitalism, can be retained because the economy and environment can be combined in ways whereby both can be enhanced, for example, reducing carbon emissions may save energy costs and reduce environmental impacts. Eco-modernisation has been criticised as a form of 'greenwashing': because it does not challenge the primacy of economic growth, it fails to tackle the impulse at the heart of the denudation of the earth's natural resource bases.

By the early 1990s, the focus was increasingly on the environmental effects of urbanisation, most notably, at the Earth Summit in Rio de Janeiro in 1992. Here, it was suggested that urbanisation was the source of many of the world's ecological and environmental problems. The prognosis was far-reaching in suggesting radical changes in patterns of urban habitation and lifestyles by reducing urban sprawl and dependence on motor vehicles. This was a recognition of the wastefulness of sprawling cities and the advantages of creating compact places. In

1990, the European Commission outlined the case for increasing urban density and encouraging the planning of compact cities. As they suggested: 'the city's economic and social importance ultimately rests on the ease for communication offered by spatial density' (Commission of the European Communities, 1990, pp 19–21). This echoes others who, in different periods of history, saw the virtues of compaction, or creating self-contained places whose inhabitants could live off their immediate hinterlands and minimise their ecological footprints. For instance, while predicated on economic growth, Ebenezer Howard's blueprint for a socially balanced city sought to enhance the urban environment, or, in Howard's (1902 [1898], p 140) terms, not to 'lessen or destroy, but ever add to its social opportunities, to its beauty, to its convenience' (see Figure 7.3).

Figure 7.3: Garden City concept

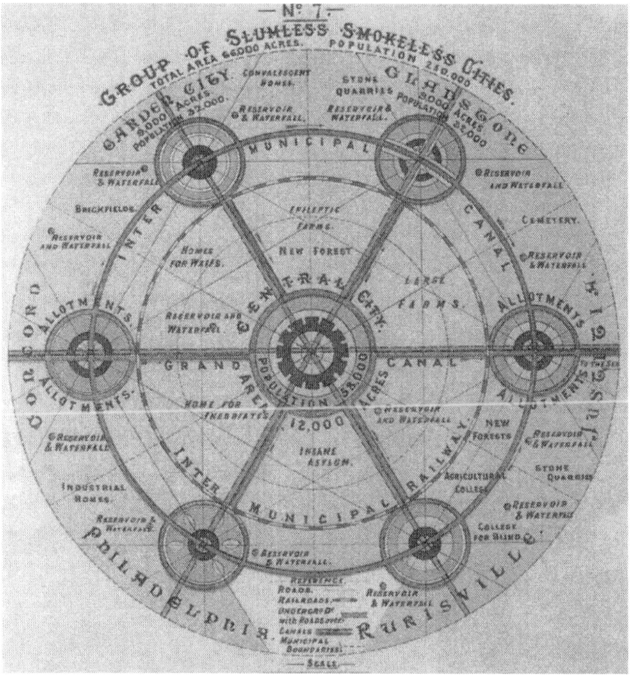

Source: http://en.wikipedia.org/wiki/File:Garden_City_Concept_by_Howard.jpg

The Garden City movement began with Ebenezer Howard setting out his vision in his 1898 book *Tomorrow: a peaceful path to real reform*, reissued in 1902 as *Garden cities of to-morrow*. The planning concept of the Garden City was a reaction against the growth, overcrowding and pollution of Victorian industrial cities, and suggested ideal towns separating housing and industry, and combining the best of the town and countryside. Howard envisioned a cooperative development in a concentric form, with civic functions, housing, schools and green areas in the centre and industry and other services on the outskirts. The value of the land was to be retained by the community. In practice, the first two garden cities of Letchworth and Welwyn Garden City (the former inaugurated in 1903; the latter in 1920) depended on private financial investment. Both struggled to provide affordable housing for the working class or to be self-sufficient in terms of employment. The Garden City concept has continued to influence planning and formed the bedrock of the post-war New Towns in the UK. Garden cities, in a different guise to provide more housing, were proposed by the UK Coalition government and may form an important element of ongoing urban development in the UK.

These views chimed with others who, in the late 20th century, were critical of decades of unchecked urban development, including the abandonment of city centres by people and investors, suburbanisation, and the design of identikit places devoid of character and a sense of place. 'Social sustainability' emerged to describe the importance of providing for more than ecological or environmental conservation, and to also ensure the 'infrastructure to support social and cultural life, social amenities, systems for citizen engagement and space for people and places to evolve' (Woodcraft, 2011, p 16). The emergence of the Congress for New Urbanism in 1992, seeking to champion a new approach to urban habitability, was indicative of a broader sense that radical changes in urban planning and place-making had to occur to (re)create cities as convivial and liveable places. New urbanist principles were a reaction against modern urbanism, seeking instead to cultivate places that Lefebvre (1991) refers to as the spontaneity of the city, where strangers intermingle and mix (see Figure 7.4). The translation of such ideas into policy and practice is evident through the planning of what Lees (2010, p 2302) refers to as 'heterospaces', or places comprising socially mixed neighbourhoods, including commercial, residential and leisure uses.

Figure 7.4: The principles of new urbanism

- *Walkability*: including pedestrian-friendly street design.
- *Connectivity*: comprising a dense network of narrow streets and an interconnected street grid.
- *Mixed use and diversity*: a mix of residential, office, retail and leisure contained within single sites, and a diversity of people of all ages, incomes, cultures and races.
- *Mixed housing*: the provision of a mix of house-types, sizes and income brackets, including low-cost housing.
- *Quality architecture and urban design*: to design beautiful places, comprising character and human comfort and creating a sense of place.
- *Traditional neighbourhood structure*: places should have a defined centre and edge and good-quality, accessible public space should be integral.
- *Increased density*: residences, shops and services should be closer together for ease of walking, and to enable a more efficient use of services and resources.
- *Smart transportation*: pedestrian-friendly design that encourages a greater use of bicycles and walking as daily transportation.
- *Sustainability*: to minimise human impact on the environment by adopting energy efficiency and more local production and respecting nature and fragile ecosystems.
- *Quality of life*: to enhance quality of life by creating places that enrich, uplift and inspire the human spirit.

(Adapted from the Congress for New Urbanism charter. Available at: http://www.cnu.org/charter)

Sustainable development and urban policy: the dimensions

While there appears to be widespread political consciousness of the social and environmental effects of urbanisation, there is less agreement about what is to be done or what the policy prognosis is or ought to be. This is reflected in the less than coherent approach by governments to the sustainable development of cities in which a plethora of policies have emerged under the banner of 'sustainability'. Some observers, such as Raco (2005), suggest that policies pay lip service to those directives that highlight equity, empowerment and environmental protection as paramount in achieving sustainable development. Instead, there is emphasis on continuing resource exploitation and urban entrepreneurship, with faith placed in conventional policy interventions to reduce environmental impact (see Imrie and Lees, 2014). These include pricing mechanisms to modify people's consumption habits and new technologies to enable the management and amelioration of negative externalities. An example of the former is the congestion charge in London and an example of the latter is the use of smart technologies in home environments to monitor and modify levels of energy consumption (see Figure 7.5).

Figure 7.5: London's congestion charge

Transport for London operates a congestion charge that covers most of Central London on weekdays. London's congestion charge was brought in to reduce congestion and carbon emissions, to ease through-traffic, and to improve the transport system. The charge was introduced in 2003 alongside other measures to improve public transport, particularly buses, as well as traffic regulation and parking provision. Revenues are supposed to be reinvested in the transport system. London's congestion charge area is one of the largest in any capital city, and it is seen as a pioneer.

The shaping of urban policy by sustainable development discourse was evident in the UK from the early 1990s and was signalled in legislation such as the Town and Country Planning Act 1990, which required local authorities to produce plans seeking to achieve sustainable outcomes. Lombardi et al (2011, p 281) note that the planning system in the UK, as the major means to address sustainable development issues in cities, defines sustainability as primarily characterised by programmes to curtail 'urban sprawl, building on brownfield sites and achieving higher densities and better mixes of use within a scheme or neighbourhood'. Here, the influence of the Congress for New Urbanism is evident, and it has shaped a raft of policy approaches, including encouraging local planning authorities to create walkable cities, to enhance the appeal of the public realm through environmental improvement programmes, to assure safety and security as part of people's well-being, and to create pedestrian places for ease of social interaction.

For some commentators, the mix of policies has been no more than 'a garnish sprinkled over other pre-existing policy commitments' (Evans et al, 2003, p 49). Instead, urban policy in England since the late 1990s has broadly followed a 'shallow greening' approach. This commits governments to economic development and the understanding that natural resources can be managed in ways whereby they can be safeguarded from depletion, while, simultaneously, being consumed by people to serve their wants and desires. The publication of the Urban White Paper (UWP) *Our towns and cities – the future: delivering an urban renaissance* (DETR, 2000, p 5) set the tone in arguing that 'Our policies, programmes and structures of governance are based on engaging local people in partnerships for change [which is] at the heart of our work on tackling social exclusion, and is central to achieving sustainable economic growth'. This was further developed in 2003 with the publication of *Sustainable communities: building for the future* (ODPM, 2003), which outlined plans to revive declining urban areas by seeking to pump-prime housing and industrial markets in areas of low demand, while seeking compact urban development by encouraging building on brownfield sites.

Building new communities was also a feature of New Labour's approach to sustainable development. The UWP outlined the rationale as 'moving towards more mixed and sustainable communities ... for improving the quality of urban life' (DETR, 2000, p 8). The subsequent publication of the Sustainable Communities Plan (SCP) in 2005 proposed four growth areas as a policy response – the Thames Gateway, Ashford, Milton Keynes and a corridor running from London to Peterborough – as part of programme to promote socially mixed places and economic sustainability. Here, the rationale was to ensure that economic growth in London and the South-East was not undermined by a lack of affordable housing that might otherwise lead to labour shortages inhibiting the expansion of key industrial sectors. One solution, in the form of new and expanding settlements, was justified by pointing to the potential of creating better-designed environments to combat social inequality and poverty in disadvantaged neighbourhoods. The objective was social mixing as a means to deconcentrate poverty and redress market failure in housing and employment (see Lees, 2014). A 'sustainable community' was defined as one whereby market failure in housing had been overturned.

This was the remit of the Mixed Communities Initiative (ODPM, 2005), one of the flagship initiatives of New Labour that followed up the sentiments of the Social Exclusion Unit's (2001, p 53) observation that 'communities function best when they contain a broad social mix'. The objective of the policy was the elimination of social deprivation by changing the mix of people in communities, primarily by extending housing choice. Manzi (2010, p 4) describes the approach as perpetuating the 'neighbourhood effects' argument 'that there are specific and cumulative locational disadvantages associated with communities where deprivation is found'. The discourse of mixed communities is seen by many academics as state-led gentrification characterised by the conversion of social housing to owner-occupation, and/or its demolition and replacement by new-build, private dwellings (Lees, 2013). The process is not confined to any one country and appears to be ubiquitous and evident in many renewal projects worldwide. One of the most extensive programmes is Homeownership Opportunities for People Everywhere (HOPE) VI in the US (see Figure 7.6).

Figure 7.6: HOPE VI programme, US

Source: Rob Imrie

The HOPE VI programme began in 1992, with formal recognition in law in 1998. As of 2005, the programme had distributed USD5.8 billion through 446 federal block grants to cities for housing development. An example of a HOPE VI revitalisation is Valencia Gardens in San Francisco, which saw the replacement of 246 dilapidated units with 260 new one-, two-, three- and four-bedroom units, comprised of 218 family flats and town house apartments and 42 one-bedroom apartments for elderly people. All family units have individual front doors facing the street and either secure backyards or upper rear decks.

Popkin (2002, p 1) describes the HOPE VI programme in the following terms:

> The Department of Housing and Urban Development (HUD) moved away from providing project-based assistance for poor families and started promoting mixed-income housing and the use of housing subsidies to prevent the concentration of troubled, low-income households. The philosophy behind the shift was similar to that driving the new approach to welfare reform a few years later. Both reforms sought to promote self-sufficiency among recipients – one by emphasizing jobs over welfare checks; the other by encouraging families to move to better, safer neighborhoods that might offer greater economic opportunities.

HOPE VI has been criticised:

> HUD's failure to provide comprehensive and accurate information about HOPE VI has created an environment in which misimpressions about the program and its basic purposes and outcomes have flourished – often with encouragement from HUD. HOPE VI plays upon the public housing program's unfairly negative reputation and an exaggerated sense of crisis about the state of public housing in general to justify a drastic model of large-scale family displacement and housing redevelopment that increasingly appears to do more harm than good. (National Housing Law Project, 2002, p ii)

Programmes such as HOPE VI have gone hand in hand with policymakers seeking to capitalise on land sales, and to repopulate and re-energise cities through property-led investments that, in the context of housing, include upscale, high-cost residences. From Sao Paulo to London and Moscow, the residential landscape of cities increasingly resembles a patchwork quilt of condominiums or high-rise-flatted developments seeking primarily to serve affluent single-person households. Central and local government administrations encourage such schemes as part of a process to attract global capital and to populate places that are otherwise semi-derelict with underutilised and, in some instances, abandoned buildings. An example is Nine Elms in Vauxhall, South-West London, described by the Nine Elms Vauxhall Partnership, the development team orchestrating the regeneration, as 'the greatest transformational story at the heart of the world's greatest city' (see Figure 7.7).

The discourse of sustainable development is increasingly oriented towards the development and management of infrastructure, and the deployment of smart technologies to enable an increase in the efficiency and reliability of different urban systems, such as housing and transportation. The notion of the 'smart city' has filtered into policy and practice as the incorporation of information and communication technologies into urban services and infrastructures. An example is the use of smart energy meters to enable cities to manage energy demand, reduce cost and, in principle, safeguard the environment. The objective is to boost the economic performance of cites, while enhancing the lifestyles of their inhabitants. The 'smart city' is shaped by technology as a means to modernise urban infrastructure, enabling people to control the complexities of human—environment interactions. Smart cities are characterised by the use of state-of-the-art digital networks and global Internet connectivity, which enable the city to perform better. There are few cities without a smart city policy, ranging from the creation of public Wi-Fi networks to the installation of a modern digital infrastructure that enables people to access information and data relating to transport.

Figure 7.7: Nine Elms, Vauxhall, London

Source: Rob Imrie

Sustainable development is also associated by academics and policymakers with seeking to create 'resilience' in cities. Planners increasingly refer to 'resilience' and, as Porter and Davoudi (2012, p 329) suggest, it 'appears to be fast replacing sustainability as the buzzword of the moment'. The notion of resilience is focused on the interrelationships between social and ecological systems, and brings to the fore the fragile interdependencies between people and their environments. Commentators note that while the notion of resilience is vague and difficult to define, it has the virtue of drawing attention to the entwined nature of ecological and social systems, and how the latter is inextricably linked to, or dependent on, the former. The development of resilience is used across institutions at different geographical scales, and is most associated with planning for energy security, climate change and responses to major civil emergencies. In the wake of the 9/11 terrorist attacks in the US, a different consciousness emerged about the fragility of human life and the vulnerability of urban infrastructure, particularly technological systems, in the event of such a precipitous occurrence.

The policy approaches adopted by different city administrations to secure and safeguard flows of ecological resources, infrastructure and services are many and varied. The 100 Resilient Cities project, pioneered by the Rockefeller Foundation, provides examples, including Christchurch, New Zealand, where three years after a devastating earthquake, it is claimed that a grassroots participatory planning process has enabled 'communities, buildings, and infrastructure and systems [to be] better prepared to withstand catastrophic events' (see: http://citiesofmigration.ca/ezine_stories/defining-urban-resilience-in-christchurch/). In January 2015, Bristol in the UK was proclaimed 'European Green Capital' in recognition of major investment in wind power and up to £300 million for energy efficiency and renewables by 2020. In contrast, Vejle in Denmark is at risk from flooding and it is predicted that low-lying residential and business areas will be underwater by 2100. The policy challenge is to regard water as a resource to be utilised as opposed to a threat to be mitigated. The city is seeking to increase its resilience by developing participative governance and implementing practical, smart technologies, such as water filtrations systems (see: http://www.100resilientcities.org/cities/entry/vejles-resilience-challenge).

Sustainable urban policy: an evaluation

It is difficult to disentangle the melange of policy programmes that claim to promote sustainable development. Barely any government urban policy proceeds without asserting its sustainability credentials to the point whereby everything and anything appears to be underpinned by, and promotes, sustainable development. There are bewildering ranges of policy and planning approaches claiming to create sustainable cities, including smart growth, new urbanism, compact cities, transition towns and eco-cities. A veritable industry has developed around policy and practice relating to sustainable city-building and place-making, characterised by the proliferation of international conferences, workshops, products, services and specialised consultancies.

Despite the widespread, popular appeal of sustainable development, including expressions of support from politicians of all political colours, there are those who suggest that the concept has failed to change the nature of urban policy. Thus, Lombardi et al (2011) note that while the UK government has incorporated sustainable development into urban renewal programmes, there is vagueness about what it entails in practice. They suggest that despite almost universal agreement that sustainable urban renewal is a good thing, 'sustainability has yet to make a serious influence on the approach to the redevelopment of land' (Lombardi et al, 2011, p 274). Giddings et al (2002, p 190) note that 'British urban policy has concentrated on economic and physical regeneration and less on environmental and social issues'. They argue that business appears to be more concerned with the marketing opportunities of a green image than embracing fundamental changes to their practices that are environmentally friendly.

For others, sustainable urban development is threatened by a number of factors, including non-localist urban development, 'growth first' policies and municipal pragmatism (see Whitehead, 2012). Non-localist developments are characterised by the proliferation of regeneration projects that while ostensibly seeking to draw in global investment to create new neighbourhoods, appear to be creating enclaves for the 'super-rich' and global business elites. Dale and Newman (2009, p 670) suggest that the benefits of redevelopment projects are not equitably shared and reflect, in part, the lack of consideration by politicians and policy officers of 'critical issues of equity and distributive justice' (see Figure 7.8). Moore and Bunce (2009, p 604) suggest a need to challenge the model of sustainable development that propagates the building of elite neighbourhoods 'in favour of social equity and social justice'. This solution requires less public reliance on private investment, and, instead, encourages community interventions in regeneration supported by major public sector resources to provide good-quality, affordable housing and related infrastructure.

Figure 7.8: Gentrification and the case of Tarlabaşı, Istanbul

Sustainable development is defined, in part, by the rebuilding of cities by property-led regeneration, breathing new life into what are otherwise old, declining areas. Here, sustainable development is to ensure that life can continue and that places are provided with the infrastructure and resources so that people's livelihoods and well-being can be assured. Too often, what transpires is a partial, particular form of regeneration based on the displacement of poor people and their replacement by upmarket, socially selective neighbourhoods.

This is the case in much of the older parts of Istanbul in Turkey that are being pulled down, with historic neighbourhoods being replaced by modernist landscapes catering to global elites. This is occurring in the name of sustainable development, or what supporters of the scheme regard as a way to boost the local economy by locking it into global flows of finance and investment in real estate. One such area is Tarlabaşı, a low-income and primarily Kurdish neighbourhood that also serves as a sanctuary for Turkey's marginalised populations.

The location of Tarlabaşı close to Central Istanbul makes it a target for gentrification, and local municipality officials and the Housing Development Administration of Istanbul declared Tarlabaşı an urban renewal area in 2006. The objective was to create a mixed community characterised by shopping malls, upscale housing units and public recreational areas. By 2012, after court battles over property rights, the project began. The renewal area encompasses a 4.9-acre part of Tarlabaşı that includes 210 historic Ottoman-era buildings, and the blighting and then demolition of buildings is a key part of the process.

Commenting on the process, the academic historian Uğur Tanyeli notes that:

> I am most dismayed by the fact that they cut out pieces of the city as if with a knife, with no regard for the history or the social fabric in these neighbourhoods. What they really mean to say is: 'There is no longer any space for lower income groups in the city centre.' (Quoted in Costanze, 2012, p 1)

It is difficult to see how this can occur in a context dominated by municipal pragmatism. For example, local authority officers seek to balance economic growth with achieving sustainability by using trade-offs that may, according to Whitehead (2012, p 40), detract from principles of sustainable development. Whitehead (2012) refers to an example of development on green-belt land between Birmingham and Coventry, where discussions by local and regional government actors and private sector agencies sought to make a trade-off between the development of the green belt and providing protected area status in other parts of the region. A similar approach is the IJ Berg development in the Netherlands, where 18,000 new dwellings are being constructed in the Ijsselmeer, a place of shallow, sheltered, nutrient-rich waters and an abundance of crustaceans and water plants. To offset the impacts, the City of Amsterdam is working with other parties to create three new nature areas (see Figure 7.9). This is not an uncommon approach to sustainable development or what Whitehead (2012) describes as the 'natural capital philosophy' approach to planning.

Figure 7.9: Organic regeneration? IJ Burg development, Amsterdam

Source: http://en.wikipedia.org/wiki/IJburg#mediaviewer/File:Amsterdam_
IJburg_20041105.jpg

IJ Burg is an urban area constructed out of artificial islands to the east of Amsterdam. The planning approach has been criticised by some as over-regulation and prescriptive planning, stifling human inventiveness and spirit. Thus, the architect Dennis Kaspori has noted that IJ Burg:

> is planned in such detail that any process that might be different is given no space. But people don't fit into this vision and they soon start using their elbows to create space. As an example, the fences around people's gardens are a particular height to encourage communal relationships and there are regulations to stop you building higher ones. After a few months the planners' dream of collective space started to collapse as people erected steel mesh and grew ivy on it to segregate themselves. (Drake, 2008)

Sustainable development can be seen as something that cannot be easily achieved because seeking to sustain ecology and the environment is irreconcilable with promoting economic growth. Some suggest that sustainable development is an empty term rendered impossible to operationalise in any practical sense. Varn (2007, p 2), for instance, regards sustainable development as a regulative ideal that is 'unachievable but nonetheless can balance, guide, and mediate our actions in practical matters'. For Stables (2013, p 182), the role of sustainable development is political and rhetorical: it encourages posturing and gestures but not substantial change. A range of commentators note that sustainable development is not progressive, but, rather, propagates the commodification of urban environments (Luke, 2005; Fry, 2009). Luke (2005) suggests that organisations that claim 'green credentials' primarily do so to enhance their sales of goods and services. Sustainable development is a product category, and is described by Dale and Newman (2009, p 669) as 'leading to further consumption rather than meaningful change'.

This state of affairs has arisen by promoting eco-modernisation, a value system that regards technology as a primary means to create an end state of 'sustainability'. For Fry (2009), however, sustainability is not an end state, but an indeterminate process, and the development and deployment of technology does not necessarily mean a greater likelihood of attaining sustainable development. A case in point is the smart city paradigm that Vanolo (2013, p 12) regards as propagating urban policies as technocratic visions of the good city 'supporting technological and ecological urban transitions'. They are premised on the power of technological and instrumental techniques to provide clean, liveable, technologically advanced cities far removed from the degradations of the industrial city. Some regard smart city policies as promoting an undesirable way of urban living characterised by a techno-rationality comprising centralised computational surveillance and control (see Batty et al, 2012).

The eco-modernising paradigm does not challenge or displace the centrality of the market economy and private sector actions as the alleged best means to achieve sustainable development. In 1994, the

British government outlined its commitment to a market-led approach to sustainable development in noting that it 'does not mean having less economic development: on the contrary, a healthy economy is better able to generate the resources to meet people's needs, and new investment and environmental improvements often go hand in hand' (UK Government, 1994, p 7). This stance was maintained throughout the New Labour years and has been exacerbated by the Coalition government's 'growth first' agenda, which Lombardi et al (2011, p 274) describe as a 'develop-at-almost-any-cost' philosophy. This reflects the broad cloth of urban policy in which sustainable development principles are weakly development and implemented, or what Lombardi et al (2011, p 274) suggest is a 'status quo' approach by the state seeking to safeguard economic growth (see Chapter Eight).

Sneddon et al (2006, p 254) note that the principles of sustainable development, as outlined by Brundtland, are not at fault for the failure 'to stem the tide of unsustainable human activities'. On almost any measure relating to social and environmental change, cities have deteriorated since Brundtland's pronouncement. For Sneddon et al (2006), this is primarily due to ineffective institutions and the failures of governments to commit to the far-reaching programmes required. They suggest that the goals of Brundtland need to be retained but developed in ways whereby a plurality of views about sustainable development is incorporated into policy. They note how the critics of sustainable development discourse, such as Whitehead (2012) and O'Conner (1994), draw attention to its capture by corporate interests and its use as a smokescreen to pursue less than sustainable development practices. Smith (2012, p 35) suggests that this is possible because the concept of sustainability 'can be moulded into forms that fit existing belief systems'. It can be whatever an actor and/or institutional culture want it to be.

Alternative visions for sustainable cities

The argument here is that policies to address sustainability in cities do not break with the 'growth first' logic and that there is a failure by policymakers to interconnect economic objectives with social and environmental goals (see Evans et al, 2009). Where such connections are made, economic objectives override social and environmental concerns, and this is particularly so since the global recession of 2008, which has ushered in an era of almost unquestioning support for economic growth as the primary goal of (urban) policy (see Chapter Eight). The World Commission on Environment and Development (Brundtland Commission) (1987) and follow-up summits and meetings about sustainable development reinforce the understanding that 'the future is able to be secured via continued economic growth' (Fry, 2009, p 42). This mentality continues to dominate urban policy even where what appear to be innovative policy experiments ensue, such as the development of new settlements labelled as eco-cities. Eco-cities are presented as the alternative to conventional urban form and lifestyles by designing out major energy use and producing zero-carbon environments.

Despite claims to integrate economic with social and environmental objectives, the evidence suggests that eco-cities are wedded to the values of eco-modernisation and promote, first and foremost, the objective of economic growth. An example is the World Bank's Eco2Cities initiative launched in 2010 and described 'as an integral part of the World Bank Urban and Local Government Strategy, to help cities in developing countries achieve greater ecological and economic sustainability' (World Bank, 2010). The approach to sustainable development advocated by the World Bank (2010, p 1) is to 'integrate ecological and economic considerations ... so that they produce cumulative and lasting advantages for cities'. Eco-city projects abound and most are characterised by top-down, technocratic management and the failure to achieve objectives. Eco-city experiments, such as Dongtan in South Korea, have never been implemented, and others, such as Masdar City in Abu Dhabi, are islands of smart technologies and high-value-added real estate that ignore the needs of the many living elsewhere in substandard dwellings (Cugurullo, 2013).

Some commentators note that an urban policy that seeks to propagate sustainable development needs to break with the illusory promises of eco-modernisation, that is, that human calculability and control through the deployment of technique, technology and management can be the panacea for urban environmental problems (Fry, 2011). Others, such as Frazier (1997), highlight the anthropogenic nature of sustainable development discourse and its inability to understand people and nature as conjoined and indissolubly intertwined. Sneddon et al (2006) suggest that there is an impasse between ideological and epistemological differences about what sustainable development is, and what it can achieve, and that this needs to be broken to move forward. They suggest 'embracing pluralism' as the way of recognising the 'complexity of sustainability dilemmas within a turbulent world' (Sneddon et al, 2006, p 253). This echoes Curry (2003), who calls for a pluralist eco-centrism that recognises the significance of nature in the city and the vitality of the non-human world.

Evans et al (2009, p 692) refer to organic regeneration as enabling people to shape places 'in their own vision' in ways whereby 'cities can become places again, rather than mere commodities'. Organic regeneration contrasts with large-scale property-led schemes that, in the view of Evans et al (2009), are insensitive to local traditions and propagate a developer-driven model that seeks speed and efficiency of outcomes. Organic regeneration is urban transformation that is 'locally grounded, slow, and piecemeal' (Evans et al, 2009, p 695). Evans et al (2009) suggest opening up opportunities for many different developers, designers and architects to participate in regeneration in order to encourage a diversity of approaches in which any parcel of land may be appropriated and shaped by numerous groups and/or individuals. The objective is to dismantle large-scale single-developer-dominated projects by providing opportunities for diverse actors, including individuals, to be provided with access to land and resources, and to encourage eclecticism rather than a singular, 'mono' approach to urban change.

A potential policy approach that has overtures of organic regeneration relates to the notion of distributed economies (Johansson et al, 2005). These entail the de-scaling of production and consumption and the use of seasonally grown produce to enable a shortening of production chains. The idea is to challenge globalisation and to sensitise producers of goods and services to respond to local market needs. A distributed economy can include urban farming to enable the reduction in transport of food produce over long distances between remote rural areas and cities, and, in doing so, to reduce reliance on fragile supply chains and help to minimise pollution. The emergence of the 'slow food' movement is also indicative of an anti-globalisation sentiment through seeking to preserve local gastronomic traditions and to encourage production and consumption that is respectful of sociocultural traditions (see Figure 7.10).

Figure 7.10: Promoting de-scaled economies and urban farming: an urban farm in downtown Chicago

Source: http://en.wikipedia.org/wiki/Urban_agriculture#mediaviewer/File:New_crops-Chicago_urban_farm.jpg

De-scaling, anti-global sentiments are particularly to the fore in the notion of 'transition culture'. This term draws attention to the necessity for local communities to be able to respond to significant global challenges, including a diminution in oil and climate change. Advocates of transition culture note that globalisation is not sustainable and that there needs to be a de-scaling of social and economic life by re-embedding people into a localisation of activities and interactions. The most popular example of the movement is transition towns, which encourage communities to plan for the demise of globalisation by developing capacities to produce local supplies of food and energy while encouraging localised consumption, often through the use of local currencies. The movement also seeks to provide low-cost housing and to provide local people with the means to shape local political decision-making about the quality of places. Grover (2009, p 1) describes the transition movement as 'non-ideological, practical and pragmatic', although others see its principles as vague and difficult to operationalise.

Conclusions

One of the most significant policy developments of the late 20th century was the rapid adoption of principles of sustainable development by a host of public and private sector organisations. By the early 2000s, no credible organisation could claim to be anything other than committed to sustainable development. From large corporations to small-scale voluntary organisations, a watchword for good, responsible practice was 'sustainability'. This was particularly so in relation to spatial development processes, and throughout the 2000s, city governments worldwide were placing sustainable development at the centre of urban policy and planning. Such planning has rarely gone beyond the propagation of an eco-modernising agenda that does not challenge the centrality of economic growth as the basis of urban development. Rather, it promotes, and perpetuates, the continued exploitation of nature.

A particular feature of urban regeneration involves gentrification and the creation of new spaces that displace the urban poor (see Lees, 2013; Slater, 2013). From Central London to Tokyo and Beijing, urban policy is implicated in low-income residents losing their homes and being replaced by high-income, often overseas, residents. Such displacements are occurring in the name of the sustainable development of urban areas, and are often dressed up as creating mixed communities, yet they do no more than supplant one social class with another. This is redolent of social cleansing and perpetuates, and even extends, social divisions and differences in cities. One could conclude that in seeking to propagate sustainable development, urban policy may be implicated in undermining the social fabric of cities and dismantling some of the socio-economic structures, such as low-cost housing, that provide the very means for people to sustain themselves.

SUMMARY

Cities have been rediscovered as places of potential for socio-economic development and the enhancement of lifestyles, and the promotion of urban renaissance policies worldwide has been a feature of policy since the early 1990s. Such policies are characterised by the adoption and development of multiple strategies, including a commitment to sustainable development. The notion of sustainable development is vague and difficult to define and operationalise. A feature of urban policy that alludes to sustainable development is the promotion of major regeneration, which, while purporting to be creating mixed communities, is likely to lead to the gentrification of neighbourhoods. City politicians and officials increasingly recognise the limits of pursuing sustainable development through globalisation, and alternative counter-movements that highlight the virtues of local, grassroots regeneration and de-scaled production systems are evident.

RECOMMENDED READING

A good overview of the subject is Wheeler and Beatley (2004), see also Krueger and Gibbs (2007). One of the best critiques of the ethics and practices of sustainable development is the work of Tony Fry, including *Design futuring* (Fry, 2009). Readers who want a trenchant critique of the sustainable communities agenda, including social mixing, should look at Mike Raco (2007) and also Flint and Raco (2012).

WEB LINKS

There are numerous websites about cities and sustainability. Some relevant sites include the Stockholm Environment Institute (see: http://www.sei-international.org), the World Cities Network (see: http://www.worldcitiesnetwork.org) and the UN Sustainable Development Platform (see: http://sustainabledevelopment.un.org/index.php?menu=1510).

8

urban recovery and the
future for cities

Introduction

This chapter considers the future for cities in a context of global economic recession and austerity measures impacting on public spending programmes. Since 2008, public sector spending has been curtailed and welfare policy programmes have been reorganised to encourage individuals to rely less on state support and more on their own capacities and resources. Urban areas, as the main places for jobs and economic development, are most likely to feel the effects of government cutbacks, with consequences for the quality of urban infrastructure and lifestyles. It is cuts to mainstream, non-spatial policy programmes on education, housing and health care that are likely to have the greatest impact on the social and economic status of people living in cities. We highlight how fiscal cutbacks in main spending programmes are changing the fortunes of people living in cities and disproportionately impacting on poor and disadvantaged people. We also discuss how the changing socio-economic and political contexts of (urban) policy are facilitating 'fire sales' of public land and assets, with politicians encouraging greater private sector involvement in the planning and development of communities.

Urban policy discourse since 2008 has been shaped by the notion of the 'Big Society', a phrase coined by Prime Minister David Cameron (2009, p 1) to describe the government's responsibility to empower and enable 'individuals, families and communities to take control of their lives'. Cameron's prognosis for a better society was a reaffirmation of what previous politicians, from J.F. Kennedy to Tony Blair, had pronounced, or, as the latter said in 2002, 'we are building an enabling state founded on the liberation of individual potential' (Blair, 2002, p 1). In the post-2008 era, such potential was signalled by the then Minister for Cities, Greg Clark, who, in December 2011, announced a series of 'City Deals'. He described the initiative as a 'bold and ambitious new idea to put cities back in charge of their own economic destiny and to seize the opportunities for growth' (Clark, 2011, p 1). Likewise, in the US, urban recovery after 2008 was defined in self-help terms, including the American Recovery and Reinvestment Act 2009, which provided an estimated USD190 billion to be invested in cities across the US. This programme, like its British counterpart, signifies a new phase of market-oriented policy in which urban futures will depend less on state subsidy and more on autarchic social and economic systems.

This seems to signify the emergence of a post-welfare urban policy, and in evaluating this proposition, we divide the rest of the chapter into five parts. First, the broader socio-political context of austerity and retrenchment of public welfare is outlined, with an evaluation of how far a 'Big Society' agenda is able to take root and redress the problems of cities. Second, focusing on the UK, we assess the urban policy programmes of austerity, and note that the primacy of 'growth first' policies is shaping spatial development around what Flint and Raco (2012, p 244) describe as 'a broader attack on the legitimacy and capacities of governments and welfare states'. The understanding of urban policy here is its marginalisation or reduction to minimal forms of state intervention, and increasing reliance on private and voluntary sector involvement in the development and delivery of urban services. Third, we outline some of the effects of austerity (urban) policy on the socio-economic fortunes of cities. Fourth, we consider alternative scenarios, or approaches, to 'growth first' that can respond to Lefebvre's (2003, p 150) observation about 'the right to the city', or the development of a socially just and democratic urbanism. We conclude by speculating on what the future is likely to be for urban policy in post-austerity times.

Global recession and the state of the cities

The period since late 2007, and ongoing at the time of writing, has been described as the Great Recession (see Bell and Blanchflower, 2010). It has witnessed the collapse in world trade and, according to Baldwin (2009, p 1), the sharpest economic downturn since records began. The recession was precipitated by defaults on mortgages and derivative products, and a diminution in lending or the supply of credit. The outcome was the collapse of industrial production, with no country or urban area unaffected. For instance, a survey for a European-funded network called the Urban Development Network Programme (URBACT) in 2009 (World Bank, 2012, p 7) suggested that 80% of the 131 cities from the 25 European Union member countries had suffered from the bankruptcy of companies, a diminution in corporate investments, the restriction of loans by banks and the reluctance of companies to take risks in times of uncertainty. The consequential changes to gross domestic product (GDP) per capita and employment in the world's major urban areas indicates that recovery is a long way off. In the US, only Dallas, Pittsburgh and Knoxville were showing signs of economic growth by 2011 (see Istrate and Nadeau, 2012). In Europe, Istrate and Nadeau's (2012, p 13) research highlights uneven development in that 'nearly all major metro areas in Germany and Austria have recovered, but none outside those countries have done so'.

Major supranational organisations, such as the International Monetary Fund (IMF) and the World Bank, suggest that the basis of urban recovery is the revitalisation of the capitalist system by restoring the vitality of the banking and industrial sectors, and reducing public debt through major deficit reduction programmes. Oosterlynck and Gonzalez (2013) report similar understandings by the Organisation for Economic Co-operation and Development (OECD) and URBACT. They show that such organisations do not question the underlying socio-political and economic relations that have precipitated the fiscal crisis. Rather, the capitalist system is presented as 'given' or beyond challenge, and as a naturalised entity that requires its restoration as a prerequisite for economic recovery. Catterell (2012, p 3) makes a similar point when referring to the period after 2008 as 'a new phase of neoliberal capitalism', which, ironically, is seeking to orchestrate recovery by reasserting, and strengthening, the very political-economic systems that led to fiscal insolvency and crisis in the first place.

The process is characterised by the privatisation of (urban) public assets and a downward squeeze on public expenditure as part of a debt reduction strategy. This is indicative of previous rounds of public sector austerity, reflecting Svara's (1990, p 3) characterisation of municipal retrenchment in expenditures in the 1980s as a 'fend-for-yourself' federalism (see also Peck, 2012). Worldwide, cities have been undergoing major programmes of public expenditure cuts, and in Toronto, over USD800 million of public funds have been cut since 2010, with the Deputy City Manager, Cam Weldon (2012, p 1), noting that the chronic structural deficit continues and will require his office 'to continue to conduct service efficiency studies'. The situation is evident across the globe, and in Manchester, UK, the council's budget was cut by £170 million between April 2011 and November 2012, resulting in the loss of 2,000 public sector jobs (Manchester City Council, 2013, p 49). The situation has since worsened, and in 2014/15, it is reported that £52 million will need to be saved from Manchester's budget, with the true cost rising to £70 million once inflation and increased demands due to population increases are accounted for (see Williams, 2013).

In other places, the cutbacks have been more extreme and exemplify the uneven nature of austerity, or what Peck (2012, p 651) refers to as 'the new urban condition'. Peck (2012) is alluding to austerity as extending previous periods of policy experimentation, including the devolution and decentralisation of administration and the creation of leaner local states by rapid reductions in budgets and the rationalisation of services. In some cities, the consequences appear to be precipitous. For instance, it is estimated that up to 40% of Detroit's street lighting has been turned off due to a mix of budget shortfalls and a lack of means to manage and maintain any stock that has failed. In February 2013, Detroit Council voted to set up a new layer of governance, the Detroit Public Lighting Authority (DPLA), charged with the task of taking 40,000 street lights out of service permanently and strategically lighting main roads and neighbourhoods based on density. One of the city council politicians, Andre Spivey, who voted in support of the DPLA, said that 'there are some blocks where citizens don't have a single working street light and other areas where no one lives and all the lights are functioning' (quoted in Craig, 2013, p 1).

This reflects a new form of urban inequality that city officials feel unable to solve given budgeting and staffing constraints. Instead, the costs and risks of managing and maintaining urban services are subject to further rounds of devolvement to new layers of, usually private, governance, leading to what Peck (2012, p 648) describes as the emergence of 'fee based systems [that] will have consequences for low income populations'. An example of a fee-based system is the 'fire sale' of Chicago's Parking Meters. In 2008, a USD one billion deal was signed between Chicago's mayor, Richard Daley, and a group of private investors led by Morgan Stanley to lease Chicago's parking meters for a 75-year period up to 2084. The company now administers Chicago's parking and has replaced the old meters with high-technology pay boxes. The sale of the meters was prompted by budget gaps in the municipality. Observations suggest that over the lifetime of the contract, the city of Chicago is forgoing USD4 billion to USD5 billion in projected revenues for the sake of a short-term windfall of USD one billion. Cohen and Farmer (2014) have described the scheme as short-changing the public because an outcome of privatisation is that parking rates have become exorbitant and the terms of the lease protecting Morgan Stanley's investment created new annual costs for the city.

A similar scenario is evident across many countries and cities, and since the early 1990s, much urban infrastructure in the UK, including school buildings, hospitals and roads, has been supplied through the Private Finance Initiative. Some commentators regard the Public Finance Initiative as 'privatisation creep' insofar that it provides lucrative contracts to private sector organisations to supply public goods and services (see Raco, 2013). Private sector firms bear the short-term costs of funding projects and lease back completed schemes to the public authority that has contacted it out. The leaseback period may be as much as 30 years. The Public Finance Initiative has the short-term advantage of attracting upfront private expenditure to provide much-needed public infrastructure, but the longer-term implication of incurring public sector debt given the often exorbitant leaseback costs (see Figure 8.1). The contradiction is that these new, privatised systems of corporate governance are part of contractual arrangements to deliver public services that appear to be costing the public sector more than if they were delivering the services themselves.

Figure 8.1: University Hospital, Coventry, UK

University Hospital in Coventry, UK, was constructed between July 2002 and early 2006 and was opened on 10 July 2006. The partners in the scheme, known as Projectco, were Innisfree Ltd, Skanska, VINCI, GE and ISS Mediclean. Skanska subsequently sold its stake to Innisfree for £66 million. The hospital cost £440 million to build, but Projectco is guaranteed an income of £3.3 billion over 30 years, including facilities contracts. This is one of the biggest Private Finance Initiatives in UK history, and it diverts public funds from patient care to infrastructure works and to serving huge long-term debts incurred as part of the private sector-led Private Finance Initiative scheme.

Austerity urban policy is also creating new and extended opportunities for other actors to replace municipal or state organisations. Allmendinger and Haughton (2009: 626) use the term 'soft spaces of governances' to describe the break-up of big government and the decentralisation of governance activities to non-governmental, voluntary sector and charitable organisations. In the UK, this involves diminishing the role of central government and replacing it with the 'Big Society', or post-welfare formations in which individuals are construed as active citizens expected to bear much more responsibility for the development and delivery of services, ranging from libraries to local, self-help, care systems. The key term shaping the policy agenda is 'localism', or decentralising government to local levels of governance, with the intent to encourage what Clarke (2013, p 492) describes as 'locally scaled action, including projects of local autonomy and self-sufficiency'. In the UK, the localism agenda was formalised by the Localism Act 2011, which includes a clause entitled 'general power of competence'. At face value, this appears to encourage local discretion and policy experimentation because it empowers local authorities to pursue whatever policy they want, free from central controls, as long as it is legal (see Figure 8.2).

Figure 8.2: Localism outlined

Localism was an important part of the UK Coalition government's attempts to transfer powers from central government to local authorities, and to provide communities with scope to influence the actions of government policymakers. The Localism Act 2011 identifies a range of objectives in seeking to create a decentralised power structure. These include:

1. lifting the burden of bureaucracy;
2. empowering communities to do things their way;
3. increasing local control of public finance;
4. diversifying the supply of public services;
5. opening up government to public scrutiny; and
6. strengthening accountability to local people.

Part of the localism agenda involves the proliferation of elected mayors, an idea derived from the US, where mayors are seen to be a positive force for local change. In 2010, the Coalition government promised to create elected mayors in the 12 largest English city authorities. While Leicester and Liverpool resolved to adopt an elected mayoral system, referendums were held in the other 10 cities and only Bristol voted in favour. In November 2014, the Coalition government announced that Manchester would be the first city outside London to get its own elected citywide mayor, covering all local authority areas in the Greater Manchester 'metro-area', with powers covering transport, housing, planning and policing. This is part of a strategy to encourage economic growth in Northern England and to reduce the gap with London, but also part of an argument to devolve powers to the regions.

While the possibility for people to gain control over decisions that influence their lives is proffered, some commentators see little evidence of localism or the 'Big Society' taking root, or the means provided by government to empower individuals in local communities (Ludwig and Ludwig, 2014). Rather, for many, the discourse of localism is a smokescreen by government to reduce state spending and the role of the public sector in providing and managing services (see Featherstone et al, 2012; Raco, 2013). The objective is the eradication of 'big government', which, so it is alleged, inhibits individuals' liberties by unnecessary and wasteful bureaucracy. Featherstone et al (2012, p 178) see nothing new in the Coalition government's stance and interpret it as the intensification of 'an anti state populist agenda' that is part of 'long standing Conservative traditions of middle class voluntarism and social responsibility'. In this interpretation, localism is the reorganisation of local authorities in ways whereby the spaces of/ for governance by non-state actors are enhanced, particularly those of private sector organisations.

Urban policy and the politics of austerity

Austerity urbanism is presented by most politicians as a 'no alternative' scenario that offers most hope for the revitalisation of urban labour and housing markets and the provision of job opportunities. Part of the process is a re-heightened emphasis on, and political support for, dismantling perceived barriers to 'growth first' policies, with planning and building regulations a target. In a series of statements, government ministers have argued that the deregulation of planning and building controls is required to encourage development activity, which will be in the vanguard of leading economic recovery. This has led to state-funded and state-directed programmes related to sustainable urbanism being dismantled, including, in England, the institutional architecture set up by successive New Labour governments from 1997. After coming to office in 2010, the Coalition government disbanded regional tiers of government, including the Regional Development Agencies and the Government Offices for the Regions. In their place, local authorities were invited to set up Local Enterprise Partnerships (LEPs), business-led organisations allegedly able to foster 'a strong environment for business growth' (BIS, 2010). LEPs' operations are not necessarily confined within local authority boundaries and they often work across them as part of a flexible mode of governance.

The Coalition government also overhauled the planning system, culminating in the publication of the National Planning Policy Framework (NPPF) in November 2012 (see Figure 8.3). The remit of the NPPF is to facilitate ease of development and speed up the planning process in the belief that to do otherwise would be to undermine the potential for economic growth. The government described the changes as making 'planning much simpler and more accessible, reducing over 1,000 pages of often impenetrable jargon into around 50 pages of clearly written guidance' (DCLG, 2012a). The NPPF introduced a presumption in favour of sustainable development, which means encouraging property investment and economic growth. Commentators note that the NPPF is no more than a carte blanche for corporate property interests to bring forward plans to build in cities, and that safeguards to check and control negative social and environmental externalities are weak. Behind the discourse of sustainable development in the NPPF is, as Ludwig and Ludwig (2014, p 245) suggest, a 'covert political objective of enabling local economic development by facilitating private sector-led growth (through ensuring fewer local objections to development proposals and more planning approvals)'.

Figure 8.3: National Planning Policy Framework (DCLG, 2012a)

The NPPF, published in 2012, simplified, shortened and consolidated national planning policy guidance into one document. It provides guidance to local planning authorities in England when considering local plans and planning applications for development. The framework sets out a presumption in favour of development that is sustainable (social, economic and environmental). A report by the House of Common Committee on Communities and Local Government in December 2014 reviews the operation of the NPPF and notes some concerns, including that the NPPF is not preventing unsustainable development. It suggests that the same weight should be given to environmental and social, as well as economic, considerations as part of 'sustainable development'. Land supply for housing is one issue identified, including the relationship with the green belt, environmental protection and the provision of appropriate infrastructure.

The reduction of planning powers has occurred alongside cutbacks to well-established urban policy programmes dating back to the early 2000s. In England and Wales, government data show that annual spending on 'core' regeneration programmes was halved in 2011/12, with a 65% reduction in the period from 2009/10 to 2011/12. Urban policy is no longer recognisable from previous periods, and there is no national programme for neighbourhood regeneration targeted at the most deprived communities, the first time since the inception of modern-day urban policy in 1969. The government's approach was criticised by the All-Party Select Committee on regeneration in 2011. Clive Betts, Committee Chair, noted that 'The Government has cut public funding for regeneration programmes dramatically and has produced no adequate "strategy" for regeneration sufficient to tackle the deep-seated problems faced by our most deprived communities' (quoted in Ramesh, 2011, p. 1). It was further observed that regeneration appeared to have been affected much more severely than other parts of the public sector, and that, combined with cuts to local authorities, it presented a real challenge to the ability to address the needs of deprived people.

The policy response has been to encourage localism, highlighting the alleged virtues of 'less government' and more community-led regeneration. In 2010, the Coalition government published a White Paper titled *Local growth* (BIS, 2010), identifying 'self-help' as significant in tackling urban problems, and exhorting local individuals and organisations to realise 'local ambitions' (see also DCLG, 2012b). The White Paper was supplemented by the DCLG (2012b), identifying the role of government as 'strategic and supportive': to enable local initiative by encouraging 'local partners … to work together to develop local solutions to local problems' (DCLG, 2012b, p 1). The document notes that the government's objective is not 'to define what regeneration is … or what measures should be used to drive it'; rather, it is up to local actors to 'develop their own regeneration strategy to address their own priorities' (DCLG, 2012b, pp 4–5). These exhortations are not without problems insofar as they fail to recognise the scaled nature of urban problems, or that a local manifestation of a problem may not necessarily be remediable through local actions or interventions, often because people do not have the resources or skills.

The reality is that the rhetoric of localism, and de-scaled urban policy, is not matched by what is happening, and the main institutional features of the localist agenda towards urban policy are characterised by a top-down agenda in which scope for local actions is prescribed by central government. Far from a break with central government's dominance in shaping local policy programmes, the Coalition's approach appears to tie local authorities into centrally defined directives. This is evident with one of the main policy approaches, City Deals, led by the government's Cities Policy Unit. The approach encourages city councils, with their LEPs, to submit competitive bids to government for financial support to bolster local economic development programmes. The City Deal policy has had two phases: the first, in mid-2012, began with eight deals with the so-called core cities in England, comprising the largest metropolitan areas in population terms (see Table 8.1); the second phase, from mid-2013, extended City Deals to a further 14 English cities. Marlow (2014) does not feel that such schemes offer local control and notes that 'far from devolution, these deals are too often a confidence trick of heavily centralised patronage'.

Other measures are primarily variations on the content of the City Deal programme, and comprise a mix of fiscal incentives to local authorities to pursue economic growth. These are based on the 'trickle down'

Table 8.1: English City Deals

Wave 1: 2012	Wave 2: 2013
Birmingham	The Black Country
Bristol	Bournemouth
Leeds	Brighton and Hove
Liverpool	Greater Cambridge
Greater Manchester	Coventry and Warwickshire
Newcastle	Hull and Humber
Nottingham	Ipswich
Sheffield	Leicester and Leicestershire
	Milton Keynes
	Greater Norwich
	Oxford and Central Oxfordshire
	Reading
	Plymouth
	Preston and Lancashire
	Southampton and Portsmouth
	Southend
	Stoke and Staffordshire
	Sunderland and the North East
	Swindon and Wiltshire
	Tees Valley

economics that dominated property-led approaches to regeneration in the 1980s and 1990s. The rationale is to provide incentives to the private sector to bring forward resources, and for local authorities to encourage development activity as a means of boosting local economic fortunes. Such measures include Tax Increment Financing, Business Rate Retention and the New Homes Bonus, all of which use fiscal incentives to attract private sector investment (see Figure 8.4). For instance, Tax Increment Financing permits local authorities to borrow money for infrastructure projects against the future growth in business rate receipts that will result from the projects. The scheme is heavily reliant on transforming land and buildings into profitable commercial ventures to attract private sector investors. The reality is that not to do so may compromise the ability of local authorities to pay back loans, and hence the scheme locks municipalities into a logic in which only the most profitable forms of urban development can enable the scheme to operate.

Figure 8.4: New Homes Bonus

The New Homes Bonus is a form of government grant to local authorities to encourage them to increase housing supply. The aim of the scheme is to provide 140,000 extra homes over a 10-year period. The New Homes Bonus is based on the amount of council tax raised from new housing, conversions and empty property brought back into use, and extra funding is provided for affordable housing. Local authorities can decide how they wish to spend their New Homes Bonus funding. In 2013, the Public Accounts Committee was concerned as to whether the New Homes Bonus was going to local authorities with the greatest housing need.

Such schemes reflect what Peck (2012) refers to as the use of a competitive funding logic and the encouragement of a grant-grabbing culture (see Chapter Four). This culture is not confined to the UK. In the US, an example of localised, competitive urban policy is the focus on community building, exemplified by the 'Strong Cities, Strong Communities' (SC) initiative. President Obama announced the initiative in July 2011 and it seeks to strengthen neighbourhoods, towns, cities and regions by enhancing the capacity of local governments to develop and execute economic strategies. The policy works by city administrations bidding for federal funds based on outlining new solutions to facilitate economic growth. The programme is concerned less with direct poverty alleviation than with providing guidance and advice to local mayors and their teams by sending in troubleshooting experts 'to help them implement their economic development visions, make more effective and efficient use of taxpayer-funded federal resources ... [and] to create jobs and revitalize communities' (White House, 2013, p 1). Adler (2013, p 1) notes that SC covers too few cities, only 10, and that projects are modest, including, in Memphis, the purchase 'of a Mississippi Riverboat as part of an effort to bring economic activity to the city's waterfront'.

The organisation of SC initiatives and other competitive urban policy programmes contributes to a denudation of local democratic processes because the austerity programmes that they produce are imposed and rarely subject to public scrutiny. Donald et al (2014, p 6) note that urban policy in US cities illustrates 'the abandonment of the democratic process' and they point to the imposition of unelected administrators in cities such as Detroit and Stockton to oversee local austerity measures that 'severely reduced the size of the public sector'. For Donald et al (2014, p 6), a new form of local governance is emerging, which they characterise as 'austerity machines', or local, propertied elites concerned with propagating economic growth and 'presenting all forms of capital investment as a good thing'. The austerity machine sees little value in the public sector and labels benefit recipients as 'undeserving' of welfare and collective social support. The potential outcomes are described by Donald et al (2014, p 9) as harmful to citizens because many urban services, ranging from day centres to libraries, have been cut back or closed down, and there is no longer a guarantee of social welfare support.

The effects of austerity (urban) policy

Debt reduction and the retrenchment of public spending mean that city officials are engaging in investment-chasing behaviour, not as a deliberative, long-term, political strategy, but more as a short-term way of alleviating financial and resource shortfalls. This is ostensibly part of the bankrolling of public policy, and it appears to be intensifying in a context whereby local authorities have no choice but to tap into the private resources of major corporate organisations. This is particularly so in relation to funding urban regeneration, which increasingly features organisations ranging from the supermarket retailers Sainsbury and Tesco to the home furnishing company IKEA. The term 'Tesco towns' has been coined by those describing the wave of urban regeneration led by major companies in which store expansion plans are usually aligned with office space and residential units (see Figure 8.5). While such schemes pre-date the economic downturn, there is evidence that local authorities are enabling private organisations to play a more active part in place-making and shaping urban environments in ways whereby the commoditisation of public space is paramount (see Imrie and Dolton, 2014).

Figure 8.5: Tesco town, Woolwich Central

Source: Rob Imrie

Opened in November 2012, Tesco 'Woolwich Central' in South-East London represents a new wave of regeneration led by major retailers in which the property development arms of retail organisations lead initiatives that, in this instance, created a new 8,000 m² store, 1,000 residential apartments, a new library and pedestrianised public spaces. It is indicative of private sector-led place-making.

In London, the redevelopment of areas such as King's Cross, Nine Elms and the International Quarter, Stratford City, is illustrative of a regeneration model whereby public land is sold to private developers for profitable use, and even where public areas are retained, the management of them is usually contracted to private sector companies, a de facto form of privatisation. While such projects are ostensibly seeking to create mixed communities, and provide a range of housing choices, they are primarily characterised by the development of upscale office, retail and residential uses aimed at global investors and individuals who are part of a globalised, professional labour market. Such regeneration is cultivating new socio-spatial patterns, including the emergence of a global housing market in London in which the marketing of new residential regeneration occurs primarily outside of the UK, and particularly in South-East Asia. Much of the new and refurbished housing stock is aimed at a 'super-rich' clientele, and Dorling (2012) notes that London is the world's capital of the super-rich, defined as 'people with $30m (£21m) or more in assets apart from their main home'.

An outcome is the exacerbation of socio-spatial inequalities, as illustrated in Figures 8.6 and 8.7. Here, contrasting residential developments show two different outcomes of a conjoined process of urban regeneration in London. One depicts multi-million pound apartments in One Hyde Park, Knightsbridge, and the other, 'sheds with beds' in Newham, primarily to cater for low-paid, usually migrant, workers. The respective developments are shaped by government policy that, on the one hand, encourages new-build, speculator-led construction aimed at wealthy people, including the 'super-rich', and, on the other, seeks to depress the level of wages, which prices many people out of decent housing and creates a demand for a new, and degrading, form of habitation, that is, the garden shed. The lack of affordable housing and/or the construction of municipal dwellings, combined with austerity cuts to welfare benefits, and income more generally, means that public policy is presiding over a housing crisis in cities in which it is estimated that homelessness has increased markedly since 2008. For instance, from April to June 2014, 2,497 people were sleeping on London's streets, a 23% increase on figures for April to June 2013 (Thames Reach, 2014).

Figure 8.6: Speculator-led regeneration: One Hyde Park, London

Source: Rob Imrie

One Hyde Park was constructed between 2009 and 2011 and it is described by its owners, Project Grande (Guernsey) Limited, as 'the most exclusive address in the world'. The development comprises a series of residential blocks and 86 apartments, and it was ready for occupation in early 2011. By mid-2013, most of the apartments were not occupied and the development is seen, by some, as emblematic of an economy whereby property is no more than an investment or shelter for savings, and not a place to be a home or to live in. The high value that can be accrued from apartments at One Hyde Park was outlined by Edmonds (2014), who reported that a five-bedroom apartment was on the rental market at £45,000 per week. One commentator, Peter York, has described the development as 'a great big global money Monopoly chip, an asset class, a bullion bar, rather than a place to live in. It has been literally twisted out of shape by the desire to achieve profitable densities' (quoted in Arlidge, 2011, p 1).

Figure 8.7: 'Sheds with beds'

Speculative investment in land and property is inflating urban land prices to the point whereby many people in London are forced to live in 'sheds with beds'. These are substandard and illegal structures that landlords charge below market rents for, and they are concentrated in areas of poverty or where low-paid work is prevalent. They have become prevalent in different cities, but are concentrated in some of the poorer parts of London.

Dawn Foster (2014, p 1) has described London's sheds with beds in the following terms:

Often little more than four walls of breeze blocks or a converted garage, with dangerous wiring and plumbing as limited as a bucket, are usually rented to the most vulnerable and ignored in society – the migrant workers, the young people close to homelessness, and destitute families, who have little option other than to accept any housing offered to them. Rents have rocketed in London, and outstripped any rise in wages and living standards everywhere else.... For people on poverty wages, without access to these sums, the landlords who don't ask for guarantors, and hundreds of pounds in fees and deposits, are their only option. In return they get appalling housing and live with the constant threat of eviction.

These figures are part of a wider trend of an increase in income inequality and poverty in cities. Public sector pay restraint has translated into both wage freezes and cuts, and there has been a marked drop in real earnings. Youth unemployment in Western countries has escalated, and the rate in the UK is 2.5 times greater than that for unemployment as a whole. It is particularly concentrated in places like London, where one in four young people are out of work, and within London, it is concentrated in the poorer parts of the city and disproportionately affects people from minority ethnic groups. The geographical unevenness of austerity is striking, and, as Beatty and Fothergill (2013, p 3) note, 'Britain's older industrial areas, a number of seaside towns and some London boroughs are hit hardest'. They further suggest that the effect of welfare reforms is to widen the gaps in prosperity between the poor and rich areas of British cities and regions.

The widening of income inequalities and the increase in displaced people on the streets have led Harvey (2001) to characterise austerity capitalism as 'capitalist accumulation through dispossession'. Here, Harvey is referring not only to the homeless or the unemployed young person, but also to the sale of land to private interests, including state involvement in dislodging the urban poor from inner-city locations to provide land for corporate property investors. The sale of public real estate to private interests is part of urban policy programmes in British local authorities, including the sale of council housing estates. Chakrabortty (2014) describes the process as a land grab in which low-rental social housing is sold off to make way for market units aimed at wealthy people. The most publicised example in the UK is the Heygate estate in South London (Lees, 2014). The local authority sold the estate to the Australian developer Lend Lease at a knockdown price, and 1,100 flats are to be demolished and replaced by 2,500 new units, of which only 70 will be for social or affordable rents. Chakrabortty (2014, p 1) suggests that this is happening because local councils have 'no other means of raising serious cash' (see also Lees, 2014).

In some cities, the impact of fiscal debt management is changing the quality of urban public environments. The sale of public assets, such as school playing fields, continues apace in Britain's inner cities, primarily to raise assets to cover financial shortfalls and budget deficits. For instance, the London Borough of Wandsworth is seeking to sell 40% of the playing fields at Elliott School in Putney for private redevelopment (see Fulcher, 2012). This is despite a public consultation that showed 96% of respondents to be against any land sale. Public space, including parks, squares and streets, are increasingly privatised or sold off as part of regeneration. While public authorities may save money in upkeep and maintenance costs, it is the erosion of collective space or places that all have the right to occupy that seems to be contrary to what the good city is or ought to be. For Mumford (1961, p 655), the challenge is 'to restore to the city the maternal, life nurturing functions, the autonomous activities, the symbiotic associations that have long been neglected or suppressed'.

These are the sentiments of those opposed to austerity urban policy, and many localised campaigns have sprung up to highlight the perceived social injustices of speculative urban development, including the loss of local shops and services and the escalation of rents on former council and socially rented housing. One example is the Focus E15 Mothers campaign, set up in Newham, East London, in 2014 to prevent the sale of large council estates to private landlords and their subsequent conversion to high-rental properties. The Focus E15 Mothers group comprises 29 single parents who faced being relocated away from their family and friends after a hostel in which they were living closed following Newham Council funding cuts. Their campaign has focused on the Carpenters estate in Newham, comprising 2,000 council housing units and earmarked for demolition and redevelopment (see Jackson, 2014). Most of the estate has been cleared of residents, and in September 2014, Focus E15 Mothers occupied a low-rise block on the estate to provide a social centre and also to draw attention to the perversity of the council maintaining empty buildings while people, like them, were forced out of the area due to the lack of affordable housing.

Beyond austerity and the right to the city

Investment in land and property has become big business in austerity times, and contemporary city-building is characterised by what appears to be an intensification of property speculation in the world's major cities. It is led by major corporate organisations, such as Qatari Diar, Mitsubishi Estate and the Westfield Development Corporation, fuelling new waves of retail-led development and residential gentrification (see Lees, 2013, 2014; Slater, 2013; Imrie and Lees, 2014). New spaces of consumption are emerging, characterised by the construction of corporate, identikit architecture, the disintegration of vibrant local community life through gentrification, and the privatisation of collective, public places. Such spatial development is actively facilitated by government policy, and much of it serves development interests by providing them with the land and legal means to shape the built environment.

This represents a continuation, even heightening, of previous trends, described by Harvey (2013, p xv) as 'rampant capitalist development' and predatory urban practices that promote 'private and quasi private interests' at the expense of the poor. The outcome, so Purcell (2002) suggests, is the decline of democracy and the disenfranchisement of different groups in the city. For Purcell (2002), significant changes in the governance of cities have reduced citizens' control of spatial development processes. These include: the rescaling of governance from local to national and supranational organisations; the shift in (urban) policy from redistributive welfare goals to promoting competition and entrepreneurialism; and the transfer of state functions to non-state, private sector and voluntary organisations. The outcome is the estrangement of many people from the centres of power and decision-making (see Harvey, 2013).

There is nothing new about this, and in the 1960s, Henri Lefebvre (1968), among other writers, drew attention to the role of property speculation in eradicating local neighbourhoods, including the dominance of exchange value, commerce and profit in shaping the spatial structure of the city. For Lefebvre (1991), the production of urban space was skewed towards powerful commercial interests and was bolstered by a system of governance able to deflect, even ignore, the demands of urban citizens. Lefebvre's (1996) prognosis was to call for the 'right to the city', or the 'demand ... [for] a transformed and renewed access to urban life'. For Lefebvre (1996, p 158), whose observations were derived, in part, from the segregation of minority ethnic groups in the *banlieues* of Paris, such access entails 'the right of the user to make known their ideas on the space and time of their activity in the urban area [and] the right to the use of the centre, a privileged place, instead of being dispersed and stuck into ghettoes'.

Lefebvre's writings are full of the possibilities of developing alternative urban lifestyles, and his work exhorts others to work for a practical, progressive urbanism. A range of writers have responded to Lefebvre's challenge in seeking to suggest forms of urban living opposed to corporate and statist interventions in housing and labour markets. Friedmann (2000, p 471) suggests that the good city ought to be predicated on 'an autonomous, self-organising civil society, active in making claims, resisting and struggling ... within a framework of democratic institutions'. This echoes self-help approaches to planning, housing and urban development, including Turner's (1976, p 154) understanding that the good city revolves around providing people with the scope to build and shape the construction of their own dwellings, 'and manage it in their own ways'.

Likewise, Amin (2006, p 1009) refers to a 'practical urban utopianism' as a basis for enhancing 'the human experience'. For Amin (2006, p 1012), such enhancement depends upon societal transformations that enable people 'to live with, perhaps even value, difference, publicise the commons, and crowd out the violence of an urbanism of exclusionary and privatised interest'. This requires the deployment and development of four principles. The first is *repair*, or what Amin refers to as the need for urban life-support systems to be subjected to democratic scrutiny. Such systems range from sanitation to the pipes supplying water, and include lighting and the entire infrastructure necessary for people to live a good life. A second is *relatedness*, or developing the habit of intercultural formation and creating a public culture based on shared space. A third is *rights*, which ensure that all citizens are able to shape urban life and 'to channel antagonism towards deliberative and agonistic disputes in the public arena capable of some degree of reconciliation or mutual recognition' (Amin, 2006, p 1019). The final principle is *re-enchantment*, which includes the provision of public spaces 'that combine pleasure with the skill of negotiating difference' (Amin, 2006, p 1019).

Amin's (2006) call for a principled urban policy is indicative of the disenchantment of many with policy and renewal programmes that are the antithesis of democracy and represent imposed policy solutions. A group called Urbanology characterises urban renewal as 'unencumbered by any social or community or human values, an engine of destruction for neighborhoods, small businesses, charities and other projects' (quote from: https://www.urbanology.com). This is indicative of an uncaring society, or one in which corporatised cultures cultivate impersonalisation and lack of concern for others. Gleeson (2014, p 145) notes that the good city is predicated on social justice and that this depends upon nurturing an enterprise of care in cities, or an atmosphere that can facilitate 'the capacities and hopes of every citizen'. For Gleeson (2014, p 21), the good city is one whereby human fulfilment and social well-being may be enhanced. He notes that this cannot be achieved by recourse to market mechanisms or the production of well-being as a commodity as those things that human beings value in an existential sense are not amenable to pricing mechanisms or market signals.

A range of writers note that a progressive urban policy needs to address who owns and controls productive assets, such as land and buildings, as it is this that shapes, in large measure, social welfare and economic well-being in cities. Imbroscio (2013b) makes a case for an approach to urban policy that is less about redistribution, where resources may be transferred from richer to poorer people and places, and more about a focus on changing one of the structural causes of urban inequality and poverty, that is, the lack of ownership and control of the means of place-shaping in cities. Instead of the state intervening to tax and transfer resources, a focus on fiscal tinkering that does little to resolve social inequality and disadvantage, Imbroscio (2013b, p 799) suggests that 'dispersing productive asset ownership' is a means to 'predistribute' resources by giving people the opportunity to be 'co-owners and thus co-profit earners'. Imbroscio (2013b) refers to this as the ownership paradigm and a basis for ensuring that the benefits of local development are shared among all members of an urban community.

Robinson (2006, p 147) also suggests that urban policy needs to break with the dominant models of city-building that revolve around an econometric logic primarily focused on 'the globalizing sectors of the economy'. Instead of looking to emulate other places by drawing on international best practice and seeking to develop city strategies that facilitate globalisation and insert cities into global flows of people and resources, Robinson (2006) notes that the future of the city will need to confront its distinctive social and political context. This may seem an obvious point but, as Robinson (2006) convincingly shows, it is overlooked by city managers in the rush to globalise. In doing so, the complexity of a city's social and economic structures may be ignored, and even threatened, by opening up local economies to global corporate networks. Ironically, internationalising urban policy may be part of a process of dismantling much that is vital about local places, and this point has been recognised by anti-globalising movements and by those seeking to maintain the diversity of local neighbourhoods (Purcell, 2002).

Conclusions

The economic crash of 2008 and beyond has changed the social and economic landscapes shaping urbanisation, and has heralded a transformation in the nature of policy interventions in the problems of cities. Politicians have focused on public debt reduction and management and this has led to the dismantling of major urban policy programmes set up in previous eras. The post-welfare policy terrain includes attempts by governments to reduce welfare spending and encourage local self help strategies, otherwise known as localism. This includes much more focus on policy experimentation, and the rapid development and dissemination of policy knowledge garnered from local experiences. Oosterlynck and Gonzalez (2013, p 1079) suggest that despite the apparent diversity of policy forms, 'little new material is in fact being presented'. Much of the old, formulaic, urban entrepreneurial approaches of the 1980s and 1990s have been recycled, and, as Clark (2009, p 75) notes, supranational organisations like the OECD are encouraging place-marketing, 'international positioning, sustainability, openness, branding, leadership, and the arts'.

In global cities such as London, place-marketing has been aligned to major privatisation programmes, including the sale of valuable public land and property, such as council housing estates. Austerity urbanism has taken debt reduction to heart through rapid 'fire sales' and the development of public–private contracts enabling corporate organisations to provide, manage and maintain key urban infrastructure, such as streetlights. The flip side of the austerity regeneration agenda is encouraging economic growth; here, the reduction of public controls on private activities has been paramount, with the belief that entrepreneurship needs to be realised as the means to promote new jobs, welfare and wealth. Any illusion of poverty alleviation programmes has disappeared, and what is left of urban policy is no more than sparse resources allocated to a variety of small-scale fiscal measures based on competitive bidding processes.

SUMMARY

The global economic crisis from 2008 has transformed the socio-economic and political context of urbanism, and has encouraged governments to reduce state spending on the social and welfare needs of citizens, with a disproportionate impact on the urban poor. Austerity is providing the context for an increase in the privatisation of urban space and the development of state-sponsored market fundamentalism encompassing self-help and localised policy experimentation. Austerity urban policy is primarily characterised by a focus on public sector debt reduction and the 'fire sale' of public assets to the private sector, including the conversion of state municipal housing stock to upscale residential dwellings. It is difficult to identify what precisely urban policy is and what it is becoming beyond a few ad hoc competitive funding programmes and exhortations by politicians for local experimentation. Austerity is part of a context whereby there is an absence of strategic steer and direction in relation to (urban) public policy.

RECOMMENDED READING

On austerity and urban policy, see the work of Crowley et al (2012) and Donald et al (2014). Chapter Six of Andrew Tallon's (2010) book, *Urban regeneration in the UK*, provides a summary of austerity and urban change in the UK context. An interesting book on the experiences of austerity in one major city is *Neoliberal urban policy and the transformation of the city: reshaping Dublin*, edited by Andrew MacLaran and Sinead Kelly (2014).

WEB LINKS

An interesting website on austerity and cities is Urban Austerity: Cities and the Politics of Crisis (see: http://www.urbanausterity.org). The Antipode Foundation's website also provides links to relevant readings about austerity urbanism (see: http://antipodefoundation.org).

postscript

The process of urbanisation is continuing apace and, according to a United Nations (2014) report, one of the most significant challenges of the mid- to late 21st century will be maintaining and managing urban areas. Such are the flows of people into cities, and the demands that they place on the provision of goods, services and jobs, that the key challenge for policymakers is *how to* govern urbanisation. This is no easy task in a globalising world in which policymakers, operating at national and/ or local levels, are struggling to deal with the urban and environmental impacts of global cycles of economic change. A response has been the shift to leaner, welfare to post-welfare, forms of governance in which citizens are encouraged to take (self-)responsibility for their lives. Policy experimentation has also proliferated, with a significant increase in inter-scalar and inter-sectoral governance between public, third sector and corporate organisations.

There appears to be less political will to invest in deprived areas, or to 'lift them out' of poverty. The mainstay of urban policy in the industrialised world is property-led regeneration, with policymakers seeking out global investment in land and property. This is the logic of neoliberalising urban policy in which the state takes the backseat in urban governance and public–private partnerships, or de facto privatisation, manage and control many services and spaces in the city. This trend is intensifying in an era of austerity politics, and whichever governments assume power over the foreseeable future, it is difficult to see any shift back to a Keynesian-style welfare state. Cities have been buffeted by the post-2007 global recession, and fiscal retrenchment has been the order of the day. Funding that might have been part of urban policy, for example, for community or social services, has experienced significant cuts and the right-wing critique of so-called 'welfare scroungers' has become stronger and more widespread.

These shifts in attitudes and values towards urban subjects are significant because they raise questions about the type of cities that are likely to emerge in the mid- to late 21st century. A theme of the book is who 'gains' and 'loses' from urban policy, and evidence suggests a shift towards social exclusion from place, and the shaping of urban spaces and opportunities that are not available to all. Should urban policy be about creating equitable cities in which a diversity of social identities can coexist and reap the social and economic dividends of urban life, or is it about liberating corporate control of space in which social and economic divisions separate those with 'the right to the city' from those without? As Lewis Mumford (1961, p 652) said, the good city is a civic structure characterised by 'human nurture and love'. This observation, if followed, identifies a moral or ethical direction for urban policy in which enhancing the freedom of people and nature in the city, beyond the strictures of the pursuit of profit or the corporate control of objects, buildings and land, is paramount.

keeping up to date

Urban policy is part of a dynamic process of change and there are continual changes to the socio-political contexts in which policy is developed and enacted, and changes to the substance of policy too. No book can hope to keep up with the fast-moving changes to urban policy and practice, and readers can do so by looking at particular newspapers, media and websites on a regular basis. Readers should not only consult sources that refer to urban policy, but also keep abreast of urban trends or information that describes current social, economic and demographic changes in cities. Some of the most useful websites include the following:

- The Urban Institute. Available at: http://www.urban.org
- City Scope. Available at: http://citiscope.org
- University of Glasgow Centre for Housing Research & Urban Studies. Available at: http://www.gla.ac.uk/subjects/urbanstudies/
- International Institute for Environment and Development. Available at: http://www.iied.org/urban
- Centre for Urban and Community Research, Goldsmiths University of London. Available at: http://www.gold.ac.uk/cucr/
- Center for Urban Policy Research. Available at: http://policy.rutgers.edu/cupr/
- The Brookings Institution. Available at: http://www.brookings.edu
- US Department of Housing and Urban Development. Available at: http://portal.hud.gov/hudportal/HUD
- United Nations, the Global Compact Cities Programme. Available at: http://citiesprogramme.com
- UN Habitat. Available at: http://unhabitat.org/safer-cities/

- ▨ UN Sustainable Cities. Available at: http:/www.un.org/en/ sustainablefuture/cities.asp
- ▨ London School of Economics Cities. Available at: http://lsecities.net
- ▨ Centre for Cities. Available at: http://www.centreforcities.org
- ▨ IPPR Housing. Available at: http://www.ippr.org/big-issues/housing

references

Adamson, D. (2010) 'Merthyr Tydfil: not workshy but let down', *The Guardian*, 2 December. Available at: http://www.theguardian.com/commentisfree/2010/dec/02/merthyr-tydfil-working-local-schemes

Addams, J. (1912) *Twenty years at Hull-House, with autobiographical notes*, New York, NY: Macmillan.

Adler, B. (2013) 'A year-one report card for Obama's Strong Cities, Strong Communities initiative', *Next City*. Available at: http://nextcity.org/daily/entry/a-year-one-report-card-for-obamas-strong-cities-strong-communities

Allen, A. (2009) 'Sustainable cities or sustainable urbanisation?', *Palette: UCL's Journal of Sustainable Cities*. Available at: www.un.org/en/sustainablefuture/cities.asp.

Allmendinger, P. and Haughton, G. (2009) 'Soft spaces, fuzzy boundaries, and metagovernance: the new spatial planning in the Thames Gateway', *Environment and Planning A*, vol 41, pp 617–33.

Amin, A. (2006) 'The good city', *Urban Studies*, vol 43, nos 5.6, pp 1009–23.

Amin, A. and Thrift, N. (2002) *Cities: reimagining the urban*, Cambridge: Polity Press.

Anderson, B. (1983) *Imagined communities: reflections on the origin and spread of nationalism*, London and New York, NY: Verso.

Arlidge, J. (2011) 'One Hyde Park: anybody home?', *The Sunday Times*, 20 November Available at: http://www.thesundaytimes.co.uk/sto/Magazine/Features/article819257.ece

Atkinson, R. (1999) 'Discourses of partnership and empowerment in contemporary British urban regeneration', *Urban Studies*, vol 36, no 1, pp 59–72.

Atkinson, R. (2000) 'Narratives of policy: the construction of urban problems and urban policy in the official discourse of British government 1968–1998', *Critical Social Policy*, vol 20, no 2, pp 211–32.

Atkinson, R. and Flint, J. (2004) 'Fortress UK? Gated communities, the spatial revolt of the elites and time–space trajectories of segregation', *Housing Studies*, vol 19, no 6, pp 875–92.

Atkinson, R. and Moon, G. (1994) *Urban policy in Britain: the city, state and the market*, Basingstoke: Macmillan.

Bachrach, P. and Baratz, M.S. (1962) 'Two faces of power', *The American Political Science Review*, vol 56, no 4, pp 947–52.

Baldwin, R. (2009) 'The great trade collapse: causes, consequences and prospects', eBook. Available at: VoxEU.org

Barnekov, T., Boyle, R. and Rich, D. (1989) *Privatism and urban policy in Britain and the United States*, Oxford: Oxford University Press.

Barton, H., Grant, M. and Guise, R. (2003) *Shaping neighbourhoods: for local health and global sustainability* (2nd edn), London: Routledge.

Bateman, T. (2012) 'With the benefit of hindsight', in D. Briggs (ed) *The English riots of 2011: a summer of discontent*, Hook: Waterside Press, pp 91–110.

Batty, M., Axhausen, K.W., Giannotti, F., Pozdnoukhov, A., Bazzani, A., Wachowicz, M., Ouzounis, G. and Portugali, Y. (2012) 'Smart cities of the future', *European Physical Journal: Special Topics*, vol 214, no 1, pp 481–518.

Bauman, Z. (1995) *Life in fragments: essays in postmodern morality*, Oxford: Blackwell.

Beatty, C. and Fothergill, S. (2013) *Hitting the poorest places hardest: the local and regional impact of welfare reform*, Sheffield: CRESR, Sheffield Hallam University.

Beauregard, R. (2003 [1993]) *Voices of decline: the postwar fate of US cities*, Cambridge, MA: Wiley Blackwell.

Beebeejaun, Y. and Grimshaw, L. (2011) 'Is the "New Deal for Communities" a new deal for equality? Getting women on board in neighbourhood governance', *Urban Studies*, vol 48, no 10, pp 1997–2011.

Belfiore, E. (2002) 'Art as a means of alleviating social exclusion: does it really work? A critique of instrumental cultural policies and social impact studies in the UK', *International Journal of Cultural Policy*, vol 8, no 1, pp 91–106.

Bell, D.N.F. and Blanchflower, D.G. (2010) 'Youth unemployment: déjà vu?', IZA Discussion Papers 4705, Institute for the Study of Labor (IZA).

Bell, E.E., Canuto, M.A. and Sharer, R.J. (eds) (2004) *Understanding early classic Copan*, Philadelphia, PA: University of Pennsylvania Museum of Archaeology and Anthropology.

BIS (Department of Business Skills and Innovation) (2010) *Local growth: realising every place's potential*, White Paper, October, London: BIS.

Blackman, T. (1995) *Urban policy in practice*, London: Routledge.

Blair, T. (2002) 'My vision for Britain', *The Observer*, 10 November. Available at: http://www.theguardian.com/politics/2002/nov/10/queensspeech2002.tonyblair

Blakeley, E.J. and Snyder, M.G. (1997) *Fortress America – gated communities in the United States*, Washington, DC: Brookings Institution.

Boland, P. (2010) '"Capital of culture – you must be having a laugh!" Challenging the official rhetoric of Liverpool as the 2008 European cultural capital', *Social and Cultural Geography*, vol 11, no 7, pp 627–45.

Bolognani, M. (2012) 'Good culture, bad culture … no culture! The implications of culture in urban regeneration in Bradford, UK', *Critical Social Policy*, vol 32, no 4, pp 618–35.

Bookchin, M. (1979) 'Ecology and revolutionary thought', *Antipode*, vol 10, no 3, pp 21–32.

Booth, C. (1889) Descriptive map of London poverty.

Bovens, L. (2008) 'The ethics of nudge', in T. Grüne-Yanoff and S.O. Hansson (eds) *Preference change: approaches from philosophy, economics and psychology*, Berlin and New York, NY: Springer, pp 207–20.

Bowsky, W. (1981) *A medieval Italian commune: Siena under the Nine, 1287–1355*, Berkeley, CA: University of California Press.

Boyer, P. (1978) *Urban masses and moral order in America, 1820–1920*, Cambridge, MA: Harvard University Press.

Brenner, N. and Schmid, C. (2014) 'The "urban age" in question', *International Journal of Urban and Regional Research*, vol 38, no 3, pp 731–55.

Briggs, A. (1965) *Victorian cities*, Berkeley, CA: University of California Press.

Brooks-Gunn, J., Duncan, G. and Aber, J.L. (eds) (1997) *Neighborhood poverty, volume 1: context and consequences for children*, New York, NY: Russell Sage Foundation.

Brownill, S. (1999) 'Turning the East End into the West End: the lessons and legacies of the London Docklands Development Corporation', in R. Imrie and H.Thomas (eds) *British urban policy*, London: Sage, pp 43–63.

Brownill, S. (2013) *London Docklands; reflections on regeneration*, London: Routledge.

Burkhalter, L. and Castells, M. (2009) 'Beyond the crisis: towards a new urban paradigm', 4th International Conference of the International Forum on Urbanism, Amsterdam/Delft.

Burton, I. (1968) 'The quality of the environment: a review', *Geographical Review*, vol 58, no 3, pp 472–81.

Callaghan, J. (1968) Local Government Grants (Social Need) Bill, 2nd Reading, *Hansard*, 2 December, vol 774, cols 1107–66.

Cameron, D. (2009) 'The Big Society', Hugo Young Memorial Lecture, 10 November.

Carson, R. (1962) *Silent spring*, Boston, MA: Houghton Mifflin.

Case, A. and Katz, L. (1991) 'The company you keep: the effects of family and neighbourhood on disadvantaged youth', NBER Working Paper 3705, National Bureau of Economic Research, Cambridge, MA.

Castells, M. (1978) *City, class and power*, London: St Martin's Press.

Catterell, B. (2012) 'Editorial', *City*, vol 16, no 1, pp 1–3.

Chadwick, E. (1984 [1842]) *The sanitary conditions of the labouring population*, Edinburgh: Edinburgh University Press.

Chakrabortty, A. (2014) 'At yacht parties in Cannes, councils have been selling our homes from under us', *The Guardian*, 14 October. Available at: http://www.theguardian.com/commentisfree/2014/oct/14/yacht-cannes-selling-homes-local-government-officials-mipim

Chant, S. (2013) 'Cities through a "gender lens": a golden "urban age" for women in the global South?', *Environment and Urbanisation*, vol 25, no 1, pp 9–29.

Clark, G. (2009) 'Leadership and governance', OPENCities Thematic Paper 1, URBACT, EU.

Clark, G. (2011) 'Launch of City Deals', Press Release, 8 December, Department for Business Innovation and Skills and Deputy Prime Minister's Office, London.

Clarke, N. (2013) 'Locality and localism: a view from British human geography', *Policy Studies* (Special Issue: Understanding Localism, part 2), vol 34, nos 5/6, pp 492–507.

Coaffee, J. (2004) 'Rings of steel, rings of concrete and rings of confidence: designing out terrorism in Central London pre and post September 11th', *International Journal of Urban and Regional Research*, vol 28, no 1, pp 201–11.

Coaffee, J. (2008) 'Sport, culture and the modern state: emerging themes in stimulating urban regeneration in the UK', *International Journal of Cultural Policy*, vol 14, no 4, pp 377–97.

Cochrane, A. (2007) *Understanding urban policy*, Oxford: Blackwell Publishing.

Cochrane, A., Peck, J. and Tickell, A. (1996) 'Manchester plays games: the local politics of globalisation', *Urban Studies*, vol 33, no 8, pp 1317–34.

Cohen, D. and Farmer, S. (2014) 'Why Chicago's botched parking meter privatization is also bad for the environment', *Next City*, 4 June. Available at: www.nextcity.org

Coleman, A. (1985) *Utopia on trial*, London: Hilary Shipman.

Commission of the European Communities (1990) 'Green Paper on the urban environment', EUR 12902 EN, Brussels CEC.

Comunian, R. (2011) 'Rethinking the creative city: the role of complexity, networks and interactions in the urban creative economy', *Urban Studies*, vol 48, no 6, pp 1157–79.

Constanze (2012) 'The looted prospect of Tarlabaşı Yenileniyor', blog post. Available at: http://www.tarlabasiistanbul.com/2012/03/the-looted-prospect-of-tarlabasi-yenileniyor/

Convention on Biological Diversity (2012) *Cities and biodiversity outlook: action and policy*, Montreal: Secretariat for the Convention on Biological Diversity.

Cook, I. (2008) 'Mobilising urban policies: the transfer of US Business Improvement Districts to England and Wales', *Urban Studies*, vol 45, no 4, pp 773–95.

Cook, I. (2009) 'Private sector involvement in urban governance: the case of Business Improvement Districts and Town Centre Management Partnerships in England', *Geoforum*, vol 40, pp 930–40.

Cozens, P.M., Pascoe, T. and Hillier, D. (2007) 'Critically reviewing the theory and practice of secured-by-design for residential new-build housing in Britain', in R. Mawby (ed) *Burglary: international library of criminology, criminal justice and penology – second series*, Aldershot: Ashgate, pp 345–61.

Craig, K. (2013) 'Detroit City Council moves forward with plan aimed at improving street lighting', *WXYZ Detroit*, ABC, 5 February. Available at: http://www.wxyz.com/news/region/detroit/detroit-city-council-moves-forward-with-plan-aimed-at-improving-street-lighting

Crone, P. (1989) *Pre-industrial societies*, Oxford: Basil Blackwell.

Crowley, L., Balaram, B. and Lee, N. (2012) *People or place? Urban policy in the age of austerity*, Lancaster: The Work Foundation, Lancaster University.

Crump, J. (2002) 'Deconcentration by demolition: public housing, poverty, and urban policy', *Environment and Planning D: Society and Space*, vol 20, no 5, pp 581–96.

Cugurullo, F. (2013) 'How to build a sandcastle: an analysis of the genesis and development of Masdar City', *Journal of Urban Technology* vol 20, no 1, pp 23–37.

Curry, P. (2003) 'Rethinking nature', *Environmental Values*, vol 12, no 3, pp 337–60.

Dahl, R. (1961) *Who governs? Democracy and power in the American city*, New Haven, CT: Yale University Press.

Daily Express (2011) 'Flaming morons: thugs and thieves terrorise Britain's streets', 9 August.

Dale, A. and Newman, L. (2009) 'Sustainable development for some: green urban development and affordability', *Local Environment*, vol 14, no 7, pp 669–81.

Davis, K. (1955) 'The origins and growth of urbanization in the world', *American Journal of Sociology*, vol 60, pp 429–37.

DCLG (Department for Communities and Local Government) (2012a) *National planning policy framework*, London: DCLG.

DCLG (2012b) *Government response to the House of Commons Communities and Local Government Committee report of session 2010–12: regeneration*, January, Cm 8264, London: The Stationery Office.

DCMS (Department for Culture, Media and Sport) (1999) *Policy Action Team 10: a report to the Social Exclusion Unit: arts and sport*, London: DCMS.

DCMS (2001) *Creative industries mapping document*, London: DCMS.

DeFilippis, J. (2001) 'The myth of social capital in community development', *Housing Policy Debate*, vol 12, no 4, pp 781–806.

DeFilippis, J., Fisher, R. and Shragge, E. (2006) 'Neither romance nor regulation: re-evaluating community', *International Journal of Urban and Regional Research*, vol 30, no 3, pp 673–89.

DeLuca, S. and Rosenbaum, J. (2010) 'Residential mobility, neighbourhoods, and poverty: results from the Chicago Gautreaux Program and the move to opportunity experiment', in C. Hartman and G. Squires (eds) *The integration debate: competing futures for American cities*, New York, NY: Routledge, pp 185–98.

Dennis, R. (1978) 'The decline of manufacturing employment in Greater London: 1966–74', *Urban Studies*, vol 15, no 1, pp 63–73.

Dennis, R. (2008) 'Urban modernity, networks and places', *History in Focus*, no 13. Available at: http://www.history.ac.uk/ihr/Focus/City/index.html

Department for Transport (2013) *Reported road casualties Great Britain 2012: Annual report*, London: Department for Transport.

Desmarais, J. (2004) 'Review – James Thomson, *City of Dreadful Night*, with drawings by Clifford Harper, London: Agraphia, 2003, 96pp', *Literary London: Interdisciplinary Studies in the Representation of London*, vol 2, no 1 (March). Available at: http://www.literarylondon.org/london-journal/march2004/desmarais.html

DETR (Department of Environment, Transport and the Regions) (2000) *Our towns and cities – the future: delivering an urban renaissance*, White Paper on Urban Policy, London: HMSO.

Dickens, C. (1866) *The adventures of Oliver Twist*, London: Chapman and Hall.

Dikeç, M. (2006) 'Guest editorial: badlands of the republic? Revolts, the French state and the question of the *banlieues*', *Environment and Planning D: Society and Space*, vol 24, pp 159–63.

Dikeç, M. (2007) *Badlands of the republic: space, politics and urban policy*, Oxford: Wiley-Blackwell.

Dillon, D. and Fanning, B. (2011) *Lessons for the Big Society: planning, regeneration and the politics of community participation*, Farnham: Ashgate.

Doering, H. (2014) 'Competing visions of community: empowerment and abandonment in the governance of coalfield regeneration', *International Journal of Urban and Regional Research*, vol 38, no 3, pp 1003–18.

Donald, B., Glasmeier, A., Gray, M. and Lobao, L. (2014) 'Austerity in the city: economic crisis and urban service decline?', *Cambridge Journal of Regions, Economy, and Society*, vol 7, no 1, pp 3–15.

Donnison, D., with Soto, P. (1980) *The good city: a study of urban development and policy in Britain*, London: Heinemann.

Dorling, D. (2012) *The population of the UK*, London: Sage.

Doyle, A.C. (1891) 'The man with the twisted lip', *Strand Magazine*, December.

Drake, D. (2008) 'The Blue House', IJburg, Amsterdam, Public Art Online. Available at: http://publicartonline.org.uk/casestudies/regeneration/bluehouse/description.php

Dublin City Council (2010) *Defining and valuing Dublin's creative industries*, Dublin: Dublin City Council.

Dublin City Council (2011) *Your city, your space: draft Dublin city public realm strategy*, Dublin: Dublin City Council.

Dyck, I. (2010) 'Geographies of disability: reflections on new body knowledges', in Chouinard, V., Hall, E., Wilton, R. (eds) *Towards enabling geographies 'Disabled' bodies and minds in society and space*, Ashgate, pp 253–63.

Edmonds, L. (2014) 'Yours for £45,000-a-WEEK', *Mail on Sunday*, 24 February. Available at: http://www.dailymail.co.uk/news/article-2566527/Yours-45-000-WEEK-Penthouse-Londons-One-Hyde-Park-expensive-rental-property-country-goes-market-2-3million-year-thats-nine-average-homes.html

Edwards, C. (2002) 'Barriers to involvement: the disconnected worlds of disability and regeneration', *Local Economy*, vol 17, no 2, pp 123–35.

Edwards, C. (2003) 'Disability and the discourses of the Single Regeneration Budget', in R. Imrie and M. Raco (eds) *Urban renaissance? New Labour, community and urban policy*, Bristol: The Policy Press, pp 163–80.

Edwards, C. (2008) 'Participative urban renewal? Disability, community and partnership in New Labour's urban policy', *Environment and Planning A*, vol 40, no 7, pp 1664–80.

Edwards, J. (1997) 'Urban policy: the victory of form over substance?', *Urban Studies*, vol 34, nos 5/6, pp 825–43.

Erlanger, S. (2012) 'French leader promises order after youths riot in a northern city', *The New York Times*. Available at: http://www.nytimes.com/2012/08/15/world/europe/hollande-pledges-order-after-rioting-in-northern-france.html?_r=0

Eshuis, J. and Edwards, A. (2013) 'Branding the city: the democratic legitimacy of a new mode of governance', *Urban Studies*, vol 50, no 5, pp 1066–82.

Etzioni, A. (1994) *The spirit of community: the reinvention of American society*, New York, NY: Touchstone.

Euchner, C. and McGovern, S. (1993) *Urban policy reconsidered: dialogues on the problems and prospects of American cities*, New York, NY: Routledge.

European Commission (2011) *Cities of tomorrow: challenges, visions, ways forward*, EC Directorate General for Regional Policy, Brussels: EC.

Evans, B., Percy, S. and Theobald, K. (2003) 'Mainstreaming sustainability into local government policymaking'. Unpublished paper vailable at: https://www.google.co.uk/?gws_rd=ssl#q=Evans,+B.,+Percy,+S.+and +Theobald,+K.+(2003)+'Mainstreaming+sustainability+into+local+g overnment+policy+making'.&spell=1

Evans, G. (2003) 'Hard-branding the cultural city: from Prado to Prada', *International Journal of Urban and Regional Research*, vol 27, no 2, pp 417–40.

Evans, G. (2005) 'Measure for measure: evaluating the evidence of culture's contribution to regeneration', *Urban Studies*, vol 42, nos 5/6, pp 1–25.

Evans, J., Jones, P. and Krueger, R. (2009) 'Organic regeneration and sustainability or can the credit crunch save our cities?', *Local Environment*, vol 14, no 7, pp 683–98.

Fainstein, N. and Fainstein, S. (eds) (1982) *Urban policy under capitalism*, Beverly Hills, CA: Sage.

Featherstone, D., Ince, A., Mackinnon, D., Strauss, K. and Cumbers, A. (2012) 'Progressive localism and the construction of political alternatives', *Transactions of the Institute of British Geographers*, vol 37, no 2, pp 177–82.

Flint, J. and Raco, M. (2012) *The future of sustainable cities: critical reflections*, Bristol: The Policy Press.

Florida, R. (2002) *The rise of the creative class: and how it's transforming work, leisure, community and everyday life*, New York, NY: Basic Books.

Foley, P. and Martin, S. (2000) 'A new deal for the community? Public participation in regeneration and local service delivery', *Policy and Politics*, vol 28, no 4, pp 479–91.

Foord, J. (2008) 'Strategies for creative industries: an international review', *Creative Industries Journal*, vol 1, no 2, pp 91–113.

Foster, D. (2014) 'Beds in sheds show who the real victims of the housing crisis are', *The Guardian*, 1 July.

Fraser, N. (1997) *Justice interruptus: critical reflections on the 'postsocialist' condition*, London: Routledge.

Frazier, J. (1997) 'Sustainable development: modern elixir or sack dress?', *Environmental Conservation*, vol 24, no 2, pp 182–93.

Friedman, M (1962) *Capitalism and freedom*, Chicago: University of Chicago Press.

Friedmann, J. (2000) 'The good city: in defense of utopian thinking', *International Journal of Urban and Regional Research*, vol 24, no 2, pp 460–72.

Fry, T. (2009) *Design futuring: sustainability, ethics and new practice*, Oxford and New York, NY: Berg.

Fry, T. (2011) *Design as politics*, Oxford: Berg.

Fulcher, M. (2012) 'Council approves Elliott School playing fields sale', *Architects Journal*. Available at: http://www.architectsjournal.co.uk/news/daily-news/council-approves-elliott-school-playing-fields-sale/8634712. article

Garcia, B. (2005) 'Deconstructing the City of Culture: the long term legacies of Glasgow 1990', *Urban Studies*, vol 42, nos 5/6, pp 841–68.

Gaskell, E. (1855) *North and South*, Bernhard Tauchnitz, Leipzig.

Geltner, G. (2012) 'Public health and the pre-modern city: a research agenda', *History Compass*, vol 10, no 3, pp 231–45.

Gibbs, L.M. (1982) *Love canal: my story*, Albany, NY: State University of New York Press.

Gibson, O. (2012) 'London Olympics triumph gives way to more sober focus on the legacy', *The Guardian*, 6 September.

Giddens, A. (1998) *The Third Way: the renewal of social democracy*, Cambridge: Polity Press.

Giddings, B., Hopwood, B. and O'Brien, G. (2002) 'Environment, economy and Society: fitting them together into sustainable development', *Sustainable Development*, vol 10, pp 187–96.

Gilchrist, A. and Taylor, M. (2011) *The short guide to community development*, Bristol: Policy Press.

Glaeser, E. (2011) *Triumph of the city*, London: Macmillan.

Glaeser, E. and Joshi-Ghani, A. (2014) *Overview – the urban imperative: toward shared prosperity,* World Bank Policy Research Working Papers, Washington, DC: World Bank.

Glasgow Herald (1928) 'Industrial Transference Board', *Glasgow Herald,* 28 May, p 13.

Gleeson, B.J. (2014) *The urban condition,* Abingdon: Routledge.

Goetz, E.G. (1996) 'The U.S. war on drugs as urban policy', *International Journal of Urban and Regional Research,* vol 20, no 3, pp 539–49.

Goetz, E. and Chapple, K. (2010) 'You gotta move: advancing the debate on the record of housing dispersal programs since 1995', *Housing Policy Debate,* vol 20, no 2, pp 209–36.

Gold, J.R. and Gold, M.M. (eds) (2011) *Olympic cities: city agendas, planning and world's games, 1896–2016,* London: Routledge.

Green, J. and Chapman, A. (1992) 'The British Community Development Project: lessons for today', *Community Development Journal,* vol 27, no 3, pp 242–58.

Grimshaw, L. (2011) 'Community work as women's work? The gendering of English neighbourhood partnerships', *Community Development Journal,* vol 46, no 3, pp 327–40.

Gripaios, P. (2002) 'The failure of regeneration policy in Britain', *Regional Studies,* vol 36, pp 568–77.

Grover, S. (2009) 'The dark side of transition towns? World changing slams transition movement'. Available at: http://www.treehugger.com/corporate-responsibility/the-dark-side-of-transition-towns-worldchanging-slams-transition-movement.html

Haack, S. (1996) *Deviant logic, fuzzy logic,* Chicago, IL: University of Chicago Press.

Haggar, R. (2013) 'Compensatory education'. Available at: http://www.earlhamsociologypages.co.uk/compensatoryed.html

Hall, P. (1982) 'Enterprise zones: a justification', *International Journal of Urban and Regional Research,* vol 6, no 3, pp 416–21.

Hall, P. (1988) *Cities of tomorrow: an intellectual history of urban planning and design,* Oxford: Wiley-Blackwell.

Harcourt, B.E. (2001) *Illusion of order: the false promise of broken windows policing,* Cambridge and London: Harvard University Press.

Harrington, M. (1962) *The other America: poverty in the United States,* New York, NY: Macmillan.

Harvey, D. (1989) 'From managerialism to entrepreneurialism: the transformation in urban governance in late capitalism', *Geografiska Annaler*, vol 71, no 1, pp 3–17.

Harvey, D. (1999) 'The environment of justice', in F. Fischer and M. Hajer (eds) *Living with nature: environmental politics as cultural discourse*, Oxford: Oxford University Press, ch 8.

Harvey, D. (2001) *Spaces of capital: towards a critical geography*, London: Routledge.

Harvey, D. (2013) *Rebel cities: from the right to the city to the urban revolution*, London and New York, NY: Verso.

Hayek, F. (1944) *The road to serfdom*, London: Routledge.

Hernstein, R.J. and Murray, C. (1994) *The bell curve: intelligence and class structure in American life*, New York, NY: Free Press.

Higgins, J., Deakin, N., Edwards, J. and Wicks, M. (1983) *Government and urban poverty: inside the policy-making process*, London: Hutchison.

Howard, E. (1902 [1898]) *Garden cities of to-morrow*, London(Originally titled *Tomorrow: a peaceful path to real reform*).

Hubbard, P. (2008) 'Here, there, everywhere: the ubiquitous geographies of heteronormativity', *Geography Compass*, vol 2, no 3, pp 640–58.

Husband, C. and Alam, Y. (2011) *Social cohesion and counter-terrorism: a policy contradiction?*, Bristol: The Policy Press.

Imbroscio, D. (2012a) 'Beyond mobility: the limits of liberal urban policy', *Journal of Urban Affairs*, vol 34, no 1, pp 1–20.

Imbroscio, D. (2012b) 'The end of (urban) liberalism: rejoinder to Professor Squires', *Journal of Urban Affairs*, vol 34, no 1, pp 35–42.

Imbroscio, D. (2013a) *Urban America reconsidered: alternatives for governance and policy* (2nd edn), Ithaca, NY: Cornell University Press.

Imbroscio, D. (2013b) 'From redistribution to ownership: toward an alternative urban policy for America's cities', *Urban Affairs Review*, vol 49, no 6, pp 787–820.

Imrie, R. (1994) 'The policies and paradoxes of 'greening' the motor vehicle in the United Kingdom', in P. Nieuwenhuis, and P. Wells (eds), *Motor vehicles in the environment*, London: Belhaven, pp 76–96.

Imrie, R. (1996) *Disability and the city*, London: Sage.

Imrie, R. (2012) 'Auto-disabilities: the case of shared space environments', *Urban Studies*, vol 50, no 16, pp 3446–62.

Imrie, R. (2013) 'Shared space and the post-politics of environmental change', *Urban Studies*, vol 50, no 16, pp 3446–62

Imrie, R. and Dolton, M. (2014) 'From supermarkets to community building: Tesco plc, sustainable place making and urban regeneration', in R. Imrie and L. Lees (eds) *Sustainable London? The future of a global city*, Bristol: Policy Press, pp 173–94.

Imrie, R. and Lees, L. (eds) (2014) *Sustainable London? The future of a global city*, Bristol: Policy Press.

Imrie, R. and Raco, M. (2003) *Urban renaissance? New Labour, community and urban policy*, Bristol: Policy Press.

Imrie, R. and Thomas, H. (1993) 'The limits of property-led regeneration', *Environment and Planning C: Government and Policy*, vol 11, no 1, pp 87–102.

Imrie, R. and Thomas, H. (1999) *British urban policy: an evaluation of the Urban Development Corporations*, London: Sage.

Istrate, E. and Nadeau, C.A. (2012) *Global metro monitor 2012: slowdown, recovery, and interdependence*, Washington, DC: The Brookings Institution.

Jackson, S. (2014) Local heroes: focus e15 mothers and the East London suffragettes. Available at: http://www.newleftproject.org/index.php/site/article_comments/local_heroes_focus_e15_mothers_and_the_east_london_suffragettes

Jacobs, J. (1961) *The death and life of great American cities*, Harmondsworth: Penguin.

Jamison, A. (2008) 'Greening the city: urban environmentalism from Mumford to Malmö', in M. Hård and T.J. Misa (eds) *Urban machinery: inside modern European cities*, Cambridge, MA: MIT Press, pp 281–98.

Jarrett, S. (2012) 'Disability in time and place', English Heritage Disability History Available at: http://www.english-heritage.org.uk/content/imported-docs/a-e/disability-in-time-and-place.pdf

Jessel, E. (2014) 'New Era Estate families face rent hikes as Benyon landlord takes over', *Hackney Citizen*, 1 July Available at: http://hackneycitizen.co.uk/2014/07/01/new-era-estate-families-rent-hikes-benyon-landlord-takes-over/

Johansson, A., Kisch, P. and Mirata, M. (2005) 'Distributed economies – a new engine for innovation', *Journal of Cleaner Production*, vol 13, nos 10/11, pp 971–9.

Johnson, M. (2005) 'Hull House'. Available at: http://www.encyclopedia.chicagohistory.org/pages/615.html

Johnston, C. and Mooney, G. (2007) '"Problem" people, "problem" spaces? New Labour and council estates', in R. Atkinson and G. Helms (eds) *Securing an urban renaissance: crime, community, and British urban policy*, Bristol: The Policy Press, pp 125–39.

Johnstone, C. and Whitehead, M. (2004) *New horizons in British urban policy: perspectives on New Labour's urban renaissance*, Farnham: Ashgate.

Jones, P. and Evans, J. (2008) *Urban regeneration in the UK: theory and practice*, London: Sage.

Jones, R., Pyke, J. and Whitehead, M. (2011) 'Governing temptation: changing behaviour in an age of libertarian paternalism', *Progress in Human Geography*, vol 35, no 4, pp 483–501.

Kane, P. (2011) *Lighting against crime*, London: ACPO (Association of Chief Police Officers).

Karsten, L. (2005) 'It all used to be better? Different generations on continuity and change in urban children's daily use of space', *Children's Geographies*, vol 3, no 3, pp 275–90.

Katz, M.B. (2010) 'Narratives of failure? Historical interpretations of federal urban policy', *City & Community*, vol 9, no 1, pp 13–22.

Kearns, A. (2003) 'Social capital, regeneration and urban policy', in R. Imrie and M. Raco (eds) *Urban renaissance? New Labour, community and urban policy*, Bristol: Policy Press, pp 37–60.

Keeble, D. (1978) 'Industrial change in the inner city and conurbation', *Transactions of the Institute of British Geographers New Series*, vol 3, no 1, pp 101–14.

Kenna, T. (2010) 'Fortress Australia? (In)Security and private governance in a gated residential estate', *Australian Geographer*, vol 41, no 4, pp 431–46.

Kleit, R.G. and Manzo, L.C. (2006) 'To move or not to move: relations to place and relocation choices HOPE VI', *Housing Policy Debate*, vol 17, no 2, pp 271–308.

Krueger, R. and Gibbs, D. (eds) (2007) *The sustainable development paradox: urban political economy in the United States and Europe*, New York, NY: Guildford Press.

Landry, C. and Bianchini, F. (1995) *The creative city*, London: DEMOS.

Larner, W. (2000) 'Neoliberalism: policy, ideology, governmentality', *Studies in Political Economy*, vol 63, pp 5–26.

Latham, A., McCormack, D., McNamara, K. and McNeill, D. (2009) *Key concepts in urban geography*, London: Sage.

Lawless, P. and Beatty, C. (2013) 'Exploring change in local regeneration areas: evidence from the New Deal Communities programme in England', *Urban Studies*, vol 50, no 5, pp 942–58.

Le Corbusier (1929) *The city of tomorrow and its planning*, London: John Rodker.

Lees, L. (2003) 'Policy (re)turns: urban policy and gentrification, gentrification and urban policy', *Environment and Planning A*, vol 35, no 4, pp 571–4.

Lees, L. (2010) 'Planning urbanity?', *Environment and Planning A*, vol 42, pp 2302–8.

Lees, L. (2012) 'Gentrification and the right to the city', in R. Lawrence, H. Turgut and P. Kellett (eds) *Requalifying the built environment: challenges and responses*, Hogrefe: Gottingen, pp 69–92.

Lees, L. (2013) 'The urban injustices of New Labour's "new urban renewal": the case of the Aylesbury Estate in London', *Antipode*, vol 46, no 4, pp 921–47.

Lees, L. (2014) 'The death of sustainable communities in London?', in R. Imrie and L. Lees (eds) *Sustainable London? The future of a global city*, Bristol: The Policy Press.

Lefebvre, H. (1968) *The right to the city*, Paris: Anthropos.

Lefebvre, H. (1991) *The production of space*, Oxford: Blackwell.

Lefebvre, H. (1996) *Writings on cities*, Cambridge, MA: Blackwell.

Lefebvre, H. (2003) *The urban revolution*, Minneapolis, MN: University of Minnesota Press.

Levitas, R. (2005) *The inclusive society? Social exclusion and New Labour* (2nd edn), Basingstoke: Palgrave Macmillan.

Lindekilde, L. (2012) 'Neo-liberal governing of "radicals": Danish radicalization prevention policies and potential iatrogenic effects', *International Journal of Conflict and Violence*, vol 6, no 1, pp 109–25.

Logan, J. and Molotch, H. (1987) *Urban fortunes: the political economy of place*, Berkeley, CA: University of California Press.

Logan, J.R., Jindricha, J., Shina, H. and Zhanga, W. (2011) 'Mapping America in 1880: the urban transition historical GIS project', *Historical Methods: A Journal of Quantitative and Interdisciplinary History*, vol 44, no 1, pp 49–60.

Lombardi, D.R., Porter, L., Barber, A. and Rogers, C.D.F. (2011) 'Conceptualising sustainability in UK urban regeneration: a discursive formation', *Urban Studies*, vol 48, no 2, pp 273–96.

Ludwig, C. and Ludwig, G. (2014) 'Empty gestures? A review of the discourses of "localism" from the practitioner's perspective', *Local Economy*, vol 29, no 3, pp 245–56.

Luke, T.W. (2005) 'Neither sustainable nor development: reconsidering sustainability in development', *Sustainable Development* (Special Issue: Critical Perspectives on Sustainable Development), vol 13, no 4, pp 228–38.

Lysgård, H.K. (2012) 'Creativity, culture and urban strategies: a fallacy in cultural urban strategies', *European Planning Studies*, vol 20, no 8, pp 1281–300.

MacLaran, A. and Kelly, S. (eds) (2014) *Neoliberal urban policy and the transformation of the city: reshaping Dublin*, Basingstoke: Palgrave Macmillan.

MacLeavy, J. (2009) '(Re)Analyzing community empowerment: rationalities and technologies of government in Bristol's New Deal for Communities', *Urban Studies*, vol 46, no 4, pp 849–75.

MacLeod, G. (2002) 'From urban entrepreneurialism to a "revanchist city"? On the spatial injustices of Glasgow's renaissance', *Antipode*, vol 34, no 3, pp 602–24.

MacLeod, G. (2011) 'Urban policies reconsidered: growth machine to post-democratic city?', *Urban Studies*, vol 48, no 12, pp 2629–60.

Malanga, S. (2004) 'The curse of the creative class', *City Journal*, Winter Available at: http://www.city-journal.org/html/14_1_the_curse.html

Manchester City Council (2013) 'Manchester City Council report for resolution', Economic Scrutiny Committee, Manchester, 17 July.

Manzi, T. (2010) 'Promoting responsibility, shaping behaviour: housing management, mixed communities and the construction of citizenship', Westminster Research, University of Westminster, London. Available at: http://www.wmin.ac.uk/westminsterresearch

Marcuse, P. (2006) 'Terrorism and the right to the secure city: safety vs. security in public spaces', in H. Berking, S. Frank, L. Frers, M. Low, L. Meier, S. Steets and S. Stoetzer, S. (eds), *Negotiating urban conflicts: interaction, space and control*, Transcript ; Piscataway, NJ, pp 289–304.

Marlow, D. (2014) 'Local growth deals 2 – the more we learn the less we know …', *PlacemakingResource*, 27 July. Available at: http://davidmarlow.placemakingresource.com/2014/07/27/local-growth-deals-2-the-more-we-learn-the-less-we-know/

Marris, P. and Rein, M. (1972) *Dilemmas of social reform: poverty and community action in the United States*, London: Routledge and Kegan Paul.

Massey, D. (1984) *Spatial divisions of labour*, London: Methuen.

Mathews, V. (2010) 'Aestheticizing space: art, gentrification and the city', *Geography Compass*, vol 4, no 6, pp 660–75.

Mayhew, H. (2008 [1851]) *London labour and the London poor*, Ware, Hertfordshire: Wordsworth Editions.

McCann, E.J. (2004) '"Best places": interurban competition, quality of life and popular media discourse', *Urban Studies*, vol 41, no 10, pp 1909–29.

McGuirk, P. (2000) 'Power and policy networks in urban governance: local government and property-led regeneration in Dublin', *Urban Studies*, vol 37, no 4, pp 651–72.

McGuirk, P. and Dowling, R. (2007) 'Understanding master-planned estates in Australian cities: a framework for research', *Urban Policy and Research*, vol 25, no 1, pp 21–38.

McGuirk, P. and Dowling, R. (2009a) 'Neoliberal privatisation? Remapping the public and the private in Sydney's masterplanned residential estates', *Political Geography*, vol 28, pp 174–85.

McGuirk, P. and Dowling, R. (2009b) 'Masterplanned residential developments: beyond iconic spaces of neoliberalism?', *Asia Pacific Viewpoint*, vol 50, pp 120–34.

Mead, W. (2011) 'The shame of the cities and the shade of Lyndon B Johnson', *The American Interest*. Available at: http://www.the-american-interest.com/2011/07/04/the-shame-of-the-cities-and-the-shade-of-lbj/

Mielke, D.P. (2011) 'Key sites of the Hittite Empire', in S.R. Steadman and G. McMahon (eds) *Oxford handbook of Ancient Anatolia (10,000–323 BC)*, Oxford: Oxford University Press, pp 1031–54.

Miles, S. (2005) '"Our Tyne": iconic regeneration and the revitalisation of identity in NewcastleGateshead', *Urban Studies*, vol 42, nos 5/6, pp 913–1028.

Miles, S. and Paddison, R. (2005) 'Introduction: the rise and rise of culture-led urban regeneration', *Urban Studies*, vol 42, nos 5-6, pp 833-839.

Mills, C.W. (1956) *The power elite*, Oxford: Oxford University Press.

Minton, A. (2006) *The privatisation of public space*, London: RICS.

Minton, A. (2009) *Ground control: fear and happiness in the twenty-first century city*, London: Penguin.

Minton, A. (2012) 'We are returning to an undemocratic model of land ownership', *The Guardian Online*, 11 June. Available at: http://www.theguardian.com/commentisfree/2012/jun/11/public-spaces-undemocratic-land-ownership

Mitchell, D. (2003) *The right to the city: social justice and the fight for public space*, New York, NY: The Guildford Press.

Mitchell, K. (2007) 'Geographies of identity: the intimate cosmopolitan', *Progress in Human Geography*, vol 31, no 5, pp 706–20.

Mol, A.P.J. and Spaargaren, G. (2000) 'Ecological modernization theory in debate: a review', 14th World Congress of Sociology, Montreal, Canada.

Montgomery, J. (2004a) 'Cultural quarters as mechanisms for urban regeneration part 1: conceptualising cultural quarters', *Planning, Practice and Research*, vol 18, no 4, pp 293–306.

Montgomery, J. (2004b) 'Cultural quarters as mechanisms for urban regeneration part 2: a review of four cultural quarters in the UK, Ireland and Australia', *Planning, Practice and Research*, vol 19, no 1, pp 3–31.

Mooney, G. (1999) 'Urban "disorders"', in S. Pile, C. Brook and G. Mooney (eds) *Unruly cities?*, London: Routledge, pp 53–92.

Mooney, G. (2007) 'Cultural policy as urban transformation? Critical reflections on Glasgow, European City of Culture 1990', *Local Economy*, vol 19, no 4, pp 327–40.

Moore, S. and Bunce, S. (2009) 'Delivering sustainable buildings and communities: eclipsing social concerns through private sector-led urban regeneration and development', *Local Environment: International Journal of Justice and Sustainability*, vol 14, no 7, pp 601–6.

Moran, M. (2012) 'Amiens riots: a police crackdown is not the answer to violence in the banlieues', *The Guardian*, 15 August. Available at: http://www.theguardian.com/commentisfree/2012/aug/15/amiens-riots-police-banlieues

Mumford, L. (1961) *The city in history*, New York, NY: Harcourt, Brace & World Inc.

Murray, C. (1984) *Losing ground, American social policy, 1950–1980*, New York, NY: Basic Books.

National Housing Law Project (2002) *False HOPE: a critical assessment of the HOPE VI public housing redevelopment program*, Oakland, CA: National Housing Law Project.

Németh, J. and Hollander, J. (2010) 'Security zones and New York City's shrinking public space', *International Journal of Urban and Regional Research,* vol 34, no 1, pp 20–34 .

Neve, P. (2000) 'The Great Temple in Boghazkoy-Hattusa', in D.C. Hopkins (ed) *Across the Anatolian Plateau: readings in the archaeology of Ancient Turkey,* Boston, MA: American School of Oriental Research, pp 77–97.

Newman, K. and Ashton, P. (2004) 'Neoliberal urban policy and new paths of neighborhood change in the American inner city', *Environment and Planning A,* vol 36, no 7, pp 1151–72.

Newman, O. (1972) *Defensible space: crime prevention through urban design,* London: MacMillan.

O'Callaghan, C. (2012) 'Urban anxieties and creative tensions in the European Capital of Culture 2005: "It couldn't just be about Cork, like"', *International Journal of Cultural Policy,* vol 18, no 2, pp 185–204.

O'Connor, J. (1973) *The fiscal crisis of the state,* New Brunswick, NJ, and London: Transaction Publishers.

O'Conner, J. (1994) 'Is sustainable capitalism possible?', in M. O'Conner (ed) *Is capitalism sustainable: political economy and the politics of ecology,* New York, NY: The Guildford Press, pp 152–75.

O'Connor, A. (1999) 'Swimming against the tide: a brief history of federal policy in poor communities', in R. Ferguson and W. Dickens (eds) *Urban problems and community development,* Washington, DC: Brookings Institution, pp 77–138.

O'Connor, A. (2001) *Poverty knowledge: social science, social policy, and the poor in twentieth-century U.S. history,* Princeton, NJ: Princeton University Press.

ODPM (Office of the Deputy Prime Minister), Social Exclusion Unit (1997) *Breaking the cycle: taking stock of progress and priorities for the future,* London: ODPM.

ODPM (2003) *Sustainable communities: building for the future,* London, HMSO.

ODPM (2005) *The mixed communities initiative: what is it?,* London, HMSO.

Odum, E.P. (1989) *Ecology and our endangered life-support systems,* Massachusetts, MA: Sinauer Associates Inc.

O'Hara, M. (2014) *Austerity bites,* Bristol: Policy Press.

Oosterlynck, S. and Gonzalez, S. (2013) '"Don't waste a crisis": opening up the city yet again for neo-liberal experimentation', *International Journal of Urban and Regional Research*, vol 37, no 3, pp 1075–82.

Owen, K.A. (2002) 'The Sydney 2000 Olympics and urban entrepreneurialism: local variations in urban governance', *Australian Geographical Studies*, vol 40, no 3, pp 323–36.

Owen, R. (1813) *A new view of society: essays on the principle of the formation of the human character*, London: W. Strange.

Pahl, R. (1975 [1970]) *Whose city?*, Harmondsworth: Penguin.

Peake, L. (1993) 'Race and sexuality: challenging the patriarchal structuring of urban social space', *Environment and Planning D: Society and Space*, vol 11, no 6, pp 415–32.

Peck, J. (2005) 'Struggling with the creative class', *International Journal of Urban and Regional Research*, vol 29, no 4, pp 740–70.

Peck, J. (2012) 'Austerity urbanism: American cities under extreme economy', *City*, vol 16, no 6, pp 626–55.

Peterson, P. (1991) 'The urban underclass and the poverty paradox', *Political Science Quarterly*, vol 106, no 4, pp 617–37.

Pile, S., Brook, C. and Mooney, G. (eds) (1999) *Unruly cities?*, London: Routledge.

Pitkänen, P. and Korpela, M. (eds) (2012) 'Characteristics of temporary transnational migration', Collected Working Papers from the EURA-NET project, Tampere, University of Tampere.

Plowden Report (1967) *Children and their primary schools*, report of the Central Advisory Council For Education (England), London: HMSO.

Pollock, V.L. and Sharp, J. (2012) 'Real participation or the tyranny of participatory practice? Public art and community involvement in the regeneration of the Raploch, Scotland', *Urban Studies*, vol 49, no 4, pp 3063–79.

Popkin, S.J. (2002) *The Hope VI program: what about the residents?*, Washington, DC: Urban Institute.

Porter, L. and Davoudi, S. (2012) 'The politics of resilience for planning: a cautionary note', *Planning Theory & Practice*, vol 13, no 2, pp 329–33.

Pounds, N. (2005) *The medieval city*, Westport, CT: Greenwood Press.

Pow, C.P. (2007) 'Constructing a new private order: gated communities and the privatisation of urban life in post-reform Shanghai', *Social and Cultural Geography*, vol 8, no 6, pp 813–33.

Powell, E. (1968) 'Rivers of blood', speech. Available at: http://www.channel4.com/news/articles/dispatches/rivers+of+blood+speech/1934152.html

Pratt, A.C. (2008) 'Creative cities: the cultural industries and the creative class', *Geografiska Annaler: Series B*, vol 90, no 2, pp 107–17.

Purcell, M. (2002) 'Excavating Lefebvre: the right to the city and its urban politics of the inhabitant', *GeoJournal*, vol 58, pp 99–108.

Putnam, R.D. (2000) *Bowling alone: the collapse and revival of American community*, New York, NY: Simon and Schuster.

Raban, J. (1974) *Soft city*, London: Harvill Press.

Raco, M. (2005) 'Sustainable development, rolled-out neoliberalism and sustainable communities', *Antipode*, vol 37, no 2, pp 324–47.

Raco, M. (2007) *Building sustainable communities*, Bristol: The Policy Press.

Raco, M. (2012) 'A growth agenda without growth: English spatial policy, sustainable communities, and the death of the neo-liberal project?', *Geojournal.*, vol 77, no 2, pp 153-65.

Raco, M. (2013) *State-led privatisation and the demise of the democratic state*, Farnham: Ashgate.

Ramesh, R. (2011) 'Deprived communities being left behind, MPs warn', *The Guardian Online*. Available at: http://www.theguardian.com/society/2011/nov/03/deprived-communities-left-behind-mps

Richardson, H. (1973) *Regional growth theory*, London: MacMillan.

Riddell, M. (2011) 'London riots: the underclass lashes out', *The Daily Telegraph*. Available at: http://www.telegraph.co.uk/news/uknews/law-and-order/8630533/Riots-the-underclass-lashes-out.html

Riis, J. (1890) *How the other half lives: studies among the tenements of New York*, New York, NY: Charles Scribner's Sons.

Robinson, F., Shaw, K. and Davidson, G. (2005) 'On the side of the angels: community involvement in the governance of neighbourhood renewal', *Local Economy*, vol 20, no 1, pp 13–26.

Robinson, J. (2006) *The ordinary city*, London: Routledge.

Robson, B. (1988) *Those inner cities*, Oxford: Oxford University Press.

Robson, B. (1994) 'No city, no civilisation', *Transactions of the Institute of British Geographers*, vol 19, no 2, pp 131–41.

Rosenbaum, J.E., Reynolds, L. and DeLuca, S. (2002) 'How do places matter? The geography of opportunity, self-efficacy, and a look inside the black box of residential mobility', *Housing Studies*, vol 17, pp 71–82.

Rowthorn, R. and Ramaswamy, R. (1997) *Deindustrialization – its causes and implications*, International Monetary Fund Working Paper WP/97/42, Washington, DC: IMF.

Schweik, S. (2009) *The ugly laws: disability in public*, New York, NY: New York University Press.

Seabrook, J. (2012) 'Cameron's attack on the "feckless poor" has a very long history', *The Guardian*, 26 June.

Sennett, R. (1996) *Flesh and stone: the body and the city in Western civilization*, New York, NY: W.W. Norton.

Shaw, K. and Robinson, F. (1998) 'Learning from experience? Reflections on two decades of British urban policy', *Town Planning Review*, vol 69, no 1, pp 49–63.

Simmel, G. (1921) 'The sociological significance of the "stranger"', in R. Park and E. Burgess (eds) *Introduction to the science of sociology*, Chicago, IL: University of Chicago Press, pp 322–7.

Sissons, A., with Brown, C. (2011) *Do enterprise zones work?*, Ideopolis policy paper, Lancaster: The Work Foundation.

Sjoberg, G. (1965) *The pre-industrial city: past and present*, New York, NY: The Free Press.

Slater, T. (2013) 'Expulsions from public housing: the hidden context of concentrated affluence', *Cities*, vol 35, pp 384–90.

Smith, A. (1776) *An inquiry into the nature and causes of the wealth of nations*, London: Methuen.

Smith, M. (2007) 'Form and meaning in the earliest cities: a new approach to ancient urban planning', *Journal of Planning History*, vol 6, no 1, pp 3–47.

Smith, P. (2012) 'Spaces of sustainable development in the Lower Hunter Regional Strategy: an application of the "cultural sociology of space"', *Geoforum*, vol 43, pp 35–43.

Sneddon, C., Howarth, R.B. and Norgaard, R.B. (2006) 'Sustainable development in a post-Brundtland world', *Ecological Economics*, vol 57, pp 253–68.

Social Exclusion Unit (2001) *A new commitment to neighbourhood renewal, national strategy action plan*, London: Cabinet Office.

Stables, A. (2013) 'The unsustainability imperative? Problems with "sustainability" and "sustainable development" as regulative ideals', *Environmental Education Research*, vol 19, no 2, pp 177–86.

Stanley, J., Stanley, J. and Hensher, D. (2012) 'Mobility, social capital and sense of community: what value?', *Urban Studies*, vol 49, no 16, pp 3595–609.

Stobaugh, J.P. (2012) *American history: observations & assessments from early settlement to today*, Green Forest, AR: Master Books.

Stone, C.N. (1980) 'Systemic power in community decision making: a restatement of stratification theory', *American Political Science Review*, vol 74, pp 978–90.

Stone, C.N. (1989) *Regime politics: governing Atlanta 1946–1988*, Lawrence, KS: University Press of Kansas.

Svara, J.H. (1990) *Official leadership in the city: patterns of conflict and cooperation*, Oxford: Oxford University Press.

Swyngedouw, E., Moulaert, F. and Rodriguez, A. (2002) 'Neoliberal urbanisation in Europe: large-scale urban development projects and the new urban policy', *Antipode*, vol 34, no 3, pp 380–404.

Tallon, A. (2010) *Urban regeneration in the UK*, Abingdon: Routledge.

Tebbit, N. (1981) Speech to Conservative Party Conference, Blackpool, October.

Teedon, P., Reid, T., Griffiths, P., Lindsay, K., Glen, S., McFadyen, A. and Cruz, P. (2009) *Secured by Design impact evaluation*, Glasgow: Glasgow Caledonian University.

Thames Reach (2014) 'Homelessness facts and figures'. Available at: http://www.thamesreach.org.uk/news-and-views/homelessness-facts-and-figures/

The Independent (2011) 'Mob rule', 9 August.

Thomas, H. (2000) *Race and planning: the UK experience*, London: Routledge.

Thomson, J. (1874) 'City of dreadful night'. Available at: http://en.wikisource.org/wiki/The_City_of_Dreadful_Night

Tickell, A. and Peck, J. (1996) 'The return of the Manchester men: men's words and men's deeds in the remaking of the local state', *Transactions of the Institute of British Geographers*, vol 21, no 4, pp 595–616.

Tonnies, F. (2001 [1887]) *Community and Civil Society* (English translation of *Gemeinschaft und Gesellschaft*), Cambridge: Cambridge University Press.

Turner, J. (1976) *Housing by people*, London: Marion Boyars Publishers.

Turok, I. (1992) 'Property-led urban regeneration: panacea or placebo?', *Environment and Planning A*, vol 24, pp 361–79.

UK Government (1994) *Sustainable development: the UK strategy*, Cm 2426, London: HMSO.

UN-HABITAT (2013) *State of women in cities 2012–13: gender and the prosperity of cities*, Nairobi: United Nations Human Settlements Programme.

United Nations (2014) *World urbanization prospects* (rev edn), Hendon, VA: United Nations Department of Economic and Social Affairs, Population Division.

Van de Mieroop, M. (1997) *The Ancient Mesopotamian city*, Oxford: Clarendon Press.

Van Ham, M., Manley, D., Bailey, N., Simpson, L. and Maclennan, D. (eds) (2012) *Neighbourhood effects research: new perspectives*, New York, NY: Springer.

Vanolo, A. (2013) 'Smartmentality: the smart city as disciplinary strategy', *Urban Studies*, vol 50, no 13, pp 1–13.

Varn, H.L. (2007) 'An ideal approach to global warming', *Inquiry Journal*, Paper 18. Available at: http://scholars.unh.edu/inquiry_2007/18

Wacquant, L. (2007) *Urban outcasts: a comparative sociology of advanced marginality*, Cambridge: Polity Press.

Wallace, A. (2010) 'New neighbourhoods, new citizens? Challenging "community" as a framework for social and moral regeneration under New Labour in the UK', *International Journal of Urban and Regional Research*, vol 34, no 4, pp 805–19.

Ward, K. (2006) '"Policies in motion", urban management and state restructuring: the trans-local expansion of Business Improvement Districts', *International Journal of Urban and Regional Research*, vol 30, no 1, pp 54–75.

Ward, K. (2007) 'Business Improvement Districts: policy origins, mobile policies and urban liveability', *Geography Compass*, vol 1, no 3, pp 657–72.

Ward, K. (2010) 'Entrepreneurial urbanism and Business Improvement Districts in the state of Wisconsin: a cosmopolitan critique', *Annals of the Association of American Geographers*, vol 100, no 5, pp 1177–96.

Warwick, E. (2012) 'Designs on security: tracing the translation of "defensible space" from a theoretical concept to a designed reality', Conference Proceedings, The Production of Place, University of East London, Docklands Campus.

Weisman, L.K. (1994) *Discrimination by design: a feminist critique of the man-made environment*, Chicago, IL: University of Illinois Press.

Weldon, C. (2012) 'Message from Cam Weldon, DCM and CFO', City of Toronto. Available at: http://www1.toronto.ca/wps/portal/contento nly?vgnextoid=0591d748c5148410VgnVCM10000071d60f89RCRD& vgnextchannel=4546e03bb8d1e310VgnVCM10000071d60f89RCRD

Wheeler, S. and Beatley, T. (2004) *The sustainable urban development reader*, London: Routledge.

Whitehead, M. (2012) 'Urban sustainability and economic development', in T. Hutton and R. Paddison (eds) *Handbook of urban economic development*, London: Sage.

White House (2013) *Strong Cities, Strong Communities initiative, 1st annual report*, Washington, DC: The White House, Council on Strong Cities, Strong Communities.

Williams, B. and Boyle, I. (2011) 'The role of property tax incentives in urban regeneration and property market failure in Dublin', *Journal of Property Tax Assessment and Administration*, vol 9, no 2, pp 5–21.

Williams, J. (2013) '£200 million: staggering new cuts facing Greater Manchester town halls', *Manchester Evening News*, 13 September. Available at: http://www.manchestereveningnews.co.uk/news/greater-manchester-news/200-million-staggering-new-cuts-5922219

Williams, R. (1985) *Keywords: a vocabulary of culture and society: revised edition*, Oxford: Oxford University Press.

Wilson, J.Q. and Kelling, G. (1982) 'Broken windows: the police and neighborhood safety', *Atlantic Monthly*, March, pp 29–38.

Wilson, W.H. (1989) *The city beautiful movement*, Baltimore, MD: Johns Hopkins University Press.

Wilson, W.J. (1978) *The declining significance of race: blacks and changing American institutions*, Chicago, IL: University of Chicago Press.

Wilson, W.J. (1987) *The truly disadvantaged: the inner city, the underclass, and public policy*, Chicago, IL: University of Chicago Press.

Wirth, L. (1938) 'Urbanism as a way of life', *American Journal of Sociology*, vol 44, pp 1–24.

Woodcraft, S., with Bacon, N., Caistor-Arendar, L. and Hackett, T. (2011) *Design for social sustainability*, London: Future Communities, The Young Foundation.

World Bank (2003) *Sustainable development in a dynamic world: transforming institutions, growth, and quality of life, world development report 2003*, New York, NY, and Oxford: World Bank and Oxford University Press.

World Bank (2010) *Eco2 cities: ecological cities as economic cities*, Washington, DC: The World Bank.

World Bank (2012) *The Great Recession and the future of cities*, Policy Research Working Paper 6256, Development Economics Department, Washington, DC: World Bank.

World Commission on Environment and Development (Brundtland Commission) (1987) *Report of the World Commission on Environment and Development: our common future*, Washington, DC: United Nations. Available at: http://www.un-documents.net/our-common-future.pdf

Wright, F.L. (1932) *The disappearing city*, New York, NY: W.F. Payson.

Yates, D. (1978) *The ungovernable city: the politics of urban problems and policy making*, Boston, MA: MIT Press.

Yelling, J. (2007) *Slums and slum clearance in Victorian London*, Abingdon: Routledge.

Young, M. and Willmott, P. (1962) *Family and kinship in East London*, London: Routledge and Kegan Paul.

Zimmerman, J. (2008) 'From brew town to cool town: neoliberalism and the creative city development strategy in Milwaukee', *Cities*, vol 25, pp 230–42.

Index